HIKING ATLANTA'S
HIDDEN FORESTS
Intown and Out

N
W   E
S

by Jonah McDonald

milestone
press

almond, nc

Milestone Press, P.O. Box 158, Almond, NC 28702

Book design by Martha Smith Design

LIBRARY OF CONGRESS CATALOGING-IN-PUBLICATION DATA

McDonald, Jonah, 1979-
 Hiking Atlanta's Hidden Forests intown and out / by Jonah McDonald.
  pages cm
 Summary: "Describes sixty hiking routes within thirty miles of downtown
Atlanta. Includes driving and hiking directions, maps, trailhead GPS coordinates,
trail highlights, and notable trees for each hike listed"-- Provided by publisher.
  ISBN 978-1-889596-29-7 (pbk. : alk. paper)
  1. Hiking--Georgia--Atlanta Region--Guidebooks. 2. Atlanta region (Ga.)--
Guidebooks. I. Title.
  GV199.42.G462A856 2014
  917.58'231--dc23
                                    2014002520

Printed in the United States on recycled paper

ACKNOWLEDGMENTS

My wife Dana is my inspiration and partner in all my projects. Without her encouragement and patience, I would never have dedicated myself to outdoor education and intown exploration. Her positive influence in my life has helped produce this guidebook.

To my family—Ron, Susan, Jesse, Cindy, Mark, Marlene, Andrea, Todd, and Buster—thank you for your support and your company on many trails. I put in long hours of work and talked your ears off about this project, and you never complained.

I am so grateful to Jim Parham and Mary Ellen Hammond of Milestone Press for sharing my vision for this project and working diligently to bring it to fruition. The final product is even better than I envisioned.

Partnering with experts has been key to this project. Thanks go to Eli Dickerson for contributions in identifying champion and sentinel trees, David Foster for support in making sure photography was well executed, Barbara Sajor and Joy Carter of the Audubon Society of Atlanta for help in integrating urban birding. I am indebted to Ranger Robby Astrove and volunteer Tom Smith of Davidson–Arabia Mountain Nature Preserve, particularly for assistance in accurately representing the Davidson–Arabia trails.

Noah Derman, Erin Hurley, Hannah and Laura MacNorlin, Jesse Stewart, Mary Ann Downey, Bill Holland, Karen Skellie, Maia, Graham and Arlie Rose Hallward, Gary Taggart Thompson, Lissa Place, Glen Satell, Sally Ferguson, Jim Tolmach, Regina Willis, Sam Chontos, Ben Fowler, and others tested hikes and took photos. Bob and Becky Lough went above and beyond with their hike testing, confirming distances to the tenth of a mile, and geotagging photos for a large number of hikes. Special thanks go to Erica Schoon, Bert Skellie, and my dog Lio, who have hiked more Atlanta trails with me than anyone except Dana.

To everyone I met while hiking the trails, thank you for sharing your local knowledge and enthusiasm for the project. I hope this guidebook meets your expectations and helps more Atlantans explore our city's hidden forests!

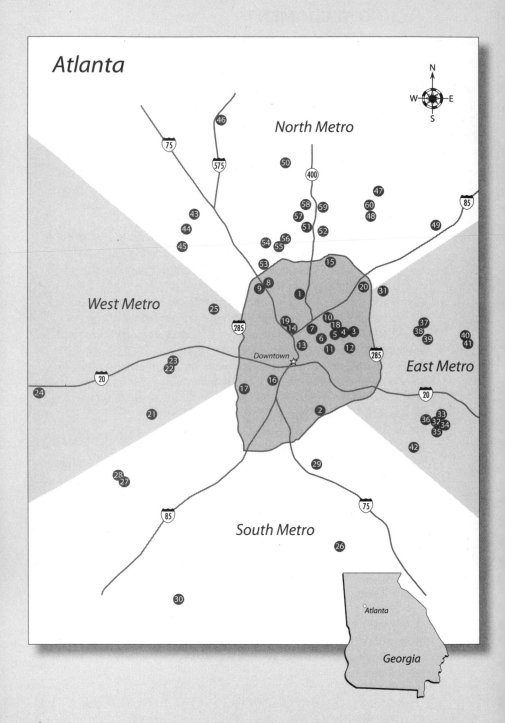

TABLE OF CONTENTS

TABLE OF CONTENTS *CONTINUED*

The bulk of Atlanta's metro area is hidden under a vast urban canopy of oak, tulip, pine, pecan, maple, hickory, and sycamore.

INTRODUCTION

Atlanta is known throughout the world as a city of Coca-Cola, sports, traffic jams, civil rights, music, and Southern culture. But if you enter the city by airplane, you may notice that—with the exception of a cluster of skyscrapers—the defining characteristic of this city with a population of five million is not concrete and metal but trees. The bulk of Atlanta's metro area is hidden under a vast urban canopy of oak, tulip, pine, pecan, maple, hickory, and sycamore.

Despite the fact that we live in a forest, most people in Atlanta believe they must drive hours to the mountains to go hiking. On the contrary, we are surrounded by hiking trails just minutes from our homes and hotels. No matter how you arrived in Atlanta—whether you grew up here, moved from another town or country, or are just visiting for the weekend—this book will introduce you to the forest trails in the city. Many of these hikes are inside the I-285 perimeter (considered "intown" by Atlantans), and all are within 30 miles of the capitol dome in downtown Atlanta.

I arrived in Atlanta by way of the Appalachian Trail. After hiking the 2,000-plus miles from Maine to Georgia and establishing my new home in the city, I continued hiking on weekends and sought out only the longest, most rugged hikes in the Southeast. I drove hundreds of miles in search of the peace and beauty that nature offers. On weekday afternoons, I sought out trails in the forests of Atlanta and wandered beside creeks, over knolls, and through some of the most impressive old-growth forests I've found anywhere. I have come to believe that short hikes, close to home, can be as life-changing as extended backpacking trips.

This guidebook can help you integrate hiking into your everyday life. The routes listed here are nestled in neighborhoods but can have the feel of remote wilderness. If you want to walk your dog after work or are in search of a Sunday afternoon excursion for your family, there's a trail close to home to explore. And if you want a full day of hiking without spending a half day in the car, Atlanta's hidden forests are a perfect place to go.

HIKING FOR EXERCISE

Hiking on forest trails is one of the best physical activities available. Walking is cardiovascular exercise that promotes overall fitness, tones muscle, burns fat, strengthens joints, and develops balance. The character of forest trails adds even more benefits to a regular "walk in the park." Because woodland trails follow the contours of the land and are rarely concrete-flat, hiking provides a more thorough muscle workout without the repetitive movements of walking on pavement. Trail surfaces—soil, wood chips, even gravel—are easier on joints than sidewalks are.

WHAT TO WEAR

Though many hikers swear by high-tech boots and specialized clothing of synthetic or woolen fabrics, the hikes in this guidebook don't require a shopping spree at an upscale outdoor retailer. Wear what you have around the house, and follow these general guidelines:

Appropriate hiking attire changes with the seasons. In warm weather, wear short sleeves, a sun hat or baseball cap, and breathable clothing that allows airflow. Though shorts are cooler, wearing lightweight pants in the summer can help you avoid annoyances such as ticks, chiggers, and poison ivy. In the winter, long sleeves and long pants are a good idea but layering is key. Wearing too many clothes while exercising can be uncomfortable and dangerous because clothing damp from sweat can lower your body temperature while you're taking breaks from your hike. It's good to be able to take off a layer as you warm up from the exercise. And it's wonderful to put that warm layer back on when you begin cooling down afterward. Much body heat is lost through the head, so a warm hat and gloves are especially effective means of staying warm in cold weather.

Shoes (the right ones) can make or break a hike. Unless you have ankle problems, athletic shoes work as well as hiking boots for any of the hikes in this book. If you seek more hiking-specific footwear, shoes marketed for trail running have more rugged and durable soles and are therefore excellent for hiking as well. Many shoe manufacturers are also now producing "light hikers" that combine the lightweight materials of sneakers with the ankle support and rugged sole of boots.

Socks are an important factor in avoiding blisters. Choose athletic or hiking socks that fit well and come up over your ankle. Most walkers prefer woolen and synthetic-blend socks because they wick away moisture, keeping your feet cool and dry.

WHAT TO BRING

The following checklist can help you leave the house prepared for your hike in any weather:

• Backpack or waist pack
• Snacks (energy bars, trail mix, and fruit are all great trail snacks)
• Water (one liter per person, at least)
• Rain gear (waterproof jacket, poncho, and/or umbrella)

- Warm layer (fleece, sweatshirt, coat, warm hat) if cold weather
- Sun hat, baseball cap, and/or sunglasses
- Insect repellent and sunscreen
- First aid kit
- Plastic bag to pack out trash
- Guidebook or map
- Cell phone
- Camera

CANINE COMPANIONS

Nearly all the hikes in this book are dog-friendly destinations (and the few that prohibit dogs are noted as such). Hiking with your pet can add to your enjoyment and safety. Bringing your dog does decrease your likelihood of seeing birds, deer, and other wildlife, but hikers with dogs often connect and strike up friendships more easily than solo hikers.

All the parks included here require your dog to be on a leash at all times, but you will undoubtedly come across hikers who are breaking the rules by walking with loose canines. Some trails in this book are used as unofficial dog parks by neighbors and local residents. Though most dogs are friendly, use common sense when approaching (or being approached by) an unleashed dog. Ask the owner if the dog is friendly, and ask him or her to leash the pet if you feel uncomfortable. Of course, you'll be following the rules yourself with your own dog!

SAFETY

Preparation, vigilance, and common sense are the foundation of safe hiking. You are in charge of your own safety while exploring the trails in this guidebook. Below are some tips that may help you as you go.

Injuries most common to hiking are minor ankle sprains, blisters, and cuts caused by a fall. Watch where you are stepping and choose appropriate footwear and socks to lessen the likelihood of falls, sprains, and blisters. Most of these can be treated on site with a small first aid kit, but some injuries might need professional attention. All of the hikes in this guidebook are in areas with thorough cell phone coverage. Call 911 if you need help.

Poison ivy is common in the Atlanta area. With its three leaves and hairy roots and vines, the uncomfortable effects of exposure make it important to learn how to identify. Wear long pants when hiking, and avoid touching the plant. If you think you have touched poison ivy, wash your skin thoroughly. Over-the-counter products such as Tecnu™ can help avoid the rash caused by poison ivy, but they must be used soon after you make contact, so it's best to have them on hand while hiking.

Hiking alone on the trails is not so different from walking alone in a large city. Pay attention to your surroundings, walk and speak with confidence, and trust your gut. Criminals are often more afraid of the forests than they are of city streets, but staying in any metro Atlanta park after dark is not recommended. Unfortunately, women need to be especially vigilant. Bring a dog, carry pepper spray, or invite a friend along. And remember, you are more likely to be mugged on a city street than in the woods.

Snakes are out there, and while there's always a chance you'll see one, it's unlikely on these well-trodden paths. Vigilance is the key to avoiding them. Stay on the trail and look where you're putting your feet—do not step blindly over a large log or rock. Pay attention when walking through marshy or open areas where snakes may choose to sun themselves. If a snake bites you, call 911 immediately.

Insects you may encounter while hiking in Atlanta during the summer months are primarily an annoyance, not a danger. Spiders, bees, hornets, wasps, and yellow jackets can best be avoided by not disturbing their homes—and staying on the trail. Mosquitoes, ticks, and chiggers can be the biggest annoyance in the forests of Atlanta. After your hike, check your body for ticks, especially in warm dark places on your body such as armpits and along waistbands and sock lines. Not all ticks carry Lyme disease, and ticks do not transmit the disease until at least 24 hours after biting you. So, search for and remove ticks quickly and put your mind at ease. Chiggers are very small insects that cause itchy bumps that last for days. It is rare to get chigger bites when walking on maintained trails. When walking through tall grasses or brush, wear long pants and shower soon after hiking to wash away any chiggers that might have found you.

LEAVE NO TRACE ETHICS

"Take only photos, leave only footprints" is an excellent motto for hikers. Atlanta intown hikers often add "and pack out trash." The Center for Outdoor Ethics promotes a philosophy that asks hikers to consider their impact on our natural places and take steps to actively "leave no trace." While hiking through the urban greenspaces in this guidebook, you will often see signs of humans—old tires, beer bottles and cans, shopping bags, and other trash. As a visitor to these trails, you can also be a steward of the land by carrying a plastic bag and packing out trash you find. For more information about Leave No Trace philosophy, visit www.lnt.org.

PUBLIC TRANSPORTATION

Atlanta is not known for public transportation, and its 16-lane superhighways have become the city's calling card. Nonetheless, the MARTA system (paired with transit systems in the surrounding counties) is extensive and inexpensive. Tourists visiting without a car and residents choosing to explore Atlanta via bus and train should use MARTA's website (www.itsmarta.com) or Google Maps' Public Transportation function (maps.google.com) to plan the trip, but each hike chapter also lists bus or train routes that will deliver you closest to the trailhead. Bicycles are welcome on MARTA trains and buses, and bringing a bike along can make these hikes even more easily accessible via public transit. Remember that the distance you'll walk or ride to the trailhead and back will increase the difficulty rating of any hike, so plan accordingly. If a hike's trailhead is more than a mile from the nearest public transport dropoff point, the entry will note that it is "not easily accessible" via public transportation.

CHAMPION & SENTINEL TREES

Each hike entry includes a list of "champion" and "sentinel" trees. Champion trees are recorded in registries across the country, based on a point system (trunk circumference [inches] + height [feet] + 1/4 average crown spread [feet] = total points). The tree (and sometimes there is more than one) of each species with the highest point total in a city, state, or the entire nation is crowned local, state, or national champion. The routes here contain many Atlanta champions and a few Georgia champions. Sentinels, for the purpose of this book, are notable trees that by virtue of their size, rarity, or some other characteristic present a memorable landmark. In a few cases the sentinel listed is not a tree but a grove of trees or a notable shrub or other plant. For each champion or sentinel, a description and GPS coordinates are provided. On trail maps, sentinels are denoted by tree icons; tree icons with halos indicate champions. Read more about champion and sentinel trees in *The Big Deal About Big Trees* (p. 15).

LAND MANAGEMENT

Each hike entry also includes the name of the agency that manages the land on which the hiking trail or trails are located. Contact information for each land management agency is listed in *Appendix C* at the back of the book.

On the trail at Davidson–Arabia Mountain Nature Preserve.

Champion tree *is a widely used term denoting the largest known living specimen or specimens of its species in a particular city, region, or country.*

THE BIG DEAL ABOUT BIG TREES

ATLANTA'S CHAMPION AND SENTINEL TREES

by Eli Dickerson

It was a cold, damp December day, and I was tromping through an old-growth section of forest at Emory University. My goal was to show a few fellow tree lovers a superb grove of the tallest beech trees in our region of Georgia. These silver-trunked giants reach more than 125 feet toward the heavens, making them "champion" or "sentinel" trees. Our small band of hikers was making slow progress across a steep north-facing slope.

Just as I was about to push our group onward toward the beech grove, my friend Jess exclaimed, "Hey, that looks like a nice-sized tulip tree up the hill!" Tulip trees are everywhere in Atlanta, but they are my favorite. I took a look and realized this was no ordinary tulip tree—it was huge! As I made my way towards it, the giant seemed to grow exponentially.

I pulled out my tape measure and touched the trunk. How big could it be? Would it be 14 feet in circumference, maybe 15 feet? I carefully took the measurement and gasped—it was 16 feet exactly. This was hands-down the largest tulip tree I'd seen in metro Atlanta, and I've measured over 250 of them. Its thick trunk rose 60 feet before sprouting any limbs. More measurements proved this tree to be over 150 feet tall. Its crown of branches had been damaged from storms in years past, but the tree was still alive and strong. How old was this majestic organism? Probably at least two centuries. I felt honored to be able to put it at the top of the list as Atlanta's new champion tulip tree.

Finding bigger trees and new champions is like being on a treasure hunt for enormous living organisms hidden in greenspaces and backyards throughout the city. Trees are nonpartisan and nondivisive. Atlantans love their trees and are proud of their neighborhoods. Atlanta's Champion Trees, the project I manage for Trees Atlanta, draws people into our hidden forests and helps celebrate the wonderful trees that are so much a part of it.

Champion tree is a widely used term denoting the largest known living specimen or specimens of its species in a particular city, region, or country. Jonah McDonald coined the term *sentinel tree,* and we both use it to describe a tree (or shrub) that is not necessarily a champion of its species but is worth noting because of its size, age, unusual features, or rarity. Not all hikes in this book have champion trees, but every single one has sentinel trees. As you walk through Atlanta's hidden forests, this guidebook will introduce you to many of the city's champion and sentinel trees, including:

- the state champion pin oak in Piedmont Park (12'6" circumference x 85' tall; p. 86)

- an Atlanta champion winged elm at the Outdoor Activity Center (8'7" circumference x 125' tall, p. 100)

- the oldest dated tree in Atlanta, a white oak in Deep Dene Park (12'5" circumference and approximately 240 years old; p. 75)

The sheer size of many champion and sentinel trees will make your jaw drop. Some stand taller than a 16-story building. In the leafless canopy of winter, you will strain to see the highest twig of these deciduous giants.

Other champion and sentinel trees noted in this book may be easily overlooked by an untrained eye. What is tall or large for a dogwood will be small for a hickory; don't assume that old equals large. Some of the biggest trees in Atlanta are oaks that grow extremely fast, adding up to six inches of girth in a single growing season! As you explore these hidden forests, you'll become more familiar with tree diversity in Atlanta. Please note also that precisely because the sentinel and champion trees identified here are some of the biggest and oldest of their species, they are more likely to die or fall. If you find that one of them has met its demise, please report it to Trees Atlanta (www.treesatlanta.org) or post a comment at www.hikingatlanta.com, the companion website to this book. Finally, here are a few tips for finding your own big trees.

To recognize a potential champion tree:

- Know how large each species grows. Remember, what is considered big for each species is relative. Get familiar with the current Atlanta Champion Tree list at www.treesatlanta.org, so you can assess the possibility that a tree might be a champion.

- Practice measuring trees. The easiest measurement is circumference. First, measure 4.5 feet up from the base of the trunk. At that height, measure the distance around the trunk in inches. Measuring height and crown spread can be a bit trickier, but the Eastern Native Tree Society (www.nativetreesociety. org) and Georgia Forestry Commission (www.gfc.state.ga.us) provide great resources to help you learn how.

To recognize an old tree:

- Note the number of limbs. Many older trees have few limbs in their crown. Limbs are often high up and are very stout.

- Calculate the "gnarliness factor." Many very old trees (centuries old) will have a contorted crown of thick, twisted limbs. Imagine what 300 years of weather events have done to these ancients!

- Look for balding bark. Many species, especially tulip trees, demonstrate a balding of their bark. Tree bark continues to grow throughout the lifespan of a tree, and many shed it as they grow older.

BIRDS YOU DON'T WANT TO MISS

ATLANTA'S RESIDENT AND MIGRATORY BIRDS

by B.E. Sajor for the Atlanta Audubon Society

When hiking in metro Atlanta, the sights and sounds of urban life are often just a footstep away. And yet...what is that bird song coming from the treetops? Was that a sparrow that flew into the brush? Look at all those ducks on the pond! Many local birdwatchers find that getting tuned into the local birdlife can make the unnatural world fade away.

In Atlanta, birds can be appreciated all year. In December 2012, when the Atlanta Audubon Society revived a metro-area Christmas Bird Count after nearly a 40-year hiatus, the participating birders—game despite a bitterly cold winter day—reported a combined total of 84 species. At any time of year, on any hike in the Atlanta area, you can be pretty sure of some remarkable bird sightings—even if they're views of familiar birds too often taken for granted. Many birds can be viewed with the naked eye, but to see the amazing details of birds' feather patterns, bills, behaviors, and other characteristics, we recommend carrying a pair of binoculars.

To help hikers focus on the wealth of intown birdlife, the Atlanta Audubon Society polled some of our regular field trip leaders and local experts. We asked them to suggest a few bird species hikers are likely to find on some of the trails included in this book. We limited suggestions to places where Atlanta Audubon tends to organize bird walks—18 of the hikes listed here—but similar habitats yield similar birds, so keep that in mind as you sample or methodically work through the 60 hikes described in this book.

Two of the hikes annotated— Kennesaw Mountain and Cochran Shoals in the Chattahoochee River National Recreation Area— are Important Bird Areas or IBAs. In the birding world, places that provide habitat considered key to the feeding and breeding of one or more species of birds are designated IBAs. These sites are part of a worldwide initiative striving to ensure the survival of bird populations.

Female pileated woodpecker.

Some of the species listed are common birds; others may seem exotic to the casual birder. We included all of them, hoping hikers will find it an appealing challenge to locate the birds listed. In fact, the pursuit of a specific species may take you back to a site to find it.

We also had to account for the fact that many birds don't stay put all year, which makes some hiking spots especially interesting to birdwatchers during certain seasons. Kennesaw Mountain, for example, is recognized as a phenomenal place to see warblers in the springtime as they migrate through Atlanta from Central and South America to breeding grounds in Georgia or much farther north. In the fall, these birds do a reverse migration equally interesting to birdwatchers, even though many of the warblers are no longer wearing their finest feathers. But that fact makes them only that much more challenging to identify.

Birds tend to be most active at dawn and dusk, and many do stay in Atlanta all year. But birds—bless their rapidly beating hearts—do not necessarily cooperate with even the most experienced birder. Consequently, no bird sighting is guaranteed. Rather, any sighting might be viewed as a gift, a precious glimpse into the parallel universe that our avian friends occupy. To help you explore that universe, we've noted birds you might see all year as well as those you're likely to see only in the winter, spring, summer, or fall. Because of Atlanta's often mild winters, we gave special attention to species and locations that may match up nicely during the coldest months of the year when wildlife seems scarce. Keep in mind, however, that because of ever-changing weather patterns and other natural phenomena, the seasons that birds recognize don't always fit precisely with our calendar. Throughout the year, please use our suggested species list as a guide, and definitely let us know about any unusual sightings at any time.

But why bother birdwatching at all? The March/April 2013 issue of *Audubon*, the national society's magazine, attempts to answer the question, "Why do birds matter?" Several answers are given, but perhaps the most notable is that birds are a barometer of the health of our environment. An abundance of birds and a good diversity of species speak of a well-conserved habitat, and the reverse is also true. When I first started birding nearly 25 years ago, seeing a loggerhead shrike on a metro Atlanta outing was fairly commonplace. Now this once abundant, endemic bird has declined dramatically in North America—by 72 percent since 1967. I don't remember the last time I saw one in the Atlanta area, and the loss causes me to feel poorer than I was years ago, despite the many species that remain to be seen.

So birds can help us monitor our local environment, but do they really enrich us in other ways as well? As you hike Atlanta's trails, consider the value added by birds' calls, colors, and activity. Keep an eye out for little birds bathing in a puddle. Look up and watch hawks catch the air currents and soar above you. Like many of us, you may find yourself immeasurably moved by birdlife. And if you'd like to know what you can do to help protect birds and their habitats, please contact the Atlanta Audubon Society.

Regardless of whether you take up the cause of birds, we wish you many enjoyable days of hiking metro Atlanta, and we can't help but wish for you some wonderful bird sightings along the trails.

INSIDE THE PERIMETER

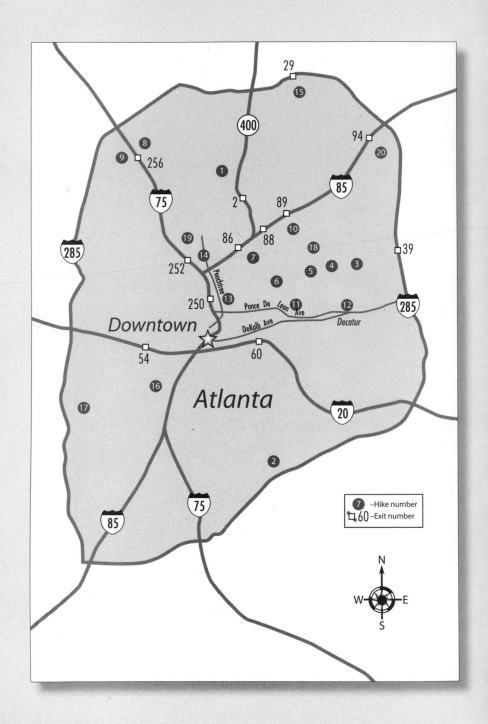

INSIDE THE PERIMETER

❶ Blue Heron Nature Preserve
❷ Constitution Lakes Park

South Fork of Peachtree Creek Greenspaces
❸ Clyde Shepherd Nature Preserve
❹ South Peachtree Creek Trail
❺ Hahn Woods & Lullwater Preserve
❻ Herbert Taylor Park
❼ Morningside Nature Preserve

Chattahoochee River National Recreation Area
❽ East Palisades
❾ West Palisades

❿ Elwyn John Wildlife Sanctuary
⓫ Frazer Forest & Deep Dene Park
⓬ Glenlake Park & Decatur Cemetery

The Beltline
⓭ Piedmont Park & Eastside Beltline Trail
⓮ Tanyard Creek Park & Northside Beltline Trail

⓯ Murphey Candler Park
⓰ Outdoor Activity Center
⓱ Cascade Springs Nature Preserve
⓲ W.D. Thompson Park
⓳ Atlanta Memorial Park
⓴ Mercer University Nature Trail

BLUE HERON NATURE PRESERVE

This small nature preserve is situated in a densely urban area of Atlanta and provides an escape from the hustle and bustle of the city. Nancy Creek, one of the larger tributaries of Peachtree Creek and the Chattahoochee River, flows through the middle of the Blue Heron Preserve and provides a good habitat for birds and other animals. The Preserve also owns the land surrounding Lake Emma, so be on the lookout for more trails being built in the area.

DISTANCE FROM DOWNTOWN • 9 MILES

BY CAR FROM PEACHTREE ROAD Drive north on Peachtree Road and turn left onto Roswell Road. Blue Heron Nature Preserve is on the right in 2 miles.

BY CAR FROM GA 400
Take exit 2 toward GA 141/ Lenox Road and go west on Lenox for 0.3 mile. Turn right onto Piedmont Road and go 0.6 mile before turning right onto Roswell Road. The Nature Preserve is on the right in 0.8 mile.

PUBLIC TRANSPORTATION Take the MARTA 5 bus to the corner of Roswell Road and Lakemoore Drive. The Nature Preserve is on this corner.

PARKING Paved parking lot; GPS N 33° 51.9747, W 84° 22.7939

ADDRESS 4055 Roswell Rd NE, Atlanta, GA 30342

HIKE DISTANCE 1-mile loop

Escape the hustle and bustle of the city in a forest habitat.

WHY THIS HIKE IS GREAT The forested area around Nancy Creek is an excellent wildlife habitat situated in the middle of Buckhead, providing a great respite from the busy city.

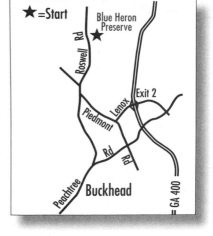

DIFFICULTY

Overall — Easy

Terrain — Hard-packed soil trails and a short section of sidewalk

Elevation change — Little or none

HOURS Dawn to dusk, year-round

DOGS Leashed dogs permitted

FACILITIES Toilets sometimes available in Beech Building if Blue Heron or Audubon staff are present

FEES & PERMITS None

LAND MANAGER Blue Heron Nature Preserve

SENTINEL TREES

Northern Red Oak · GPS N 33° 51.9953, W 84° 22.7866
- 12'12" circumference
- The largest tree in the nature preserve, this northern red oak welcomes you to the woods at the very beginning of the hike. The thick white stripes on its bark are one of the most prominent identifying marks of the species.

Water Oak · GPS N 33° 52.1119, W 84° 22.7824
- Double-trunk; larger trunk has 8'7" circumference
- Water oaks are the fastest growing species of oak in Georgia; this one was originally two separate trees before they grew together. Its size makes it easy to spot on the right side of the trail.

Green Ash · GPS N 33° 52.0990, W 84° 22.7811
- Triple-trunk; largest trunk has 7'8" circumference.
- Ash trees commonly grow on floodplains around creeks. This one is on the left side of the trail before you reach the boardwalk.

HIKE

Start the hike across the parking lot from the Beech Building and walk through the wood arbor next to the map and information kiosk.

Almost immediately beyond an outdoor classroom, pass the sentinel northern red oak on the right. In 0.1 mile, cross a bridge and follow the trail up onto a raised ridge. Go right on the trail along the ridge parallel to Nancy Creek, and walk 100 yards farther to where the trail meets Rickenbacker Drive. Go left on the road and cross the bridge over the creek, then make a left onto the trail at a map kiosk.

Following the trail, hike through a stand of river birches with very flaky bark. In less than 100 yards, pass a U.S. Geological Survey Stream Monitoring Station, then come to a junction with a trail on the right and a creek access trail on the left. To the right is the sentinel double-trunk water oak.

Continue on the main trail parallel to the creek, and you will pass the sentinel triple-trunk white ash on your left.

In less than 50 yards, go straight onto a boardwalk at the next junction, pass through a picnic pavilion, then reach a junction in a clearing near the community garden. Go left, pass between the birding information kiosk and the Nancy Creek Tunnel Cap and go right at the next junction.

In 100 yards, reach a map kiosk and the sidewalk along Roswell Road. Turn left and walk the sidewalk across a bridge over Nancy Creek (from the bridge, there is a view of a small waterfall) and continue on the sidewalk past the Nature Preserve driveway. Keep your eye out for turtles where the sidewalk skirts the pond.

Just before reaching Lakemoore Drive, turn left onto a crushed gravel path. At the spillway, cross the road to reach Mill Trail. Walk up the stone stairs and follow the path for 0.1 mile to an overlook above a small waterfall. Turn back and cross the road to rejoin the main trail. Go right, pass a pond overlook, and continue on the mulched path to the reach Rickenbacker Drive. Turn left on the road and walk 0.1 mile to a gravel path that leads downhill, back to the parking lot to finish the hike.

BIRDS TO LOOK FOR

BLUE HERON NATURE PRESERVE

All Year: belted kingfisher, Canada goose, great blue heron, mallard duck, red-headed woodpecker
Winter and Spring: cedar waxwing

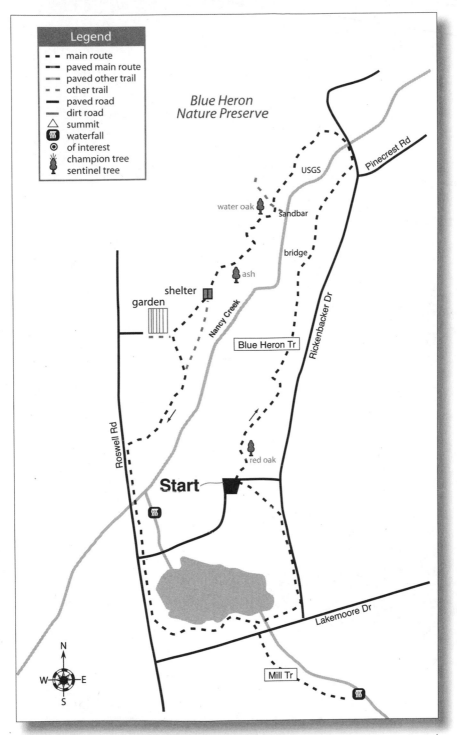

Nature now thrives at Constitution Lakes.

CONSTITUTION LAKES PARK

Situated in an industrial area of south DeKalb County, Constitution Lakes is one of DeKalb's newest parks and also one of its most secluded and beautiful. There is something for everyone here—a handicapped-accessible paved multi-use path, a boardwalk with views of the lake and wetlands, and a trail with many unusual pieces of "found object" artwork. Be on the lookout for new trails being built on the west side of the lakes. Having reclaimed what was once a brick mine and factory, nature now thrives at Constitution Lakes.

DISTANCE FROM DOWNTOWN ATLANTA • 6 MILES

BY CAR FROM I-20 From downtown Atlanta, take I-20 east to exit 60A for US 23S/Moreland Ave. Take the exit and turn onto Moreland. Continue 4.3 miles, then turn left at the traffic light at S. River Industrial Boulevard. Immediately on your right will be the entrance to Constitution Lakes Park. Drive 500 feet on the gravel road to the parking area near the information kiosk.

PUBLIC TRANSPORTATION Take the 4 Thomasville/Moreland Ave bus south on Moreland Avenue and get off at the intersection of Moreland and Constitution Road. Walk south on Moreland for just under 1 mile, making a left turn onto S River Industrial Boulevard, and then an immediate right at the sign for Constitution Lakes Park. The trailhead is 500 feet down a gravel road from the park entrance.

PARKING Gravel parking area just beyond the park entrance; GPS N 33° 40.9550, W 84° 20.6840

ADDRESS 1305 S. River Industrial Boulevard SE, Atlanta, GA 30315

HIKE DISTANCE 2.25-mile lollipop loop

WHY THIS HIKE IS GREAT The beauty of the lake and wetlands (which provide refuge for many animals and plants in this industrial area) and the unusual artwork on Doll's Head Trail are great reasons to spend an afternoon here.

DIFFICULTY

Overall — Easy

Terrain — First 0.5 mile is concrete path and boardwalks, other trails are hard-packed soil; some trails are narrow, others can be muddy after rain.

Elevation change — Very little

HOURS 7 am to sunset, year-round

DOGS Leashed dogs permitted

FACILITIES Portable toilets in parking lot; information kiosks along concrete path and boardwalk

FEES & PERMITS None

LAND MANAGER DeKalb County Parks & Recreation

SENTINEL TREES

Willow Oak – GPS N 33° 40.8299, W 84° 20.1515
- 9'6" circumference
- This willow oak growing at the water's edge is one of the larger trees in this park. Willow oaks like wet areas and are easily identified by their long, skinny leaves.

City Champion Willow Oak – GPS N 33° 40.8932, W 84° 20.1958
- 16'2" circumference, 119' tall, 122' crown spread (344 champion points)
- This park is mostly very young forest, but that doesn't mean there aren't a few large (and possibly old) trees here as well. This one stands rooted on a mound of earth in the middle of the Doll's Head Trail section of the park and just happens to be the second largest willow oak known in Atlanta. The largest is a whopping 2 feet bigger around and sits behind a small home in Avondale Estates, where it shades three houses.

BIRDS TO LOOK FOR

CONSTITUTION LAKES PARK

Winter & Spring: cedar waxwing
Summer: green heron, yellow-crowned night heron
Fall: great egret, osprey

Water Oak & Sweetgum – GPS N 33° 40.8992, W 84° 20.7127

- 9'7" and 9'9" circumferences, respectively
- About 30 feet to the right of the new trail on the west side of the lake, these two mature hardwood trees are growing so close together that they intertwine. Despite the fact that they are different species, they are almost exactly the same size.

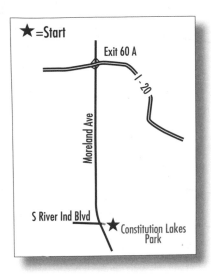

HIKE

Begin your hike at the information kiosk where the concrete multi-use path begins. Walk past the motor vehicle barrier and continue on the multi-use path for 0.5 mile until you reach the boardwalk next to the lake. As you walk along the multi-use path, you'll pass an information sign about Native Americans next to the second bench you see. This sign introduces you to Soapstone Ridge, of which you'll have a good view shortly. The next set of benches is paired with another information sign about early settlers. The forest surrounding the multi-use path is a young forest containing trees common to bottomlands—red maple, loblolly pine, box elder, willow and water oak, and an occasional beech and redbud. Don't get confused by the small trails to the left off the path; these simply lead into the surrounding neighborhoods.

At the boardwalk, you'll pass a stately willow oak on your right. Walk straight ahead onto the boardwalk, and stop to look at the view from the octagon platform. The lake and wetlands were created when a brick mine and factory closed and the mine crater filled with water; that was when the land began to go back to nature. This park is a great reminder that industrial degradation does not always end in ugliness. Nevertheless, you'll probably see some trash on the boardwalk—you can help by picking up and carrying out any bottles or cans you see lying around. You might also see anglers on the boardwalk.

After taking in the view from the octagon, turn right and walk to the end of the boardwalk, where you have another view of the wetlands. Walk quietly and you may see some turtles sunning themselves on a log in warm weather.

When you're ready, backtrack and turn right before leaving the boardwalk. As you walk down this section, look beyond the lake and you'll see Soapstone Ridge, a major geological formation just south of the South River valley you're walking through now. The ridge is named for the soapstone that Native Americans used to make bowls. Civil War ruins and Native American artifacts have been found on the ridge.

Continue straight where the boardwalk ends and walk along the dirt path surrounded by tall grasses and vines that make the trail feel a little like a tunnel. River cane, a native bamboo species, grows along the trail on your right. You'll emerge from this section of the trail at a junction with the Doll's Head Trail on your right. If you continue straight, you'll end up paralleling the railroad tracks on a trail that's not officially part of the park but leads to a railroad trestle over the South River. Turn right onto Doll's Head Trail. Pass an old well and trough. Pass a spur that leads to the railroad trail on the left, then reach a junction with Doll's Head Trail loop.

Turn left to start the Doll's Head loop. Doll's Head Trail is created by hikers and Constitution Lakes volunteers recycling trash found in the park to create "found object" art installations. Sometimes creepy, sometimes beautiful, sometimes thought-provoking, always intriguing, this trail is one of a kind. Follow the small winding path past small art projects.

After 0.1 mile, reach a junction at the other end of Doll's Head Trail. Go left, then right to make a small loop. After the right turn where a proposed boardwalk will connect this trail with others on the west side of the lake, pass the first sentinel willow oak on the left at the water's edge.

Back at the Doll's Head Trail junction, stay left and pass more art installations, along with bricks and tiles that hikers can write notes on. At a large willow oak (on the left) and a pile of bricks with writing on them (on the right), stand with your back to the willow oak on your left and you'll see another majestic champion willow oak—the second largest in Atlanta.

Continue on the trail to the junction with the other half of the loop. Stay left to reach the main trail and turn left to return to the boardwalk. From the boardwalk, a right turn onto the multi-use path with take you back to the parking area.

INSIDER TIP

NEW DEVELOPMENTS AT CONSTITUTION LAKES PARK

A major new trail project is underway at Constitution Lakes that will connect the east and west sides of the lakes. A recently built soft-surface trail will soon lead to an observation platform and a boardwalk crossing the lake near the South River; the boardwalk will connect with the small loop trail on the south end of Doll's Head Trail. When these western trails are complete, the recommended loop will start on the soft-surface trail and end via the paved multi-use path.

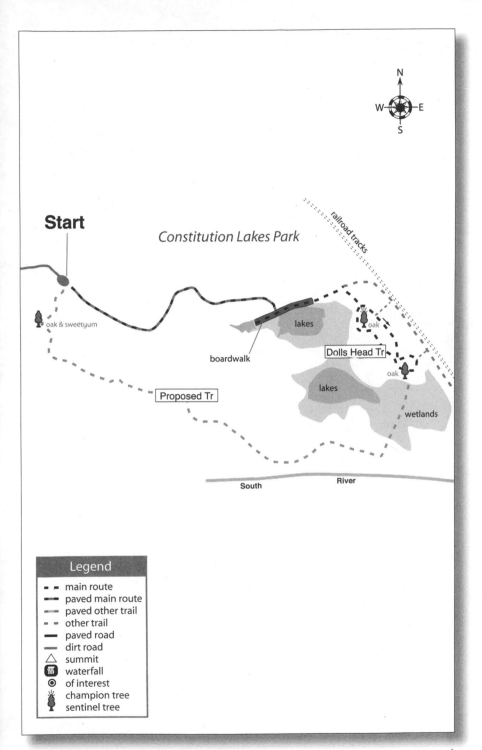

Start

Constitution Lakes Park

railroad tracks

oak & sweetgum

lakes

boardwalk

oak

Dolls Head Tr

Proposed Tr

lakes

oak

wetlands

South   River

Legend

- - main route
— paved main route
— paved other trail
- - other trail
— paved road
— dirt road
△ summit
🌊 waterfall
◉ of interest
🌲 champion tree
🌲 sentinel tree

Early in the year the calls of spring peepers, leopard frogs, and bull frogs create an amazing orchestral sound that's really something to hear.

CLYDE SHEPHERD NATURE PRESERVE

SOUTH FORK OF PEACHTREE CREEK GREENSPACES

Formerly known as South Peachtree Creek Nature Preserve, this park owes its existence to the creek itself. Local city and county governments prohibit new construction on floodplains, so the bottomlands of the South Fork of Peachtree Creek have been preserved (thanks to a generous donor and a group of dedicated volunteers) as a natural area of forested trails. With over 30 acres of land and more than 2 miles of trails, including this 1.5-mile loop, it is home to many species of frogs and birds. Early in the year the calls of spring peepers, leopard frogs, and bullfrogs create an amazing orchestral sound. It's really something to hear, and at times it can be deafening.

DISTANCE FROM DOWNTOWN ATLANTA • 9 MILES

BY CAR FROM I-85 Take North Druid Hills exit east toward Decatur. After approximately 3 miles, go right on US 78 at North DeKalb Mall. Pass the mall and continue uphill past a QuikTrip gas station. At the intersection of Highway 78, North Decatur Road, and Medlock Road, take a right on Medlock and drive 0.5 mile to an elementary school. Turn right on Wood Trail Lane. Go through one stop sign and continue another 0.2 mile to the Clyde Shepherd Nature Preserve entrance.

BY CAR FROM I-285 Take US 78 (Stone Mountain Freeway exit) west toward Decatur until you reach its intersection with North Decatur Road and Medlock Road. Then follow directions above.

PUBLIC TRANSPORTATION Both the 75 Tucker bus and 123 N. DeKalb Mall/Belvedere bus will drop you off on Scott Boulevard, 0.8 mile from the entrance to the Clyde Shepherd Nature Preservo.

PARKING Street parking on Pine Bluff Drive; GPS N 33° 48.3665, W 84° 17.0411

ADDRESS 2580 Pine Bluff Drive, Decatur, GA 30033

HIKE DISTANCE 1.5-mile loop

WHY THIS HIKE IS GREAT Diverse ecological zones feature a wide variety of wildlife, particularly birds and frogs, with several wildlife-viewing platforms.

DIFFICULTY
Overall — Easy

Terrain — Hard-packed trails and boardwalks; some overgrowth of brush in summer

Elevation change — Almost completely flat, with only two small hills on Forest Trail

HOURS Dawn to dusk, year-round

DOGS Leashed dogs permitted

FACILITIES No toilets; small covered pavilion, wildlife-viewing platform, two outdoor classrooms

FEES & PERMITS None

LAND MANAGER Clyde Shepherd Nature Preserve

SENTINEL TREES
Tulip Tree – GPS N 33°48.3500, W 84°16.9660
- 120' tall, 10.5' circumference
- Notice the bark at the base of this tree. Though mature tulip trees are known for deeply grooved bark, the outer bark of this tree has been flaking off at the base as is common among older tulip trees. Note the interesting pattern left on the smoother inner bark. This tree is sometimes called tulip poplar, yellow poplar, or just plain poplar, though is not a true poplar at all.

BIRDS TO LOOK FOR

CLYDE SHEPHERD NATURE PRESERVE

Spring: Baltimore oriole, blackpoll warbler, blue-winged teal, hooded warbler, northern parula warbler, orchard oriole, rose-breasted grosbeak, wood duck, wood thrush, yellow warbler

Hardwood Grove –
GPS N 33°48.3666, W 84°16.9500

- A sign along the Forest Trail tells about the ecology of mature forests. Stop here and marvel at this grove of relic hardwoods—including **tulip tree, sweetgum, beech, northern red oak,** and **red maple**—at the edge of the preserve. The large diagonal tree trunk on your right seems to be alive until you look up and see that the canopy has been cut off. It's been dead for years, though it still provides excellent wildlife habitat.

Loblolly Pine Grove – GPS N 33°48.4000, W 84°16.9166

- Loblolly was originally a word that meant a thick mush or gruel. It later came to describe a marsh. Though we usually think of pines as mountaintop trees, loblolly pines—as their name indicates—thrive in the lowlands. This grove of loblolly pines grows on a floodplain, just on the edge of wetlands.

HIKE

Begin your hike on Forest Trail, at the right (south) entrance of the preserve. This trail winds through a mature hardwood forest (the first sentinel grove of this hike) where you'll see large beech, sweetgum, oak, and tulip trees. Find the sentinel tulip tree 15 feet to your right as you pass the first large tree (a water oak) on the left side of the trail.

The route undulates over small rises before reaching the first trail junction at Raccoon Rock. Turn left at the junction and walk 50 feet to an outdoor classroom and an intersection with Pine Trail. You'll be standing in the middle of the second sentinel grove—a stand of loblolly pine that has little underbrush and a soft cushion of pine straw under your feet.

Continue straight on Beaver Pond Trail over a boardwalk until you reach a small bridge and junction with a spur trail to a bird blind. The bird blind is a nice side trip, as it allows you to stand closer to the center of the wetlands than at any other viewing location. To continue from the intersection of Beaver Pond Trail and the Bird Blind spur, cross the bridge and walk along the boardwalk, which offers another view of the wetlands at a repurposed lifeguard chair. At the end of the boardwalk you'll reach an elevated viewing platform with excellent views of the entire wetlands.

Passing the viewing platform, you'll see the preserve's tool shed ahead and a bird garden on your left. Look for a short wooden footbridge and turn right to begin Outer Loop Trail. This trail winds through an area that until recently was covered with invasive English ivy. Volunteers have put in a great deal of work to rid this section of the ivy. Look around you and you'll see Chinese privet, another invasive plant.

At the northwest corner of the preserve property (Pine Bluff Drive will be on your left) the trail turns right over a makeshift boardwalk, across a small wooden footbridge, to a T-junction with Creek Trail. Turn right (turning left leads to private property) to continue your hike parallel to the South Fork of Peachtree Creek. On your left there are several short access spurs leading to sandy beaches along the creek. The first spur is the easiest way to get to the creek and a flat, sandy beach for stream exploration. Because this section of creek is adjacent to a mall and a highway, you'll see some trash in the area. Consider helping the park volunteers by packing some out with you.

Continuing on Creek Trail, just before entering a bamboo grove you'll see two small trails to your right. The first is unmaintained and leads to an old bird blind. The second takes you to the edge of what in some seasons is a pond and in other seasons is wetland meadow. Across the wetlands you can see the bird blind and viewing platforms you visited on Beaver Pond Trail.

Walking on Creek Trail through the bamboo grove, you'll pass a junction with Pine Trail. Beyond this junction, continue to a junction with Meadow Trail. Turn right (continuing straight will walk you out of the preserve and into the parking lot of an auto dealership) and follow Meadow Trail through a smaller wetland area and onto a long boardwalk. Pass a boardwalk intersection with Pine Trail and continue left to where the boardwalk ends.

Continue straight to rejoin Forest Trail and exit the preserve, or follow a small footpath to the right that leads up and over Indian Rock and Raccoon Rock before meeting the intersection of Forest Trail and Beaver Bond Trail at the outdoor classroom. From here, follow either trail to exit the preserve and end the hike.

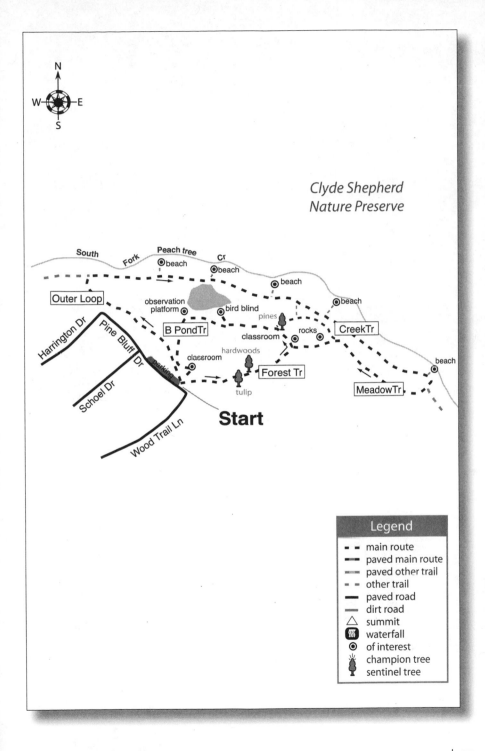

Clyde Shepherd
Nature Preserve

This bridge provides a view of the old Decatur Waterworks ruins, which until recently were covered with invasive plant growth and graffiti.

SOUTH PEACHTREE CREEK TRAIL

SOUTH FORK OF PEACHTREE CREEK GREENSPACES

The PATH Foundation's South Peachtree Creek Trail provides access to a web of trails and three parks. Between Ira Melton, Mason Mill, and Medlock Parks, at the confluence of Burnt Fork and South Fork of Peachtree Creeks, is a lush forest with several miles of interconnecting footpaths. The development of the multi-use trail has included a reclamation of the ruins of the old Decatur Waterworks, which until recently was covered in invasive plant growth and graffiti. Now it is an interesting historical artifact and work of urban art.

DISTANCE FROM DOWNTOWN ATLANTA • 8 MILES

BY CAR FROM I-85 Take exit 89 and drive south on North Druid Hills Road for 3.2 miles before turning right onto Willivee Drive. In 0.7 mile turn left onto Scott Circle. Trailhead parking is on your left just before passing the baseball fields.

BY CAR FROM I-285 Take exit 39A toward Atlanta/Decatur and merge onto US 78. Merge with US 29, then continue 0.5 mile before making a right onto Medlock Road at a 6-way intersection. In 0.5 mile turn left onto Lancelot Drive, then right on Scott Circle. Medlock Park will be on your right, and trailhead parking is near the baseball fields.

BY CAR FROM PONCE DE LEON AVENUE Take Ponce de Leon Avenue east toward Decatur and turn left onto Scott Boulevard. In 2 miles, turn left onto Medlock Road at a 6-way intersection. In 0.5 mile turn left onto Lancelot Drive, then right on Scott Circle. Medlock Park will be on your right, and trailhead parking is near the baseball fields.

PUBLIC TRANSPORTATION The 19, 36, and 123 MARTA buses will all let you off within 1 mile of the trailhead. This hike can also be accessed from the Ira Melton Park entrance on Desmond Drive and from Mason Mill Park on McConnell Drive.

PARKING Paved parking area near baseball fields;
GPS N 33° 48.1697, W 84° 17.7786

ADDRESS 981 Scott Circle, Decatur, GA 30033

HIKE DISTANCE 3.25-mile loop

WHY THIS HIKE IS GREAT This greenspace provides a very diverse hiking environment, including an extended boardwalk, a paved multi-use path, creeks, a historic waterworks site, and peaceful forests.

DIFFICULTY

Overall — Easy

Terrain — The multi-use PATH Foundation trail for which this hike is named is 1.5 miles long; other trails on this route are hard-packed soil; there is one rockhopping creek crossing.

Elevation change — Steep but short ascents and descents

HOURS Dawn to dusk, year-round

DOGS Leashed dogs permitted

FACILITIES Toilets near baseball fields

FEES & PERMITS None

LAND MANAGER PATH Foundation

SENTINEL TREES

City Champion River Birch – GPS N 33° 48.3144, W 84° 17.8158
- 9' circumference, 71.9' tall, 50.2' crown spread (181.4 champion points)
- On the right just before the boardwalk, this is the first large multi-trunked tree at the creek's edge. You can tell the species by its dark bark which becomes flaky with age; river birch prefer to be near water and thrive on creek banks.

Hophornbeam Grove – GPS N 33° 48.3770, W 84° 17.9780
- Hophornbeam is a small-to-medium-sized native identified by brownish bark that shreds in vertical strips along the trunk. In summer, look for characteristic finely (doubly) serrated simple leaves.

BIRDS TO LOOK FOR

SOUTH PEACHTREE CREEK TRAIL

All Year: brown thrasher, Eastern bluebird, mourning dove, red-bellied woodpecker, red-shouldered hawk

Mockernut Hickory –
GPS N 33° 48.3924, W 84° 18.0060

- 6" circumference
- This tree's oddly-shaped lower trunk (likely from storm damage early in its life) stands out among the taller straight-trunked trees. *Tomentosa* ("hairy") is the species name—an apt description of the leaves, which upon examination reveal their fuzzy nature.

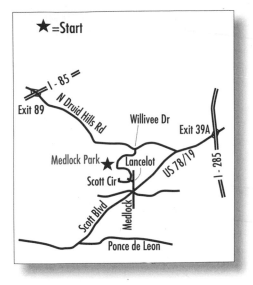

HIKE

This route includes both a paved multi-use trail that is very easy to follow and hard-packed soil trails that have many twists, turns, and junctions. The hike generally keeps to the largest trails, so when in doubt, choose the more well-worn trail.

The PATH Foundation multi-use trail begins at the far left side of the parking lot, to the left of the baseball fields. Walk 0.2 mile to reach a boardwalk. Just before the boardwalk to the right is a small dirt path leading to the creek. The first multi-trunked tree you come to at the creek's edge is a city champion river birch. Continue onto the boardwalk and pass a community garden before crossing Willivee Road at the crosswalk.

The boardwalk continues on the other side of the road. Cross a bridge over the creek in 0.1 mile, then look to your left to see the sentinel hophornbeam grove. You'll reach a boardwalk exit on the right in another 0.1 mile. Across from the exit, next to a small observation deck with a bench, is the sentinel mockernut hickory. After looking at the sentinel tree, turn right to leave the boardwalk and hike steeply uphill. Go right on the steepest trail until it levels off and arrives at a junction with a red-blazed trail. Go left and walk 0.1 mile to another junction with the boardwalk. Instead of entering the boardwalk continue straight, down the hill, and turn left under the bridge.

Walk 0.1 mile on the wide yellow-blazed trail as it follows the creek and curves right. Just before dipping down to a low point, turn right onto a smaller trail and hike uphill, staying on this trail past a junction with a yellow blaze and another junction with a red blaze. In 0.1 mile, reach another junction with the yellow-blazed trail on your left. Continue straight (parallel with the multi-use path) another 10 yards, then turn left and hike downhill toward the creek.

Parallel the creek for 0.1 mile, then stay to the left as the main trail curves away from the water to the right, crests a small hump, and enters a young pine forest. Stay left as the trail crests another slightly larger hump and reaches a junction with two trails that run along the ridge. Turn left on the trail just over the crest of the hump and walk 50 yards to a sandy beach on the creek's edge where you can hop across on cinder blocks and concrete-filled tires to enter Ira Melton Park.

After crossing the creek, turn right and stay right (along the creek's edge) at the first two junctions. To your right are views of the old Decatur Waterworks.

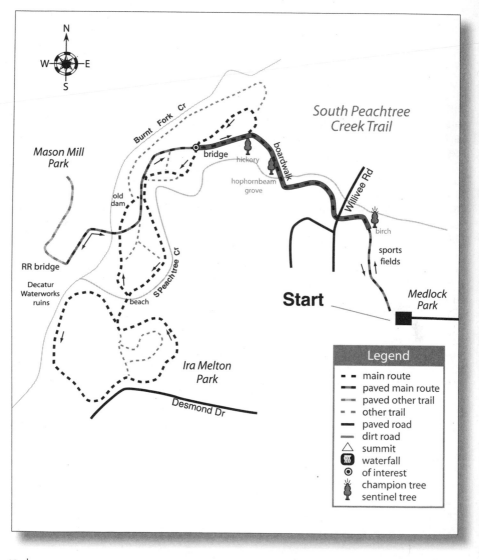

Stay on the main trail (generally parallel to the creek) past several small trail junctions until the trail curves left at the entrance to Ira Melton Park (at Desmond Drive). Turn left and parallel the road for 0.1 mile before reaching a junction with a trail on the left. Continue straight and the trail soon ascends just enough out of the floodplain to allow larger trees to grow. You will walk through an area with larger hardwood trees for 0.2 mile before reaching a double junction at which you should stay right twice. This takes you back, past a junction on your left, to the creek crossing where you entered Ira Melton Park.

Cross the creek, turn left on the trail, and stay left at the next two junctions before coming to an open area near two large beech trees (one of them has a small rope swing attached to its branches). Just after the beech trees stay left and arrive at the paved multi-use path.

A side trip to the old Decatur Waterworks and railroad bridge is a worthwhile 0.3-mile walk. Cross the bridge over Burnt Fork Creek to the left and follow the path past the waterworks ruins on your left. The path winds up to the railroad bridge where you'll be treated to views of the graffiti-covered ruins.

Backtrack to the bridge over Burnt Fork Creek, then turn left onto the soft-surface trail immediately beyond it. This leads past a stone bench to an old dam—a nice place to soak your feet and have a snack. Then hike steeply uphill to the right, following blue blazes, to reach the multi-use path.

Turn left on the paved trail and follow it for 0.75 mile back to the parking area in Medlock Park to end the hike.

Hahn Woods & Lullwater Preserve

South Fork of Peachtree Creek Greenspaces

Beautiful Lullwater Preserve sits in the center of the Emory University campus. At Lullwater you'll see people out for a stroll or jog, but Hahn Woods is the place for hikers. A narrow trail along the banks South Fork of Peachtree Creek connects the two greenspaces; the entire area is reserved for Emory faculty, staff, and students only. Along the trail are city champion trees, the ruins of two mills, and a suspension bridge.

Distance from Downtown Atlanta • 7 miles

By car from I-85 Take exit 89 and turn right onto North Druid Hills Road. Drive for 1.6 miles, then turn right onto Lavista Road. In 0.5 mile turn left onto Houston Mill Road. Hahn Woods is on the right in 0.9 mile, just after crossing the bridge over the South Fork of Peachtree Creek.

Public Transportation Take the MARTA 6 Emory bus to the corner of Clifton Road and Houston Mill Road. Walk 0.4 mile north on Houston Mill Road to Hahn Woods.

Parking Circular gravel parking area; GPS N 33° 48.2276, W 84° 19.3840

Address 866 Houston Mill Road, Atlanta, GA 30329

Hike Distance 2.5-mile figure-8 loop

Why this hike is great The Hahn Woods route into Lullwater Preserve adds adventure to what is typically a simple stroll in the park.

Crossing the suspension bridge in Lullwater Preserve.

DIFFICULTY

Overall — Easy

Terrain — Hard-packed soil trails and one short section of pavement; can be overgrown and muddy in summer; the last leg includes a suspension bridge and a sewer pipe that also serves as a bridge; trails in Lullwater Preserve are either paved or crushed gravel.

Elevation change — After a short downhill from the Hahn Woods parking circle, this hike has almost no elevation change.

HOURS

November through March: 8 am to 5 pm
April through October: 8 am to 7 pm

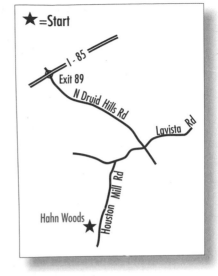

DOGS Leashed dogs permitted

FACILITIES No toilets; map kiosk at entrance, suspension bridge in Lullwater Preserve

FEES & PERMITS Visitation restricted to Emory University faculty, staff, and students.

LAND MANAGER Emory University

SENTINEL TREES

City Champion Loblolly Pine – GPS N 33° 48.2000, W 84° 19.0500
- 10'11" circumference, 117' tall, 48' crown spread (260 champion points)
- Loblolly pine trees are the most common pines in Atlanta, but specimens this large are rare; this is one of only four known loblollies in the city with a circumference of over 10 feet. Though not extremely tall, it racks up enough big tree points to have a place on the city champion tree list.

River Birch – GPS N 33° 48.1166, W 84° 18.9166
- 6' circumference, 60' tall
- A water-loving species, river birch are restricted to the banks of perennial (year-round) streams and are easily identified by their peeling and shredding bark. Crossing the suspension bridge over the South Fork of Peachtree Creek, you can see what this tree looks like from 30 feet up.

City Champion Ironwood – GPS N 33° 48.1500, W 84° 18.9500
- 3'8" circumference, 51' tall, 38' crown spread (105 champion points)
- Ironwoods prefer moist woods and creekside habitats, both of which are

present throughout Lullwater Preserve and Hahn Woods. They resemble beech trees but have undulating, almost wavy bark. If you tap gently on the trunk you can tell how it gets its name—it has the densest wood in the forest. This particular tree is the largest known specimen within the perimeter.

HIKE

Start your hike on the trail to the left of the map kiosk. This 0.1-mile trail curves back to the other side of the parking circle, then turns right and switchbacks down the hill. Take the left fork when the trail splits, then turn right to parallel the creek. Pass a concrete overlook platform on your left and continue straight.

Go left to stay next to the creek when the trail splits again. Hike 0.1 mile, crossing a small footbridge and climbing two small sets of stairs to reach the bottom of the longer staircase that leads up the parking area to the right. Continue straight on the broken and uneven concrete path, then walk under the Houston Mill Road bridge to reach the historic Houston Mill (which is now a waterfall).

Continue straight along the path that parallels the creek for 0.5 mile before reaching the suspension bridge. Keep an eye out for mountain laurel growing next to the trail. When the trail splits you can take either fork, as they reconnect shortly; the city champion loblolly pine can be found on the right fork, just before the trails reconnect.

Walk under the suspension bridge and continue another 0.1 mile to a waterfall pouring over a small dam near where the Lullwater Preserve paved path begins. Go straight onto the pavement and walk 0.25 mile along the lakeshore to the next junction.

Go straight onto the gravel path and continue to circle the lake. In 0.3 mile, stay straight at another junction then keep an eye out for steps leading down onto the floodplain on your left in less than 75 yards. Follow this mulched trail down the steps and through a privet thicket for 0.3 mile until you return to the junction near the waterfall at the edge of the lake. From here, the loop route that follows can be fairly overgrown in the summer months. If you prefer, you can retrace your steps and return to the Hahn Woods parking area.

INSIDER TIP

PROTECTED GREENSPACES FOR OBSERVATION AND RESEARCH

Hahn Woods and Lullwater are true forest research preserves, set aside by Emory University for preservation and study. Together they comprise one of the last old-growth forests in metro Atlanta. Stewards of the preserve are working hard to heal and restore overused areas. If you walk here, resist the urge to explore on any side trails you may see. Be sure to stay on the beaten path to avoid disturbing rare and fragile plants.

Rejoin the paved path and continue straight on the pavement, up the hill. Above you to your left is the Emory University President's residence. In 0.1 mile, turn right onto the suspension bridge and cross the creek. Below on your left on the near side of the creek is the sentinel river birch. Turn left on the other side of the bridge and walk 0.25 mile to another trail junction. Midway between the bridge and this junction is the city champion ironwood on the left next to the creek. When you reach the junction, turn left and walk downhill.

In 100 yards cross a feeder creek on a sewage pipe, which can be slippery even in dry weather. Walk another 0.25 mile, pass the old Houston Mill ruin, then reach Houston Mill Road. Carefully cross the road (there is no crosswalk) and turn left, crossing the bridge and turning right into the Hahn Woods parking area to finish your hike.

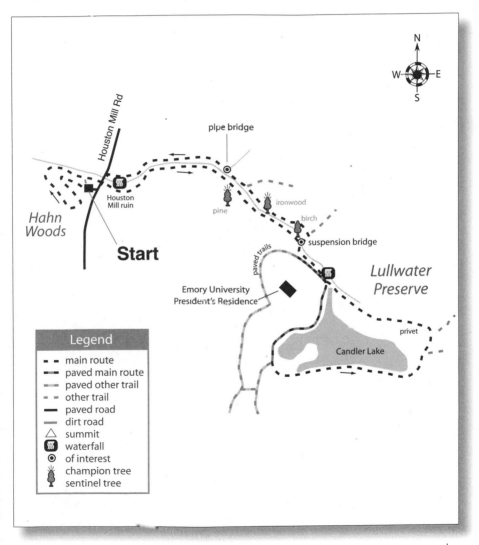

HERBERT TAYLOR PARK

SOUTH FORK OF PEACHTREE CREEK GREENSPACES

This contiguous park and nature preserve duo in the Morningside neighborhood is a real gem of a place to walk; the northern half of the loop described here is in Herbert Taylor Park, and the southern half is in Daniel Johnson Nature Preserve. You'll follow Rock Creek and the South Fork of Peachtree Creek through stands of old-growth hardwoods, hanging vines of muscadine grapes, and fields of jewelweed. Herons and ducks are often seen along the creeks. The trails are well-maintained, thanks to many neighbors who care for the park.

DISTANCE FROM DOWNTOWN ATLANTA • 6 MILES

BY CAR FROM I-85 Take exit 89 and go south on North Druid Hills Road. In less than half a mile turn right onto Briarcliff Road. Continue 1.8 miles and turn right on Johnson Road, across from the Kroger Shopping Center. Drive half a mile and turn left onto Pasadena Avenue. In one block you'll come to the intersection with Beech Valley Road and the entrance to Herbert Taylor Park at an information kiosk.

PUBLIC TRANSPORTATION The 16 Noble Bus will drop you off on Johnson Road, 0.2 mile from the entrance to Herbert Taylor Park.

PARKING Park on the street along Beech Valley Road; GPS N 33° 47.9183, W 84° 20.5572

ADDRESS 1385 Beech Valley Road NE, Atlanta, GA 30306

It's hard to find a section of intown forest as beautiful as this one.

HIKE DISTANCE 1.5-mile loop

WHY THIS HIKE IS GREAT Trees and streams! This loop takes you though some of the largest and oldest stands of hardwoods in the city, and because the park is flanked by two streams, there are excellent opportunities for wading. It's hard to find a section of intown forest as beautiful as this one.

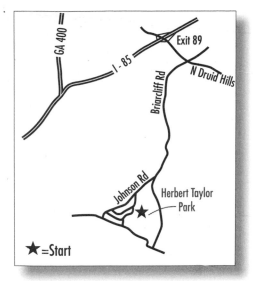

DIFFICULTY

Overall — Easy

Terrain — Hard-packed soil and gravel trails; several short footbridges

Elevation change — Most trails are flat, with a few short uphills in the southeast corner of the park.

HOURS 6 am to sunset, year-round

DOGS Leashed dogs permitted

FACILITIES No toilets; trail maps posted throughout the park

FEES & PERMITS None

LAND MANAGER City of Atlanta Office of Parks

SENTINEL TREES

City Champion Black Cherry – GPS N 33° 47.9500, W 84° 20.4166
- 7'7" circumference, 111' tall, 44' crown spread (212 champion points)
- This is one of only a few cherry trees located in the park. Cherry wood is prized for its strong and beautiful reddish color; most large old cherry trees were logged years ago for lumber. This one is likely at least 100 years old and somehow survived both the ax and the chainsaw.

Shumard Oak – GPS N 33° 47.8859, W 84° 20.5080
- 10'6" circumference, 132' tall
- Shumard oaks prefer lowlands where their roots can be near a steady water source. The ones in this park grow taller than any others documented in the area, up to 14 stories—almost twice as tall as the trees in an average front yard.

City Champion Silver Maple – GPS N 33° 47.9833, W 84° 20.4333
- 13'6" circumference, 102' tall, 91' crown spread (286 champion points)
- Silver maples are restricted almost entirely to floodplains. Their close relatives, red maples, can be found in both wet and drier areas. This giant tree has been a city champion since 2005.

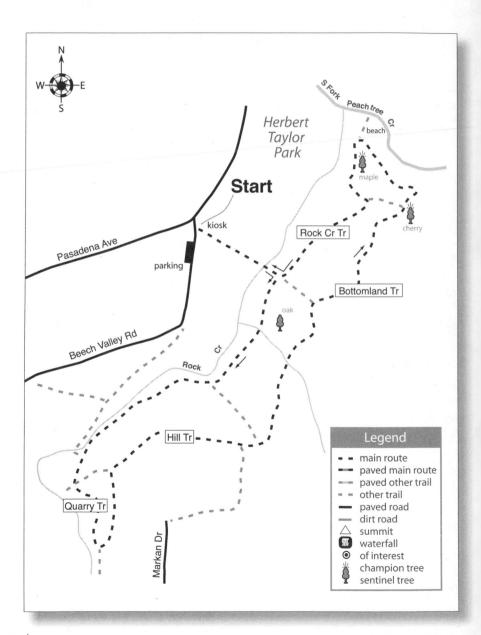

Hike

Start your hike at the information kiosk at the corner of Beech Valley Road and Pasadena Avenue. Follow the trail into the park through tall grasses and over a bridge across Rock Creek. Approach quietly, as herons are known to fish in this section of the creek. On the far side of the bridge, turn right onto Rock Creek Trail, a wide gravel path. As you follow Rock Creek Trail to its conclusion, notice the old-growth trees around you. You will also pass an unusual mound on your left. Some people speculate on a possible connection to Native American mounds in other areas of the Southeast, but there is no evidence to prove this hypothesis. On the mound is the sentinel shumard oak.

At the end of Rock Creek Trail you'll reach a small bench next to a particularly scenic section of Rock Creek. Turn left onto Quarry Trail toward an old quarry with steep walls. After only about 50 feet, take the trail fork curving to the left to climb to the rim of the quarry (the trail continuing straight leads to private property). Once on the quarry rim, follow the small path between the fence and rim until Hill Trail branches off to the right.

Continue on Hill Trail past several small spur trails until the path reaches a flat bottomland area and the trail name changes, though the trail itself stays the same. On Bottomland Trail, you'll pass the mound again on your left and cross several small wooden footbridges. After the second footbridge you'll be close to the South Fork of Peachtree Creek, and you'll reach several small paths branching off from Bottomland Trail. Here you'll find the Atlanta champion black cherry tree on your right, across from a side trail on the left. Stay on the main trail until it reaches Rock Creek Trail. Make a right to visit a sandy beach along the creek. At the entrance to the beach area, look up to see some healthy muscadine vines. This is also a nice area for taking off your shoes and wading through the water.

After spending some time at the creek, walk back along Rock Creek Trail, passing the city champion silver maple tree with its small granite marker on the left. Beyond the silver maple, continue hiking the same trail until you reach the bridge over Rock Creek. Turn right and cross the bridge to exit the park and end the hike.

Mountain wildflowers flourish in one of the largest nature preserves inside the perimeter.

MORNINGSIDE NATURE PRESERVE

SOUTH FORK OF PEACHTREE CREEK GREENSPACES

For a long time Morningside Nature Preserve was known only to those in the neighborhood who had found its unassuming entrance on a small local street. Then the City of Atlanta built a parking area and main entrance to the greenspace which opened a whole new area to hikers. The preserve now contains a long stairway through the forest canopy, a suspension bridge over the South Fork of Peachtree Creek, and many trails through piedmont hills. Trillium and other flowers flourish in this preserve.

DISTANCE FROM DOWNTOWN ATLANTA • 6 MILES

BY CAR FROM I-85 NORTH Take exit 86 for GA 13N toward Buford Highway, then the Monroe Drive exit toward Piedmont Road South. Turn left onto Monroe Drive, which becomes Piedmont Circle. At the light turn right onto Piedmont Road and then immediately left onto Cheshire Bridge Road. Turn right on Lenox Road in 1 mile. Cross the railroad tracks, and the Morningside Nature Preserve parking area is clearly marked on your right.

BY CAR FROM I-85 SOUTH Take exit 88 and go south on Cheshire Bridge Road. After a half mile turn left onto Woodland Avenue. Make the first right onto Lenox Road, cross the railroad tracks, and the parking area is clearly marked on your right.

PUBLIC TRANSPORTATION Take either the MARTA 27 or 30 bus to the corner of Cheshire Bridge Road and Woodland Avenue, which is 0.4 mile from the parking area and trailhead.

PARKING Gravel parking area; GPS N 33° 48.585′, W 84° 21.1274

ADDRESS 2020 Lenox Road NE, Atlanta, GA 30306

HIKE DISTANCE 2-mile double loop

WHY THIS HIKE IS GREAT This is one of the largest nature preserves inside the perimeter, and offers a high-level view of the forest canopy for free.

DIFFICULTY

Overall — Easy

Terrain — Hard-packed soil trails, boardwalks, stairs, and a suspension bridge

Elevation change — Hike starts with a short but steep climb and includes several other ascents and descents

HOURS 6 am to 11 pm, year-round

DOGS Leashed dogs permitted

FACILITIES No toilets; water fountain in the parking lot

FEES & PERMITS None

LAND MANAGER City of Atlanta Office of Parks

SENTINEL TREES

Black Willow – GPS N 33° 48.5025, W 84° 21.3296
- The largest of these trees measures 2'7" in circumference
- The small trees on the left side of the trail are sentinels not for their size but for their importance in the ecosystem. Willows grow in low places near creeks and other water sources, providing shade and habitat for birds and animals who need water, and their roots help prevent erosion.

Sweetgum – GPS N 33° 48.4606, W 84° 21.5086
- 9'6" circumference
- Often seen as an annoyance because of the many spiky seedpods they drop, sweetgum trees thrive in the Atlanta climate. This one is on the right just before a trail junction, surrounded by invasive English ivy. Identify sweetgum trees by their seedpods and their star-shaped leaves.

White Oak – GPS N 33° 48.4373, W 84° 21.4502
- 10'6" circumference
- Probably the largest tree in the preserve, but not by much. Most of the large hardwoods near it are similar age and size, but white oaks grow fast and this one is about a foot bigger around than the others. Find it 15 feet off the trail on the right as you ascend the ridge; look for flaky bark plates high up on its trunk.

HIKE

Neighbors of the Morningside Nature Preserve access this park primarily through its Wellbourne Drive entrance, which is situated in the middle of a thriving residential neighborhood. However, the route in this book uses the newer entrance in front of a Georgia Power substation adjacent to a CSX railroad track.

From the parking area looking up the hill, you'll see a trail paralleling the woods' edge on the left side of the cleared area beneath the power lines. The trail climbs the hill under tree cover. Begin your hike at the information kiosk next to the parking area. Follow the trail into the woods, crossing a wooden footbridge. Continue up the hill and pass a couple of side trails on your right. When you see a Private Property sign and a small trail marker with an arrow, bear right and continue up the hill until you come to a wooden fence where the trail turns right, through the cleared area beneath the power lines. The view down the hill is rather industrial, but look next to the trail for wildflowers and blackberries.

As you re-enter the forest, you'll come to a wooden stairway leading down off the hill. Check out the forest canopy as you descend the stairs; you'll see maple, oak, tulip, and linden trees among others. This view is equal in height to the canopy tour at the Atlanta Botanical Gardens.

Below the stairs, continue along a boardwalk through the South Fork of Peachtree Creek floodplain. When the boardwalk ends, turn left to begin walking parallel to the creek through a narrow clearing surrounded by forest. Immediately after turning left you'll pass the sentinel black willow trees on the left with branches hanging over the trail.

In less than 0.25 mile you'll arrive at a large suspension bridge spanning the creek. Cross the bridge and take a look. Like so many inner-city streams, despite the efforts of local volunteers, this one is sometimes choked with kudzu and discarded junk. But the South Fork of Peachtree Creek's sandy banks and serpentine path are still beautiful, especially when viewed from above.

Beyond the bridge, reach a 4-way trail junction. Turn right to follow the path parallel to the creek. Cross a bridge, then pass a trail leading up the hill to your left. This trail connects to a loop trail slightly smaller than the one this route uses. You will soon pass another trail leading uphill to the left. Continue straight on, and just beyond this junction you'll see a path to the right. This short spur leads to a large flat sandy area along the creek—a good place to take off your shoes and dip your toes in the water if you're so inclined.

Continuing on the main trail, you'll notice a change in the terrain as it turns away from the creek; as you leave its primary floodplain there are larger boulders and trees.

In another 0.25 mile you'll pass the sentinel sweetgum tree on the right just before a junction with a trail leading up the hill to the left. If you continue straight, you'll come to the Wellbourne Drive trailhead. Turn left here and begin climbing the ridge.

Immediately you'll notice piedmont terrain and flora—a reminder that Atlanta rests in the foothills of the Appalachians. Trillium and other mountain wildflowers can be found here.

After hiking uphill for 0.1 mile, just before the trail curves to the right, you'll pass the sentinel white oak about 15 feet off the trail to the right. Continue hiking up and over the ridge for 0.2 mile until you reach a junction with a trail on the left at a partially demolished footbridge. Before carefully crossing the footbridge, look to your right. In the spring, Japanese azaleas light up the woods with their bright colors. We're used to seeing these non-native flowering bushes in city lawns, but it's a special treat to come upon such stunning color in the deep green of the forest.

The trail ascends again, and you'll soon come to a junction with a trail on the left that descends the ridge and takes you back to the suspension bridge. Instead, continue up the ridge until the forest ends and you find yourself under power lines. Turn right and follow a gravel access road to the top of the ridge where you'll be treated (on a clear day) to a view of the "pencil tower"—the Bank of America Plaza, the tallest building in Atlanta and the ninth tallest in the United States.

Turn around and descend the steep access road beneath the power lines. At the end of this trail, bear left and you'll be at the suspension bridge. Cross the bridge and hike back toward the parking area.

When you arrive at the start of the boardwalk, look to the left for a small trail that continues to parallel the creek. This trail can be muddy after rain and overgrown in the height of the summer, so follow the boardwalk and stairs back to your car if you choose. Otherwise, take the trail to the left. You'll pass a field with a radio tower and utility building and then ascend out of the creek floodplain parallel to the CSX railroad track. As you emerge from the forest you'll see the electrical substation and parking area to your right. Follow the railroad tracks to Lenox Road, turn right, and you'll be back at the parking area to end the hike.

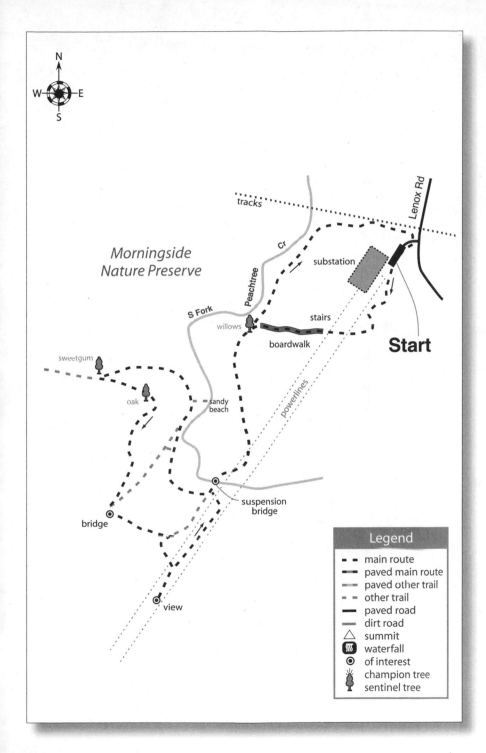

N
W E
S

Morningside
Nature Preserve

tracks

Lenox Rd

Cr

Peachtree

substation

S Fork

willows

stairs

boardwalk

Start

sweetgum

oak

sandy
beach

powerlines

suspension
bridge

bridge

view

Legend

- - - main route
— — paved main route
— — paved other trail
- - other trail
— paved road
— dirt road
△ summit
🌀 waterfall
◉ of interest
🎄 champion tree
🎄 sentinel tree

*Wildlife abounds and plant life is diverse—
a hike not to miss.*

EAST PALISADES

CHATTAHOOCHEE RIVER NATIONAL RECREATION AREA

Of all the hikes within Atlanta's perimeter, East Palisades Trail is the most similar to trails in the Appalachian Mountains. This route passes through many ecological zones, including a remarkable bamboo grove. Wildlife abounds and plant life is diverse, including several city champion trees—it's a hike not to miss.

DISTANCE FROM DOWNTOWN ATLANTA • 11 MILES

BY CAR FROM I-75 Take exit 256 and drive east on Mt. Paran Road for 0.4 mile. Turn left at the first light onto Harris Trail and go 0.6 mile before taking the next left onto Whitewater Creek Road. Just before Whitewater Creek Road curves left, turn right into the park entrance and drive 0.3 mile on a gravel road to the parking area.

PUBLIC TRANSPORTATION *This hike is not easily accessible by public transportation.* Take the MARTA 12 Howell Mill/Cumberland bus to the corner of Northside Parkway and Mt. Paran Road. From here, the trailhead is 1.3 mile.

PARKING Gravel parking area; GPS N 33° 52.6700, W 84° 26.5224

ADDRESS 4001 Whitewater Creek Road NW, Atlanta, GA 30327

HIKE DISTANCE 4.25-mile lollipop loop

WHY THIS HIKE IS GREAT There are not one but two fabulous destinations at the end of this beautiful walk beside the Chattahoochee River: a bamboo forest and a peaceful rocky overlook above the river.

DIFFICULTY

Overall— Moderate

Terrain— Hard-packed soil trails; can be muddy in wet weather

Elevation change— Several extended ascents and descents, some quite steep

HOURS Dawn to dusk, year-round

DOGS Leashed dogs permitted

FACILITIES No toilets; map signs at most trail junctions

FEES & PERMITS $3 daily park pass—cash only at on-site kiosk (kiosks are often out of service)—or $25 annual park pass which can be purchased online

LAND MANAGER Chattahoochee River National River Recreation Area

SENTINEL TREES AND PLANTS

City Champion River Birch – GPS N 33° 52.8876, W 84° 26.5669
- 8'5" circumference, 83.5' tall, 53.3' crown spread (199.3 champion points)
- River birch is the only birch commonly found in the metro area. It has bark that curls outward and must be near a permanent water source to survive. Among many big river birch in this park, this one may be the largest.

City Champion Pawpaw – GPS N 33° 53.1392, W 84° 26.5774
- 1'7" circumference, 36.5' tall, 11' crown spread (59.6 champion points)
- No other tree native to North America produces a fruit as large as the pawpaw. It often grows no higher than 15 or 20 feet but can produce a six-inch, kidney-shaped fruit said to taste like a blend of papaya, mango, banana, and pineapple.

Mountain Laurel – GPS N 33° 53.4510, W 84° 26.2614
- Though common to the North Georgia mountains, mountain laurel is not common in Atlanta. It likes acidic, rocky soils and steep slopes—exactly the habitat in the creek hollow at East Palisades. Visit in late spring, when the gorgeous pink and white flowers put on quite a show.

INSIDER TIP

CONNECTING EAST AND WEST PALISADES

Willing to do a little urban walking, rock scrambling, and off-trail exploration? If you are, you can connect *West Palisades* (p. 64) and this route to make an 8-mile loop. Overgrown social trails connect the East Palisades Whitewater Creek parking area to the Cobb Parkway Bridge and West Palisades parking area. Dog-walking trails along the river behind two apartment complexes connect the West Palisades trails to the Powers Ferry Road bridge. A riverside trail beyond Ray's on the River leads back into the East Palisades unit. Good luck, adventurers!

HIKE

From the parking area, start the hike on the trail next to the creek and cross the bridge. Turn left and cross another bridge.

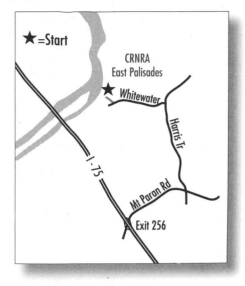

After 0.2 mile you'll cross a third bridge. In another 0.1 mile the city champion river birch is about 20 feet off the trail on your right, just beyond a large sycamore tree on the same side.

In 0.2 mile, cross a bridge over Charlie's Trapping Creek and turn left at the junction just after the bridge.

In 0.2 mile, just before the next junction, the city champion pawpaw tree is on your left at the water's edge, next to a wooden post. Turn left at the junction. In less than 75 yards turn right at a junction, hike up a steep hill, and turn right at a second junction. The trail winds uphill for the next 0.35 mile. Continue straight at a junction and map sign halfway up the hill. When you reach the ridgeline, the trail curves to the right. In 0.15 mile turn left at a junction, then stay left at two more successive junctions. The trail descends on a steep set of stairs to an overlook platform that provides nice views of the river.

Facing the overlook continue to the right, passing through a mountain laurel thicket. Turn left at two successive junctions and hike 0.25 mile downhill to a reach Cabin Creek. Cross a bridge and pass several large sentinel mountain laurels on the left. Stay left at a junction with a small trail on the right, then hop across a small creek and walk uphill for a few steps and turn left on a wider trail that used to be a forest road.

Continue straight at the next junction, then hike downhill to a bridge before reaching the foundation of an old building by the river's edge. Turn right and cross a bridge after 0.1 mile. In another 0.2 mile you'll reach an astonishing bamboo grove. The bamboo grows tall and thick and is an excellent place for photographs and exploration.

Continue past the bamboo grove for 0.1 mile, following the trail up the rocks to a natural overlook over the river. This is a great place to have lunch or a snack and is the turnaround point on this hike.

Return the way you came, passing the bamboo. At the old foundation, turn left on the old forest road. After the trail turns right and you hop across the small creek, you'll come to a junction with a board laid across Cabin Creek (if you reach the large wooden bridge, you've gone too far). Cross the creek to the small trail on the opposite bank and turn left to follow the creek into the hollow.

The small trail hugs the bank of the creek for 0.25 mile, then curves away from the creek to the right and uphill for 0.1 mile to reach a junction with the main trail. Turn left on this old roadbed and hike uphill. Turn right when the trail splits and hike uphill for another 100 yards until the trail reaches the gravel Indian Trail Road.

Turn right and walk along Indian Trail Road for 0.2 mile to reach Indian Trail parking area. Go straight through the parking area and continue on the trail next to the fee station and information kiosk.

In 0.15 mile you'll pass an old patio on your right, then go steeply downhill for 0.25 mile. Continue straight at the first junction, then turn right at the next. Cross a bridge and hike along Whitewater Creek for 0.1 mile back to the large bridge you crossed at the start. Cross the bridge and go left to reach the parking area and finish the hike.

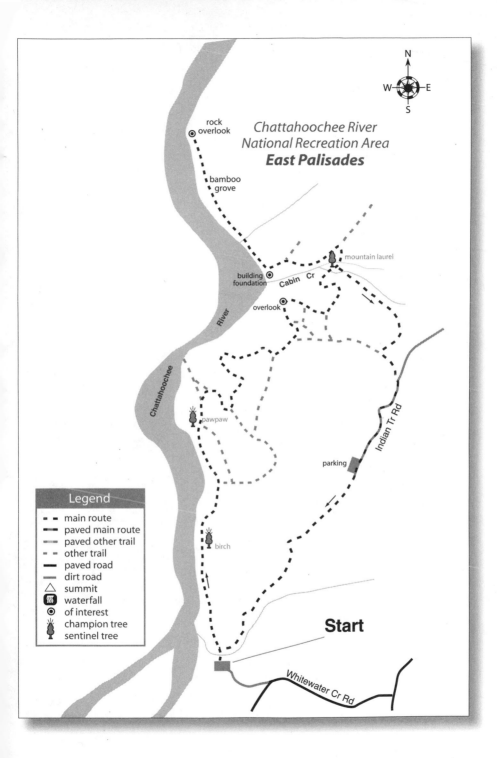

Chattahoochee River
National Recreation Area
East Palisades

Legend
- - - main route
- - - paved main route
- - - paved other trail
- - - other trail
--- paved road
--- dirt road
△ summit
♨ waterfall
◉ of interest
🌳 champion tree
🌳 sentinel tree

rock overlook
bamboo grove
mountain laurel
building foundation Cabin Cr
overlook
River
Chattahoochee
pawpaw
parking
Indian Tr Rd
birch
Start
Whitewater Cr Rd

WEST PALISADES

CHATTAHOOCHEE RIVER NATIONAL RECREATION AREA

On beautiful warm weekends, Atlantans flock to the West Palisades unit of the Chattahoochee National Recreation Area for hiking, swimming, and rafting. This trail includes a section of paved multi-use path, beautiful forest trails, and one of the best swimming holes the river has to offer. A famous way station for people "tubing the Hooch," the jumping rock and beach at the apex of this loop is teeming with people on summer afternoons. If you dare risk the cold waters of the Chattahoochee, bring your swimsuit on this hike.

DISTANCE FROM DOWNTOWN ATLANTA • 11 MILES

BY CAR FROM I-75 Take exit 256 for Mt. Paran Road and go west on Mt. Paran, then north on Northside Parkway. Continue 1 mile (Northside Parkway becomes Cobb Parkway), cross the bridge over the Chattahoochee, and make the first left at the sign "Paces Mill: Chattahoochee National Recreation Area." This road curves you around and under the Cobb Parkway bridge to reach the Paces Mill parking area.

PUBLIC TRANSPORTATION Take the MARTA 12 Howell Mill/Cumberland bus to the corner of Cobb Parkway and Paces Mill Road. The trailhead is less than a half mile from the bus stop.

PARKING Large paved parking area; GPS N 33° 52.2321, W 84° 27.2385

ADDRESS 4210 Cobb Parkway SE, Atlanta, GA 30339

HIKE DISTANCE 4.25-mile lollipop loop

On warm weekends, Atlantans flock to the river for hiking, swimming, and rafting.

HIKING ATLANTA'S HIDDEN FORESTS

WHY THIS HIKE IS GREAT This is an excellent wildflower hike and leads to one of the most popular sites along the Chattahoochee River—with a swimming hole, jumping rock, and swinging rope.

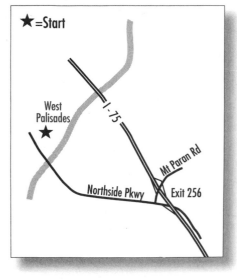

DIFFICULTY

Overall — Moderate

Terrain — Includes 0.5 mile of the paved Rottenwood Creek/Bob Callan multi-use trail; other trails are hard-packed soil and gravel

Elevation change — Several very steep ascents and descents

HOURS Dawn to dusk, year-round

DOGS Leashed dogs permitted

FACILITIES Toilets, water fountains, boat ramp, picnic area, maps at each trail junction

FEES & PERMITS $3 daily park pass—cash only at on-site kiosk (kiosks are often out of service)—or $25 annual park pass which can be purchased online

LAND MANAGER Chattahoochee River National River Recreation Area

SENTINEL TREES

Northern Red Oak – GPS N 33° 52.6702, W 84° 26.7706
- 11'0" circumference
- This large tree at the river's edge raises several interesting questions. Why is its base so thick while its crown is quite small? Is it significantly older than the others around it and was it damaged by winds or lightning, or is it a younger tree whose location near the river induced it to put on extra girth at its base? Either way, it's impressively large compared to its neighbors.

Northern Red Oaks – GPS N 33° 53.0199, W 84° 26.7667
- 9'4" and 8'11" circumferences, respectively
- These two northern red oaks are a good comparative study in tree growth. Though of similar age, the first of them is more gnarled and twisted, having probably taken a lightning hit earlier in its life. What other differences do you notice between these "twin" sentinels?

Loblolly Pine – GPS N 33° 53.3035, W 84° 26.6342

- 11'5" circumference
- One of the older loblolly pines on this section of the river, this specimen suffered significant fire damage at one time in its life. The scar remains, but the tree has healed itself and continues to grow straight, tall, and thick.

HIKE

Start your hike on the Rottenwood Creek Multi-Use Trail at the far end of the parking lot, next to a large grassy field. Walk on this path for 0.5 mile, under the I-75 bridge, to a footbridge over Rottenwood Creek. After crossing the bridge, turn right off the paved path onto a hard-packed soil trail that parallels the Chattahoochee River.

In 0.1 mile, pass a sentinel northern red oak on your right. Then, in 0.2 mile, reach a rock outcrop with a great view of the river. Continue past the outcrop for 0.1 mile to a junction. Turn left and hike uphill for 0.2 mile to another junction. Turn right and continue hiking uphill to a junction at the top of the ridge in 0.1 mile. Turn right.

Hike along the ridge for 0.4 miles, passing two small trails on the right. Fifty yards down the first of these two small trails are two sentinel northern red oaks. With the exception of this short diversion to see the sentinel trees, continue straight on the main path as it descends. Just as the trail becomes an asphalt path, turn right and hike downhill to a junction with a small trail on the left in 0.1 mile. Go straight, then hike uphill for 0.1 mile to another junction. Turn right onto the wide gravel roadbed. The roadbed becomes paved as it begins a steep descent.

Pass two trail junctions on your way down the hill. When the roadbed splits, stay left to reach the bathhouse and a trail junction. Turn right in front of the bathhouse, and pass a bench and the beach across from the swimming hole and jumping rock. In the summer, this area is often packed with people floating the river in boats and tubes.

Continue hiking with the river on your left. At a junction in 100 yards, stay straight on the single-track path parallel to the river. Almost immediately, you'll come to the sentinel loblolly pine with fire damage on its far side. Continue hiking for 0.1 mile to a junction. Bear left, cross a bridge and short boardwalk, then turn right at the next junction. Look out for trillium and buckeye in this area.

After crossing another bridge, turn left at a junction and hike uphill for 0.1 mile to the roadbed trail. Turn left and continue hiking uphill, back the way you originally came.

In 0.1 mile, turn left and hike downhill. In 0.2 mile, turn left. In 0.4 mile, turn left and hike downhill (if you go straight here, the trail is exceedingly steep and leads you to the Rottenwood Creek Multi-Use Trail).

In 0.1 mile, reach another junction. Turn right and hike 0.3 mile back to a junction with the Rottenwood Creek Multi-Use Trail. Turn right onto the paved path, cross the bridge to your right, and hike 0.5 mile back to the parking area.

HIKING ATLANTA'S HIDDEN FORESTS

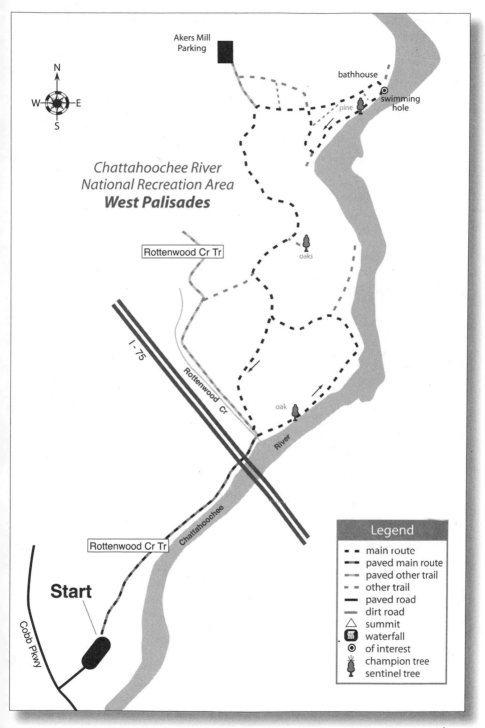

Akers Mill
Parking

bathhouse

N
W—E
S

swimming
hole

pine

Chattahoochee River
National Recreation Area
West Palisades

Rottenwood Cr Tr

oaks

I-75

Rottenwood Cr

oak

River

Chattahoochee

Rottenwood Cr Tr

Start

Cobb Pkwy

Legend

- - - main route
━ ━ paved main route
━━ paved other trail
- - other trail
━━ paved road
━━ dirt road
△ summit
♨ waterfall
◉ of interest
♣ champion tree
♣ sentinel tree

ELWYN JOHN WILDLIFE SANCTUARY

Well-known in its own neighborhood for years, Elwyn John has only recently begun to receive care and maintenance. Trails are being blazed, wooden benches and structures built, and invasive plants cleared. This wildlife sanctuary is home to many old trees, with one particularly impressive tulip tree to be found on an off-trail excursion. Expect trails to be less than obvious, often overgrown, and without signage. With each visit you'll find more developed trails that facilitate human enjoyment of this greenspace.

DISTANCE FROM DOWNTOWN ATLANTA • 8 MILES

BY CAR FROM I-85 Take exit 89 for GA 42 and go east onto North Druid Hills Road. Drive 0.5 mile, then turn right at a traffic light onto Kittredge Park Road. Follow this road for 0.2 miles and park near the swimming pool and baseball field.

PUBLIC TRANSPORTATION Take the 16 Noble MARTA bus to the corner of North Druid Hills Road and Briarcliff Road. Walk 0.2 mile east on North Druid Hills Road and turn right onto Kittredge Park Road. Walk 0.2 mile to the parking lot and trailhead next to the swimming pool and baseball field.

PARKING Paved parking lot next to swimming pool and baseball field; GPS N 33° 49.4761, W 84° 19.7029

This sentinel beech shades a great resting spot.

ADDRESS 1400 Kittredge Park Road NE, Atlanta, GA 30329

HIKE DISTANCE 1-mile figure-8 loop

WHY THIS HIKE IS GREAT For intown explorers used to a manicured landscape, Elwyn John can be a thrilling place to visit. Trail blazing is just beginning, and the old-growth trees and quiet creekside setting will excite any nature-lover.

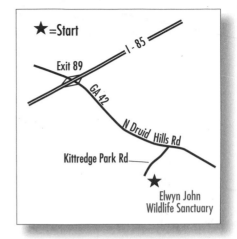

DIFFICULTY

Overall — Easy

Terrain — Trails are hard-packed soil; not all are well maintained, and one section of this hike follows a flagged route that is not on a trail; may be overgrown and muddy

Elevation change — Rolling hills and several short ascents and descents

HOURS 7 am to sunset, year-round

DOGS Leashed dogs permitted

FACILITIES No toilets; observation platform and several benches

FEES & PERMITS None

LAND MANAGER City of Atlanta Office of Parks

SENTINEL TREES

White Oak – GPS N 33° 49.4480, W 84° 19.5270
- 9'3" circumference
- One of several large oaks in this area of the park, this one is close enough to the trail that you can get a feel for its size and age. The trees here have been protected from logging by the ravine's steep banks.

Beech – GPS N 33° 49.4440, W 84° 19.5190
- 9'4" circumference
- Both this beech and the one farther into the ravine are old and majestic trees. Their smooth gray bark makes them stand out in the forest—and often invites pocket knife graffiti as can be seen on this tree.

Tulip Tree – GPS N 33° 49.3680, W 84° 19.6560

- 11'4" circumference
- The most impressive tree in this wildlife sanctuary is notable for its size, age, and bent shape. Though no official trail leads to it, it is often visited by hikers.

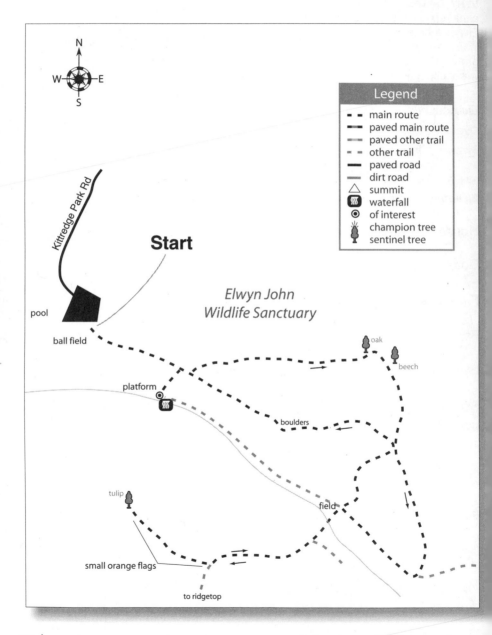

HIKE

Park near the swimming pool and begin by walking downhill past the barrier on the paved service road. Pass the baseball field, and in 0.1 mile take the path on your right to visit a small observation platform where you can view the creek and a small cascade. Returning to the service road, continue straight across it and hike up the hill on a smaller trail.

You'll pass two benches and a picnic area before the trail turns right at a third bench in 0.1 mile. Look into the ravine on your left and you'll see several large trees — tulip tree, white oak, and beech. Also on your left just before the third bench is the sentinel white oak. Behind the bench is the sentinel beech.

After viewing the sentinel trees, follow the trail to the right and hike 0.1 mile to another junction. Turn left and hike another 0.1 mile (past another bench) to a T-intersection where you'll make a right. The trail ends at an open field in 0.1 mile.

The next part of the hike is an out-and-back spur that leads to the impressive sentinel tulip tree. The trails on this spur are not fully developed, but the destination makes it worth the trip. Crude steps lead down to the creek on your left. Cross the creek and walk a couple of dozen yards on the small path uphill through English ivy to reach an old roadbed. Turn right and walk uphill, ignoring the Private Property sign on a tree — it dates to a time before the land was converted to public use. In 100 yards the path curves to the left. Just before the Beware of the Dog sign, look for small orange flags on the right leading to the sentinel tulip tree.

Follow the flags and turn right off the main path, making your way down and up a small gully; then the route skirts the ridge about 100 yards to the enormous and bent sentinel tulip tree. After viewing the tree, retrace your steps to the roadbed. If you'd like to extend your hike, turn right and hike uphill on the old road to the top of the ridge and a nice grove of trees and flowering bushes. To return to the main trail, hike back down the hill and re-cross the creek to continue your hike.

On the other side of the creek, standing with the field on your left, go straight on the trail in front of you. It switchbacks uphill past a bench to a junction in 0.1 mile. Turn left and hike 100 yards to where the trail ends at a cluster of boulders. Just beyond the boulders is an old paved circular driveway. Hike along the pavement to the right, and you'll reach the parking lot in 0.15 miles to end the hike.

A treasure reminiscent of the majesty of great piedmont forests before Atlanta was settled.

FRAZER FOREST & DEEP DENE PARK

If you love the old-growth timber of the Joyce Kilmer Memorial Forest in North Carolina, you'll find Atlanta's closest equivalent in these two small adjoining forests. Tulip trees and oaks in Frazer Forest and Deep Dene stretch their branches skyward on massive ancient trunks. Hidden in the eastern corner of the city, this area is a treasure reminiscent of the majesty of great piedmont forests before Atlanta was settled.

DISTANCE FROM DOWNTOWN ATLANTA • 11 MILES

BY CAR FROM PONCE DE LEON AVENUE From Peachtree Street, travel east on Ponce de Leon. One block after passing Clifton Road, the turn for the Fernbank Museum of Natural History, make a hard right onto South Ponce de Leon and then an immediate left into the Frazer Center driveway.

BY CAR FROM DECATUR Travel west on Ponce de Leon Avenue. One block after passing Lakeshore Drive, make a left onto South Ponce de Leon and then an immediate left into the Frazer Center driveway. Follow the driveway past the garden and up the hill to the main parking area.

PUBLIC TRANSPORTATION Take the 2 Ponce de Leon/Moreland bus east on Ponce de Leon Avenue and get off in Dellwood Park, just after passing Clifton Road. Walk across the park to the Frazer Center entrance and up the driveway to the trailhead in the main parking area.

PARKING Paved parking area near the main Frazer Center buildings; GPS N 33° 46.100, W 84° 19.698

ADDRESS 1815 South Ponce de Leon Avenue, Atlanta, GA 30307

HIKE DISTANCE 2.5-mile figure-8 loop

WHY THIS HIKE IS GREAT You'll see one of the oldest and best preserved areas of old-growth hardwood in metro Atlanta, with particularly large tulip trees.

DIFFICULTY

Overall — Easy

Terrain — Mostly wide, hard-packed soil trails with some bridges, stone stairs, and asphalt

Elevation change — Regularly undulating trails and several stone stairs and creek crossings; no extended uphill climbs

HOURS 6 am to 8 pm, year-round

DOGS Leashed dogs permitted

FACILITIES No toilets; maps and information signs are posted throughout Deep Dene Park

FEES & PERMITS None

LAND MANAGER DeKalb County Parks and Frazer Center

SENTINEL TREES

Twin Tulip Trees – GPS N 33° 46.2140, W 84° 19.7580
- 13'10" circumference and 9'9" circumference
- These "twin" trees grow just beside the trail where it makes a sharp right turn. They both have thick trunks and soar over 140 feet into the sky; being rooted in a low part of the forest and the constant water source of the creek have helped them grow big and tall. From the trail, look at the twin on the right. At 13 feet circumference, it's big—but would you believe the largest tulip poplar in Atlanta is another 3 feet larger in circumference and 20 feet taller?

INSIDER TIP

ALTERNATE STARTS FOR FRAZER FOREST & DEEP DENE PARK

You can begin this hike from many different points on the route. The south entrance to the Frazer Center (at Ridgewood Road) is often closed, but can sometimes be used as an alternate entrance to the property. Park along Lakeshore Drive between Cator Woolford Gardens and the west end of Deep Dene Park, or along North Ponce de Leon Avenue on the east end. Want to extend your walk beyond the described route? Walk west on Ponce de Leon to reach several other (less forested) sections of the Olmsted Linear Parks and connections to Candler Park and Freedom Park.

White Oak –
GPS N 33° 46.3269, W 84° 19.2246

- 12'5" circumference
- Look for this large tree on the right as you walk down stone steps toward a bridge. This is the largest white oak in Deep Dene Park and is also the oldest dated tree in Atlanta. Researchers from Fernbank Museum and Kennesaw State University cored the tree to retrieve a sample of wood in which they counted approximately 240 annual growth rings in the spring of 2011. This tree predates the signing of the Declaration of Independence.

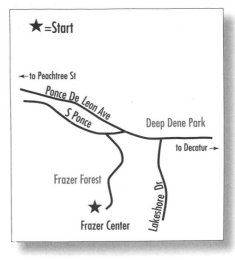

City Champion Redbud – GPS N 33° 46.2363, W 84° 19.5701

- 3'6" circumference, 27.5' tall, 36' crown spread (78.5 champion points)
- One of the oldest redbud trees in Atlanta, you'll find this triple-trunk tree directly across from a bridge in the Cator Woolford Gardens. Redbud trees, a small species, are one of the more prevalent understory trees in Atlanta. It wouldn't be surprising if Atlanta celebrated the Redbud Festival alongside the famous Dogwood Festival. If you visit this tree in the spring when it's in bloom, sample its flowers—they are delicious.

HIKE

Enter the Frazer Forest trails at a small trailhead on the west side of the main parking lot, across from the Frazer Center buildings. On your left is a sign listing the forest's hours and asking owners to leash and clean up after their dogs. On your right is a black chain-link fence.

This forest is laced with trails so there are many possible hiking routes; the one described here will wind you past some of the most beautiful sights. If at any time you feel you are off the recommended path, staying generally to the right (northeast) should lead you to the Frazer Center driveway near the Cator Woolford Gardens and the next leg of the hike.

Walk 50 feet down the path until you come to the first trail junction. Turn left here and walk another 50 feet to the next junction where you'll turn left again. Pass a large tulip tree on your right and step over a log across the trail. You'll come to another junction with a small trail on the left. Turn right and continue down the hill.

The next junction is at the edge of a ravine. To the left the trail leads to Harold Avenue and a rope swing surrounded by bamboo. Turn right here to follow the edge of the ravine.

When the main trail turns right away from the ravine, turn left on the smaller trail and hike downhill. At the bottom, turn right at a 4-way trail junction toward a fallen tree with a large root ball. Continue along the streambed. Just before the enormous sentinel double-trunked tulip tree, follow the trail to the right along the creek, then left and up a short hill before turning left onto the main trail at the top.

In less than 100 yards you'll reach a small parking area and the Frazer Center driveway. Turn left onto the asphalt and continue downhill, watching out for vehicles. In 150 feet you'll see stone steps on the right (often covered with leaves and easy to miss) that lead to a small hemlock grove. Hemlock trees in Georgia are being destroyed by the invasive woolly adelgid bug, so this secluded grove may someday be a relic of the great hemlock forests of the southern Appalachians.

Past the stone steps, turn right into the Cator Woolford Gardens parking area and follow the path into the gardens on your left. Though there are many paths in the garden, maintain your current general direction toward the rear of the gardens (away from the buildings), then turn right after a small stone bridge. Follow the stone streambed on your right, cross another bridge, and continue left past the bench, then left across another bridge so the creek is on your right. Follow the trail next to the creek, then immediately turn left, up the hill and out of the garden.

At the top of the hill you'll pass a chain across the path and emerge onto the sidewalk along Lakeshore Drive. Turn left on Lakeshore and cross Ponce de Leon Avenue at the crosswalk to enter the west end of Deep Dene Park.

Re-enter the woods on a mulched trail next to a map of the park at the far side of the paved circular path and walk past several large tulip trees. Just past a large one labeled with a sign, look for another tulip tree with a small sign at its base that identifies it as the tallest tree in Atlanta.

Just past a bench on your right turn left onto Creekside Path and follow this trail for 0.1 mile as it leads you on several crossings of the creek via stone steps. When Creekside Path meets up with the main trail, turn left and continue until just before a bridge and information sign. Turn left here and walk down the steps, over the creek, and uphill.

At the first junction turn right (towards the stone bridge), then right again at the next junction. At a park map next to a large stone bridge, turn right and go across. Stay left after the bridge, then right toward the open field called the Mead.

Circle the Mead to the left (clockwise) on the paved path, staying to the right when the paved multi-use path branches off to the left. After a sign that contains a description of the Mead, turn left onto a mulched trail, downhill, then left at a junction with two signs (a map of the park and an information sign about the Vale).

Turn left, up the hill, at a junction just past a bench and follow this trail 0.3 mile back to the west end of Deep Dene Park, past several spur trails that lead to the multi-use path along Ponce de Leon Avenue. As you go down stone steps toward a bridge, the sentinel white oak is on the right.

Retrace your steps across Ponce de Leon and up Lakeshore Drive to the path that leads back into Cator Woolford Gardens. At the bottom of the hill turn left and walk parallel to the creek until you come to a bridge on the right. Across from the bridge on your left is the city champion redbud tree. Cross the bridge, then turn right into the garden parking area. Walk left up the Frazer Center driveway, turning right into the small gravel parking area and back onto the mulched trail.

Once in the woods, turn left at the first 4-way trail junction and continue uphill, making a left at the next main junction. This trail will lead you back to the parking lot to end the hike.

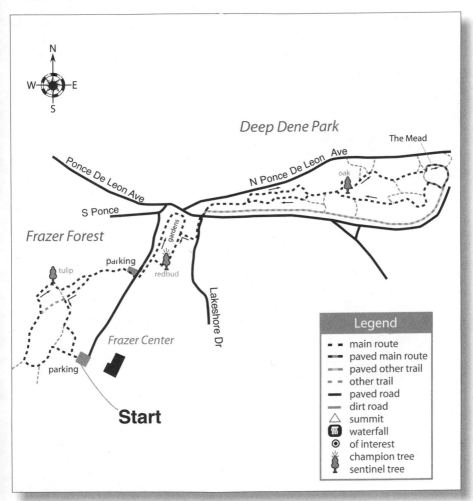

There's something for everyone in the family on this hike.

GLENLAKE PARK & DECATUR CEMETERY

This hike leads you through a manicured park with a playground to an urban forest along a small stream, into a historic cemetery full of large, ancient trees, and finally through a modern cemetery. The route will never bore you; there's something for everyone in the family—even a dog park along the way.

DISTANCE FROM DOWNTOWN ATLANTA • 7 MILES

BY CAR FROM DEKALB AVENUE Drive east on DeKalb Avenue, which changes names to Howard Avenue when you enter the City of Decatur. Turn left on Commerce Drive and drive 0.8 mile before turning left again onto Church Street. Glenlake Park is on your right in 0.4 mile.

PUBLIC TRANSPORTATION Take the Blue MARTA train eastbound. Get off at the Decatur Station and walk 0.6 miles on Church Street to Glenlake Park. You can also begin this hike from the cemetery entrance on Commerce Drive (next to Kroger).

PARKING Paved parking lot next to the tennis center in Glenlake Park; GPS N 33° 46.9796, W 84° 17.4725

ADDRESS 1211 Church Street, Decatur, GA 30030

HIKE DISTANCE 1.5-mile loop

WHY THIS HIKE IS GREAT This diverse walk through Decatur's largest greenspace leads past ancient trees and gravestones, through forest trails, and around manicured playing fields.

DIFFICULTY

Overall—Easy

Terrain—Mostly asphalt or gravel trails with a short section of hard-packed soil

Elevation change—The cemetery and park are quite hilly, and the trail has many short ups and downs.

HOURS Dawn to dusk, year-round

DOGS Leashed dogs permitted; a dog park in Glenlake Park

FACILITIES Toilets, water fountains, playground, outdoor workout equipment, sports fields, and picnic areas in Glenlake Park

FEES & PERMITS None

LAND MANAGER City of Decatur

SENTINEL TREES

City Champion Pignut Hickory – GPS N 33° 46.9850, W 84° 17.3960
- 9'6" circumference, 116' tall, 78' crown spread (250 champion points)
- The most impressive feature of this tree is its girth. Hickories grow notoriously slowly, putting on very little new wood each year; this one is over 9 feet in circumference. The nuts contain edible meat, but are hard to get to before the forest animals find them.

City Champion Eastern Red Cedar – GPS N 33° 46.6833, W 84° 17.4916
- 7' circumference, 72' tall, 33' crown spread (164 champion points)
- This tree is in the historic portion of the Decatur Cemetery. Easily identified by their shredding/peeling, lighter-colored bark and scaly, needle-like leaves, eastern red cedars make great cemetery trees because they thrive in full sun. The trunk of this one has engulfed a granite grave marker at its base.

BIRDS TO LOOK FOR

GLENLAKE PARK & DECATUR CEMETERY

All Year: brown-headed nuthatch, Eastern bluebird, red-headed woodpecker, red-shouldered hawk

City Champion Virginia Pine –
GPS N 33° 46.9560, W 84° 17.4783

- 4'6" circumference, 68' tall, 32' crown spread (130 champion points)
- Of all native pines in the Southeast, Virginia pine has the shortest needles and smallest cones. They grow larger in the North Georgia mountains but rarely get this tall in metro Atlanta, which is why this one is city champion. Find it by looking for the largest and tallest tree near the gate of the fence separating Glenlake Park from Decatur Cemetery.

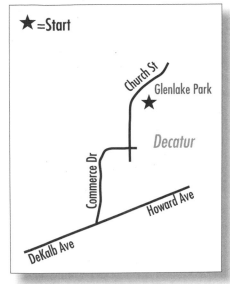

HIKE

Begin your hike on the paved path to the right of the tennis center and cross the bridge in front of you. After crossing the bridge, pass an outdoor workout station on your right and continue straight past a junction that leads to the basketball court on the right. Pass another junction on your left and hike uphill for another 0.1 mile where you'll cross a gravel drive and continue straight on a gravel path that becomes paved and curves around the outfield of a baseball diamond. Stop at the baseball field and look to the south (right) for a great view of the cemetery.

Pass a junction leading out of the park on your left and continue to circle the baseball diamond. Descend the hill and pass the city champion pignut hickory on your left. Pass a dog park and open field. At the bottom of the hill, turn left and cross the bridge.

In another 0.1 mile, cross a bridge just before the path meets a larger multi-use path. Make a right and then an immediate left onto a faint path through the grass on the right bank of the creek. This trail becomes much more obvious in 50 feet and leads through a mature forest of tulip and sweetgum trees. Cross a long bridge over the creek, then follow either fork as the trail splits to go around or through the meadow ahead. At the end of the meadow turn right and cross another bridge, following the gravel path into the cemetery.

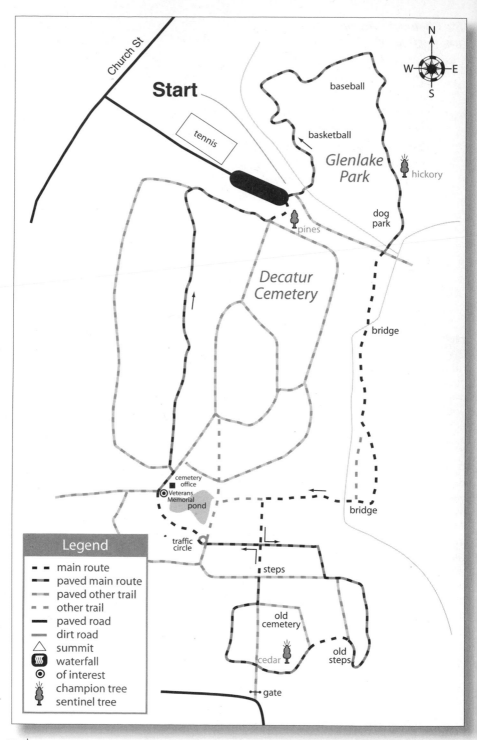

Start

Church St

tennis

baseball

basketball

N
W — E
S

Glenlake
Park

hickory

dog
park

pines

Decatur
Cemetery

bridge

cemetery
office

Veterans
Memorial
pond

bridge

traffic
circle

steps

old
cemetery

cedar

old
steps

gate

Legend

- - - main route
- - - paved main route
- - - paved other trail
- - - other trail
— paved road
— dirt road
△ summit
▩ waterfall
◉ of interest
♣ champion tree
♣ sentinel tree

HIKING ATLANTA'S HIDDEN FORESTS

When the line of trees on the left ends, look for a small path through the graves to the left and follow this to a small gravel road at the base of a set of stairs. Turn left onto this road and walk another 0.1 mile into the older section of Decatur Cemetery. Take a left at the first fork in the road, then another left when the road splits again. Look around for old gravestones that have been weathered by the years and overgrown with trees. The path curves to the right past a stand of large bamboo and then circles back up the hill.

After the path turns up the hill, turn left onto an old set of steps and walk under the trees, past grave markers, to another small road. Turn left, passing hand-carved gravestones of Revolutionary War veterans at the corner on your right. It's worth spending some time in this part of the cemetery as the old graves are particularly interesting; also, the champion red cedar is in this section. Continue walking on the road to reach an intersection with a larger road that leads to a gazebo on your right. Continue past this intersection, curve to the right, and reach the main drive at the top of a flight of stairs. Walk down these stairs and turn left onto the gravel drive, which leads you to a small traffic circle.

Cross the traffic circle and walk onto the grass past a weeping willow and around the left bank of the pond to the stairs on the opposite side. Continue up the stairs and path to a veterans' memorial and another nice view of the cemetery. At the memorial continue right toward the Cemetery Office; before reaching the office make a left onto the first road and then an immediate right.

Walk 0.2 mile through a newer section of the cemetery past rows of mature water oaks, then turn right at a T-intersection. In less than 0.1 mile reach a "Walk There! Decatur" sign and city champion Virginia pine grove. Turn left off the path and pass through the gate to re-enter Glenlake Park at the parking lot where this hike began.

Thousands of children and many adults have climbed on the low-hanging limbs of the "Climbing Magnolia."

PIEDMONT PARK & EASTSIDE BELTLINE TRAIL

THE BELTLINE

Piedmont Park is often called the Central Park of Atlanta. Not surprising, since its creators, the Olmsted brothers, also designed Central Park in New York City. Though most people know Piedmont Park for its open lawns that host music, art festivals, and outdoor movies, the forests of Piedmont Park have a special magic. This hike can introduce you to forested areas of the park you may not be familiar with—Lake Clara Meer, the new Six Springs Wetland, the Northwoods, and the Beltline path.

DISTANCE FROM DOWNTOWN ATLANTA • 4 MILES

BY CAR FROM I-75 Take exit 250 toward 10th Street/14th Street/Georgia Tech, merge onto Williams Street, and make a right at the first light onto 10th Street. Drive 1.3 miles and make a left onto Monroe Drive. In 0.6 miles, turn left onto Worchester Drive, then make an immediate left onto Evelyn Street, towards the Piedmont Park (SAGE) parking deck. Enter the deck and park inside.

PUBLIC TRANSPORTATION Take the Red or Gold MARTA train line to the Midtown Station. Exit the station on 10th Street and walk east for 1 mile on 10th to reach Piedmont Park (the hike starts near Magnolia Hall in the park), or ride the 27 Cheshire Bridge/Lindbergh Station bus from 10th Street to the corner of Piedmont Avenue and 14th Street and walk through the park to Magnolia Hall.

PARKING Park at the SAGE Parking Facility ($2 per hour); GPS N 33° 47.3566, W 84° 22.3613

ADDRESS 1345 Piedmont Road NE, Atlanta, GA 30309

HIKE DISTANCE 2.5-mile loop

WHY THIS HIKE IS GREAT Even for people very familiar with Piedmont Park, it's a great introduction to newly accessible forest areas of the park, as well as a section of the new Beltline path.

DIFFICULTY

Overall — Easy

Terrain — Paved or hard-packed gravel trails, with plans underway to pave most trails on this hike

Elevation change — A few short steep sections of trail, but mostly level

HOURS 6 am to 11 pm, year-round; Six Springs Wetland Trail open 6 am to sunset

DOGS Leashed dogs permitted; off-leash dog park adjacent to the route

FACILITIES Toilets, parking deck, many map and information kiosks, water fountains, picnic tables, benches, playgrounds, dog park

FEES & PERMITS None

LAND MANAGER City of Atlanta Office of Parks

SENTINEL TREES

"Climbing Magnolia" – GPS N 33° 47.1030, W 84° 22.3840
- 10'8" circumference, 56' tall
- This is a southern magnolia. Thousands of children and many adults have climbed on its massive, low-hanging limbs; over time because of this its bark has become smooth and polished.

State Champion Pin Oak – GPS N 33° 47.1370, W 84° 22.4850
- 12'6" circumference, 85' tall, 96' crown spread (259 champion points)
- Planted by humans less than 100 years ago, this tree thrives because of good growing conditions and little competition. It's visible from the front entrance of the Greystone Building.

BIRDS TO LOOK FOR

PIEDMONT PARK & EASTSIDE BELTLINE TRAIL

All Year: Cooper's hawk, red-bellied woodpecker, red-shouldered hawk, red-tailed hawk
Winter: white-throated sparrow, yellow-bellied sapsucker, yellow-rumped warbler

Six Springs Sentinel Grove –
GPS N 33° 47.2260, W 84° 22.2900

- Includes oak, tulip tree, beech, and winged elm
- A remnant of a much larger forest, this grove was spared from development in the mid-1800s, likely because of its steep topography and swampy bottomland. There is probably higher tree and plant diversity in this one 5-acre patch than the other 180 acres of Piedmont Park combined.

HIKE

Start the hike at the interactive kiosk in the Welcome Plaza behind Magnolia Hall. If you parked in the parking deck, exit through the lowest level to reach the Welcome Plaza.

Cross the plaza and head down the stairs. Turn right, then make a hard left onto the smaller path that leads steeply down the hill.

In 0.1 mile at the bottom of the hill, continue straight, past the boardwalk and semi-circle viewing area on your right. Walk through the underpass and you'll see Clear Creek on your right. This creek begins in the Inman Park neighborhood but flows underground until this point, where it emerges from its man-made tunnel.

After another 0.1 mile, pass a ramp and staircase on your left that lead up to the Legacy Fountain and Grand Arbor (where you can also find toilets). The trail continues alongside Clear Creek for 0.2 mile before ending at Westminster Drive. Turn right and immediately right again onto Eastside Beltline Trail. Cross the bridge over Clear Creek, then continue farther through an old railroad cut where you can see evidence of blasting marks from when the rock was removed.

The Beltline often has art installations along its route, so be on the lookout for interesting works of art. In 0.1 mile pass under power lines where you'll see a view of the Atlanta skyline ahead. Continue another 0.1 mile and carefully cross Evelyn Street, which leads to the parking deck. In 0.2 mile more you'll come to the Park Drive underpass, painted with a colorful mural.

Immediately after passing under the bridge turn right on a small informal trail to connect back to the Piedmont Park path between the dog park and orchard. Turn left on this paved path and walk 0.1 mile, past the orchard and children's garden. Just beyond the children's garden on the left and a set of stairs on the right, follow the path to the right as it curves around the Meadow and up the hill.

In 0.1 mile, at the top of the hill above the Meadow, turn right and walk to the intersection with the park's main road. There is a bridge in front of you, and the sentinel Climbing Magnolia is to your right.

After visiting the Climbing Magnolia, turn left and walk the small gravel path between the lakeshore and the main road. You'll pass several large water and willow oaks on your right before you come to stairs leading down to a lake overlook platform in 0.1 mile. Go down these stairs and turn left onto a gravel path right along the water's edge.

Pass a second platform and hike up a ramp onto a short boardwalk. After 0.25 mile along the water's edge, you'll reach the main dock, where you'll sometimes see weddings or other special events. Follow the circular path and continue up the far stairs near the historic visitor center.

At the top of the stairs turn right on the sidewalk between the road and the lakeshore. When the sidewalk splits in 0.2 mile, go left and stay on the main path toward the historic Greystone Building. This path leads into the Mayor's Grove, which includes a monument to the mayors of Atlanta and a tree planted in honor of each one, plus a nearby playground.

As you near the Greystone Building you'll see the state champion pin oak on your left. Continue to the front of the Greystone Building and turn right, passing the playground on your right and toilets and a water fountain on your left. After passing the restrooms turn left and walk across the bridge and past the gazebo, noticing the bald cypress growing on the lakeshore to your left.

After the bridge turn left onto the sidewalk, pass the Climbing Magnolia again, and continue through a grove of cypress trees.

At the end of the lake turn right at a small obelisk with information signs and a map. Walk up two steps, cross the road, and walk down a longer flight of stairs toward the dog park.

Turn left at the bottom of the stairs and make an immediate left onto the gravel Six Springs Wetland Trail and into a sentinel relic grove containing a great diversity of species of mature trees common in piedmont forests: oak, tulip tree, sourwood, beech, and others.

Cross a small footbridge and then a boardwalk before crossing a drainage waterfall after 0.1 mile. Just before climbing the stairs onto the main boardwalk you'll pass the stump of a white oak tree that fell in 2010 and dated back to antebellum times.

Take a left after ascending the stairs onto the boardwalk. At the end of the boardwalk turn left and walk 50 yards up the steep hill. At the top of the hill make a hard right and continue up the stairs to the Welcome Plaza where the hike ends.

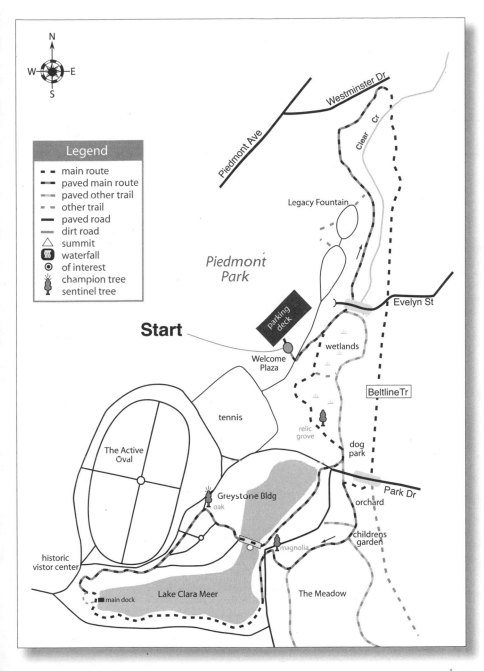

TANYARD CREEK PARK & NORTHSIDE BELTLINE TRAIL

THE BELTLINE

The Beltline is an exciting part of the vision for Atlanta's future, and you can experience a unique forested part of it on the Northside Beltline Trail. Though it is a paved urban trail situated between a golf course and a residential neighborhood, sections of it make you forget you are in the middle of the city. The route leads through a mature hardwood forest, past the largest white ash in the state, and parallels the scenic Tanyard Creek.

DISTANCE FROM DOWNTOWN ATLANTA • 6 MILES

BY CAR FROM I-75 Take exit 252A for Northside Drive and go north on Northside for 0.4 mile before turning right onto Collier Road. In 0.6 mile, turn left onto Dellwood Drive. In 0.3 mile, park on the side of the road near the corner of Dellwood Drive and South Colonial Homes Circle, across from the Bobby Jones Golf Course.

PUBLIC TRANSPORTATION Take the MARTA 110 bus to the corner of Peachtree Road and Colonial Homes Drive. The trailhead is 0.4 miles west on Colonial Homes Drive.

PARKING Street parking near the corner of Dellwood Drive and South Colonial Homes Circle; GPS N 33° 48.8095, W 84° 23.8445

The Beltline is an exciting part of the vision for Atlanta's future.

ADDRESS 290 South Colonial Homes Circle NW, Atlanta, GA 30309

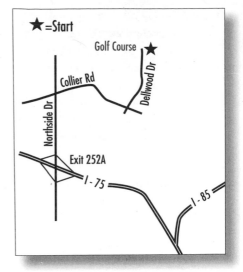

HIKE DISTANCE 2.25 miles out & back

WHY THIS HIKE IS GREAT It's easy, accessible, an excellent way to experience nature in the city, and has not one but two state champion trees on the route.

DIFFICULTY

Overall — Easy

Terrain — Paved multi-use path

Elevation change — Almost none

HOURS 6 am to 11 pm, year-round

DOGS Leashed dogs permitted

FACILITIES No toilets; playgrounds and picnic areas

FEES & PERMITS None

LAND MANAGER The Atlanta Beltline

SENTINEL TREES

State Champion Basswood – GPS N 33° 48.6905, W 84° 24.1333
- 8'5" circumference, 113' tall, 48' crown spread (226 champion points)
- This tree is only 50 yards from the champion white ash, very close to the paved path, and easily identified by the remnants of a broken-off side trunk. Basswoods have darker bark than most trees here and slightly heart-shaped leaves with serrated edges.

Silverbell – GPS N 33° 48.6696, W 84° 24.0991
- 1'8" circumference, 47' tall
- You'll find this tree in a grove of silverbells beside the champion white ash. This slice of forest has quite a lot of diversity for an urban park; when this was a homestead, this portion of the land must somehow have managed to thrive mostly untouched for many decades. You can identify silverbell trees by their subtle vertical striping on the bark. They are much smaller than the towering ash, basswood, and tulip trees here.

State Champion White Ash – GPS N 33° 48.665, W 84° 24.100
- 14' circumference, 132' tall, 56' crown spread (314 champion points)
- It's hard to miss this tree as it is the largest in the park and stands less than a foot from the paved path. White ash is common, but an ash of this size is quite remarkable. In fact, it is the largest of its species in all of Georgia. It stands on an old homestead site that was acquired by the city in the early 2000s. This section of the park is probably a relic of a much older forest that was never cut by the previous landowners.

Hike

Start your hike at the Dellwood Drive entrance to the Northside Beltline Trail. The paved multi-use path skirts the Bobby Jones Golf Course for 0.4 mile before crossing the creek on a metal bridge.

At 0.1 mile past the bridge, pass the state champion basswood, then the sentinel silverbell and the state champion white ash in quick succession on the right, just before a trail junction leading to Overbrook Drive and Collier Road.

After another 0.1 mile, the path leads under Collier Road and past a rocky and scenic section of Tanyard Creek. Pass a junction on the right across from a bench, cross a small bridge, then reach a bridge crossing the creek on your left and a junction on your right. Stay straight on the paved path, and you'll pass a playground and picnic area on your right in 0.2 mile.

Cross another bridge, then hike 0.1 mile to the railroad trestle that you'll pass under on a covered boardwalk.

Just after passing under the railroad trestle, reach a junction at Ardmore Park (you'll see a playground on your left). Go right and continue 0.15 mile through a forest of mature sycamore, tulip, and sweetgum trees to the end of the path at a development called The Reserve at City Park.

Turn around and follow the multi-use path back to Ardmore Park, turn left, cross under the railroad trestle, and follow the path back to the Dellwood Drive entrance to finish your hike.

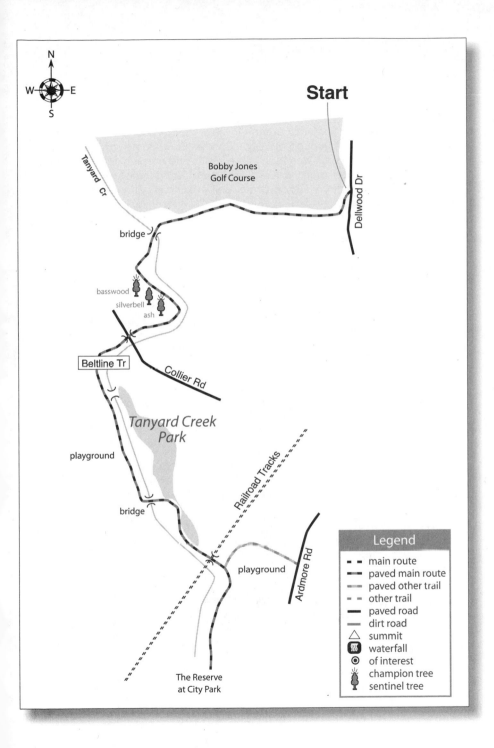

MURPHEY CANDLER PARK

Watching the reflection of clouds on the lake's surface is just the beginning of a beautiful hike through Murphey Candler Park. Best known for its youth baseball program, the park was built in the 1950s and now includes a 1.5-mile loop through hardwood forest, wetland areas, and along the lakeshore. It connects with the PATH Foundation's Nancy Creek Trail which can add a 1.6-mile paved extension to your hike.

DISTANCE FROM DOWNTOWN ATLANTA • 16 MILES

BY CAR FROM I-285 Take exit 29 and go south on Ashford Dunwoody Road. After 0.9 mile, turn left onto West Nancy Creek Drive. In 0.4, reach a parking lot on the left at the corner of West Nancy Creek Drive and Candler Lake West.

PUBLIC TRANSPORTATION *This hike is not easily accessible by public transportation.* Take the MARTA Red Line to the Medical Center Station and walk 2 miles along Lake Hearn Drive, Ashford Dunwoody Road, and West Nancy Creek Drive to reach the trailhead.

PARKING Paved parking area at the corner of West Nancy Creek Drive and Candler Lake West (during baseball season, consider parking just north on Candler Lake West if the West Nancy Creek lot is full); GPS N 33° 54.5797, W 84° 19.5675

Lake, wetlands, and forests—this hike has something for you.

ADDRESS 1600 W Nancy Creek Drive NE, Atlanta, GA 30319

HIKE DISTANCE 1.5-mile loop

WHY THIS HIKE IS GREAT Whether you are interested in the lake, wetlands, creeks, or forests, Murphey Candler has something for you. It's a perfect place to bring kids, walk your dog, go on a trail run, or just hike with a friend.

DIFFICULTY

Overall — Easy

Terrain — Hard-packed soil trails, wooden bridges, some paved paths

Elevation change — Minimal elevation change

HOURS 7 am to sunset, year-round

DOGS Leashed dogs permitted

FACILITIES Seasonal toilets near baseball fields; picnic areas and playground

FEES & PERMITS None

LAND MANAGER Murphey Candler Park Conservancy

SENTINEL TREES

Northern Red Oak – GPS N 33° 54.7281, W 84° 19.5493
- 6'5" circumference (closest trunk)
- Though not quite champion level in terms of size, this is a decent-sized northern red oak for this park. You can always spot this species by the lighter colored vertical ridges on the bark that look like stripes from a distance. All trees in the red oak family have leaves with pointed tips as well. Look for these pointed leaves on the tree in the warmer months, or search on the ground in winter to find them. This tree grows to the right of the trail, across from a small side trail leading to the park's swimming pool.

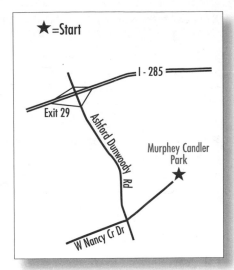

Big Leaf Magnolias – GPS N 33° 54.921, W 84° 19.619
- 2' circumference
- You'll find these sentinel trees about 20 feet down a small path to the right. Big leaf magnolia is one of a handful of native magnolias here in the Piedmont region of Georgia. All of these species are deciduous, meaning they drop their leaves in winter. There are several in this area and they have the biggest leaves of any tree in the forest.

Cottonwood – GPS N 33° 54.9330, W 84° 19.5119
- 10'8" circumference
- Cottonwood trees are water-loving species and almost always grow near a permanent water source. This one occupies a low wet spot at the edge of the lake, just before you cross a bridge. Cottonwoods grow quickly, so don't be fooled by the large girth of this tree—it may in fact be only a few decades old.

HIKE

From the parking lot walk toward the lake, then turn left onto the asphalt path along the lakeshore. Pass several picnic pavilions, then come to a junction with a side trail to the swimming pool on the left after 0.2 mile. The sentinel northern red oak is on your right. It has two trunks and is the oldest tree in this area of the park.

Continue straight, then go right at a junction in 0.1 mile, cross a bridge, stay right when the trail splits, then cross another bridge.

Not far beyond the bridge a small side trail leads down to the water; 20 feet down this path are the sentinel big leaf magnolias. Continue straight at this junction and in 0.15 mile the trail dips to the floodplain and a junction. Go left, cross several small footbridges, stay right at another junction, then cross a bridge over Nancy Creek.

After the bridge walk a boardwalk, then follow the trail to the right. At a junction in 0.1 mile continue straight past a loblolly pine stump on your right (count the rings to see how old the tree was; one count was 81). In another 0.1 mile, cross a small bridge, pass a sentinel cottonwood tree on your right, then cross a larger bridge.

BIRDS TO LOOK FOR

MURPHEY CANDLER PARK

Winter: American goldfinch, brown-headed nuthatch, Eastern towhee, golden-crowned kinglet, house finch, ruby-crowned kinglet

Just past a parking area on your left, the trail splits. Continue on either fork 0.2 mile until you reach the lakeshore. Pass a bench and picnic tables, continuing through an open area for another 0.1 mile. The sewer access points have been painted like birds' heads (duck, Canada goose, and cardinal). Cross a large bridge and the path becomes paved. In 0.1 mile, stay right at a parking lot, pass an overlook platform and turn right, crossing the dam on a sidewalk that leads to the parking area where you began the hike.

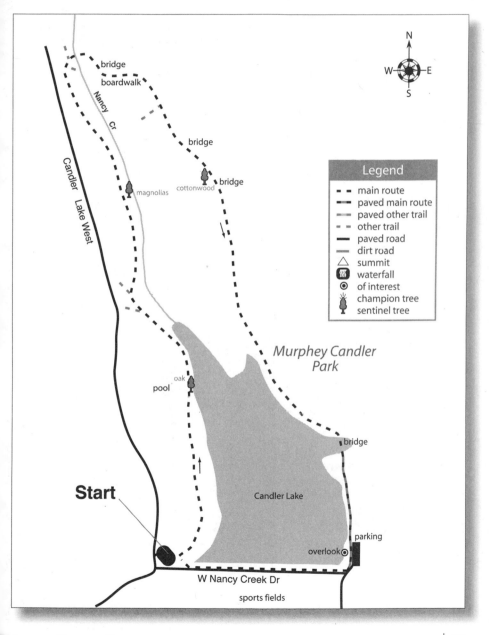

OUTDOOR ACTIVITY CENTER

This fabulous greenspace in the heart of Atlanta was once a flagship of the Atlanta Park system. Though it contains a nature center, ropes course, outdoor classrooms, and a network of interconnecting trails, budget cuts resulted in the city's neglect of the property. Now run by the nonprofit West Atlanta Watershed Alliance, the Outdoor Activity Center is again becoming a center for outdoor activity. The surrounding neighborhood is crumbling and full of boarded-up homes, but the trails within the Center's boundaries are a great community resource. On this hike you'll see many large trees, wildflowers, wildlife, and even the historic field where the Black Crackers, Atlanta's Negro League baseball team, used to practice.

DISTANCE FROM DOWNTOWN ATLANTA • 4 MILES

BY CAR FROM I-20

Take exit 54 for Langhorn Street and go south on Langhorn. At the traffic light in 0.6 mile, turn right onto Ralph David Abernathy Boulevard which immediately becomes Cascade Road. Follow Cascade Road for 0.5 mile, then turn left onto Beecher Street. Turn right on Gaston Street, then left onto Richland Road. The Outdoor Activity Center will be on your right.

PUBLIC TRANSPORTATION

The MARTA 68 bus will take you to the corner of Beecher Street and Rochelle Drive, 0.3 mile from the trailhead. The MARTA 71 bus will take you to the corner of Richland Road and Cascade Road, 0.3 mile from the trailhead. Or you can take

The so-called Grandfather Beech is thought to date from the Civil War.

the Gold train to the Oakland City station and walk 1.5 mile to the trailhead.

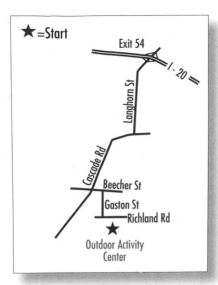

PARKING Fenced gravel parking area; GPS N 33° 43.8397, W 84° 26.0875

ADDRESS 1472 Richland Road SW, Atlanta, GA 30310

HIKE DISTANCE 1.5-mile loop

WHY THIS HIKE IS GREAT This walk will introduce you to one of the city's best hidden greenspaces along with some interesting city history.

DIFFICULTY

Overall — Easy

Terrain — Hard-packed soil trails and one low-lying area of soft ground

Elevation change — Back loop includes a short ascent and descent; other trails are mostly level

HOURS Monday through Saturday, 9 am to 4 pm.
Because this park is staffed by volunteers, it is worth calling to confirm hours before visiting: 404-752-5385.

DOGS Leashed dogs permitted; off-leash dog park located adjacent to the hike route

FACILITIES Toilets, nature center, outdoor classroom, challenge course

FEES & PERMITS None

LAND MANAGER City of Atlanta Office of Parks

SENTINEL TREES

White Oak – GPS N 33° 43.6140, W 84° 26.1790
  • 13'4" circumference
  • The largest tree in the Outdoor Activity Center forest, this white oak is on the left just after crossing an old bridge. Its size and age are a testament to the many years this forest has been protected.

"Grandfather Beech" – GPS N 33° 43.7256, W 84° 26.0467
- 10'4" circumference
- The centerpiece of this urban forest, the so-called Grandfather Beech is labeled as a Civil War-era tree. The graffiti on its trunk is more than 10 feet up, giving some credence to the claim of its more than 150 years of age.

City Champion Winged Elm – GPS N 33° 43.7400, W 84° 26.074
- 8'7" circumference, 125' tall
- This tree stands in one of the lowest spots in the forest along a creekbed near a key trail junction. Elms used to make up a larger percentage of the forest across the eastern U.S., but were decimated by the invasive Dutch elm disease. Winged elms seem to particularly like the piedmont and have maintained a stronger presence than the common American elms from years ago. This individual happens to be a city champion tree. You can identify it by small serrated leaves and corky "wings" along some branch tips.

HIKE

Start your hike in the parking lot in front of the building. Follow the trail to the right of the front door of the Nature Center building, past the composting demonstration area, the outdoor classrooms, and challenge course to a gate at the right rear of the fenced area. You might have to go into the building and ask whoever is working to unlock the gate for you.

After passing through the gate, stay straight for 0.1 mile, then cross a bridge to reach a trail junction. Turn right immediately after the bridge. Bear left at a ruined bridge on your right, and the trail ascends the ridge. Just after passing an observation platform and plaque, make a hard right on a trail that leads to the sentinel white oak. Cross an old, rickety bridge and you'll see the oak on your left. Turn around here and return to the main trail.

Continue straight on the main route. In just over 100 yards, reach an overlook with three benches. Just after this overlook, turn right on a small trail that leads 50 yards uphill to an open area that used to be the practice field for Atlanta's Negro League baseball team, the Atlanta Black Crackers. After visiting the field, return to the main trail and turn right to continue the loop.

In 0.1 mile, reach a platform and benches surrounding the sentinel known as Grandfather Beech. Go right at the tree and reach another junction in 100 yards. Turn left, descending for 0.1 mile to cross an area of the floodplain that can be soggy. In another 0.1 mile, the trail switchbacks to the left around a large white oak.

Pass two gates to the fenced area on your right, then walk along a short boardwalk.

Pass a granite signpost and cross two small bridges after the boardwalk ends. At the next junction, look to your right to see the city champion winged elm. Then turn right and walk 0.1 mile back to the first bridge you crossed on this hike. Turn right, cross the bridge, then go right to return to the fenced area in 0.1 mile. Follow the trail on the left to return to the parking lot.

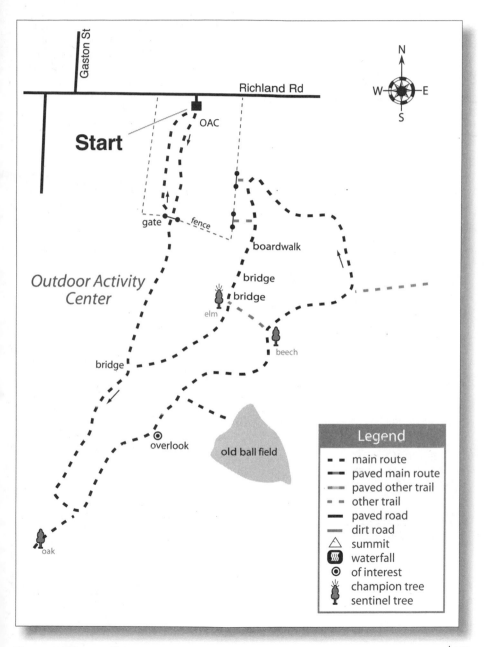

CASCADE SPRINGS NATURE PRESERVE

Most people have no clue that Cascade Springs Nature Preserve exists, but thanks to a small group of dedicated volunteers, it is open to the general public. You may never have heard of this 140-acre greenspace at the confluence of Turkeyfoot Creek and Utoy Creek, but it was once the home of a spa and nature retreat and has been drawing visitors for years. The remains of the resort, spring house (where the water from the eponymous spring was bottled and sold in the early 1900s), and farming terraces are still visible.

DISTANCE FROM DOWNTOWN ATLANTA • 7 MILES

BY CAR FROM I-20
Take exit 54 and go south on Langhorn Street. At the traffic light in 0.6 mile, turn right onto Ralph David Abernathy Boulevard which immediately becomes Cascade Road. Continue for 3.3 miles and turn left into the gated Nature Preserve parking area at a traffic light at Veltre Circle.

PUBLIC TRANSPORTATION
Take the MARTA 71 bus to the front gate of the nature preserve on Cascade Road.

PARKING Gravel parking area; GPS N 33° 43.1772, W 84° 28.8667

ADDRESS 2852 Cascade Road SW, Atlanta, GA 30311

HIKE DISTANCE 2-mile loop

You'll see old-growth trees, impressive boulders, and a waterfall.

WHY THIS HIKE IS GREAT One of the most impressive forests in the Atlanta, this preserve is a hidden gem where you'll see old-growth trees, impressive boulders, and a waterfall.

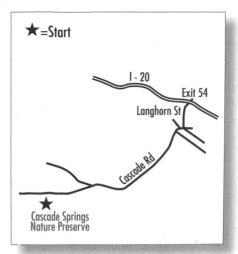

★=Start

I - 20

Exit 54

Langhorn St

Cascade Rd

★
Cascade Springs
Nature Preserve

DIFFICULTY

Overall — Easy

Terrain — Hard-packed soil trails that can be overgrown in the summer

Elevation change — Rolling hills but no major ascents or descents

HOURS *Summer:* Weekdays 7:30 am to 3 pm, weekends 7:30 am to 7:30 pm
Winter: Weekdays 7:30 am to 3 pm, weekends 7:30 am to 6 pm

DOGS Leashed dogs permitted

FACILITIES No toilets; several picnic areas

FEES & PERMITS None

LAND MANAGER City of Atlanta Office of Parks

SENTINEL TREES

State Champion Sourwood – GPS N 33° 43.1130, W 84° 28.9030
- 6'2" circumference, 99' tall, 38' crown spread (183 champion points)
- Normally sourwood is a mid-story tree, but this one reaches all the way to the top of the canopy. At 99 feet, it is one of the tallest known sourwoods in the state. Find it beside the frog pond.

Big Leaf Magnolia – GPS N 33° 43.1830, W 84° 28.6860
- 2'6" circumference, 83' tall
- Many people are familiar with the evergreen southern magnolias planted across Atlanta, but we also have a few native magnolias in our piedmont forests; these trees are deciduous, losing their leaves annually. Big leaf magnolias are common in this park. Their leaves grow up to 3.5 feet, the largest of any native tree in the country.

Beech – GPS N 33° 42.9341, W 84° 28.7364

- 11' circumference
- This massive beech with pale gray bark is one of the most memorable trees in the forest. Its branches hold the remains of an old tree house or deer stand, and the graffiti carved into its trunk are now significantly higher than a human can reach.

HIKE

Start the hike on the boardwalk next to the water fountain. Continue on the paved path when the boardwalk ends, passing the ruins of the old Cascade Inn, a nature resort from the 1920s, on your left.

Cross the bridge over Turkeyfoot Creek and inspect the spring house that once provided crystal clear drinking water. If you take the paved path to the right and continue for a short distance on a dirt trail at the end of it, you'll come to a frog pond and the state champion sourwood tree. Back at the spring house, follow the yellow posts along the creek for 0.15 mile. At the end of the boardwalk just past a ruined spring house, the sentinel big leaf magnolia is across the creek on your left. After the sentinel tree you'll come to a waterfall.

At the waterfall, hike uphill on the trail to a bench, then make a hard right to continue on Ridge Trail. This trail winds through rolling hills past a large white oak on the left to reach a junction with Spring Trail in 0.3 mile. Go left to stay on Ridge Trail and hike uphill for a few more yards to reach another junction. Stay left on Ridge Trail and pass two more large white oak trees.

In 0.45 mile stay left at a junction and hike 0.1 mile to another junction. Just before reaching a T-junction (near the sentinel beech tree), look for a small side trail on the left. This side trail leads 0.1 mile to an interesting rock formation just beyond a hole in the chain-link fence that borders the Nature Preserve. Return to the main trail and turn left, then left again to loop through an area of large boulders, passing the enormous and beautiful sentinel beech tree on your left. When this trail loops back to the main trail, turn left. In less than 75 yards turn left on a small trail.

Descend to the Utoy Creek floodplain and reach a gravel maintenance road in 0.1 mile. Turn right and hike along Utoy Creek for 0.1 mile, pass a junction with a small trail below a large hillside rock outcrop, and continue straight along the creek 0.1 mile more to the next junction. Keep your eye out, as these trails are not well maintained and can sometimes be hidden by brush. Turn right and follow this trail uphill to meet up with the main loop trail in 0.1 mile. Turn right and hike to a junction signed for Terrace Trail. Turn left and follow Terrace Trail for 0.2 mile to a junction with Spring Trail. Turn left and hike 0.15 mile to return to the spring house near Turkeyfoot Creek. Continue straight, cross the bridge, and walk the paved path back up the hill to the parking area to end the hike.

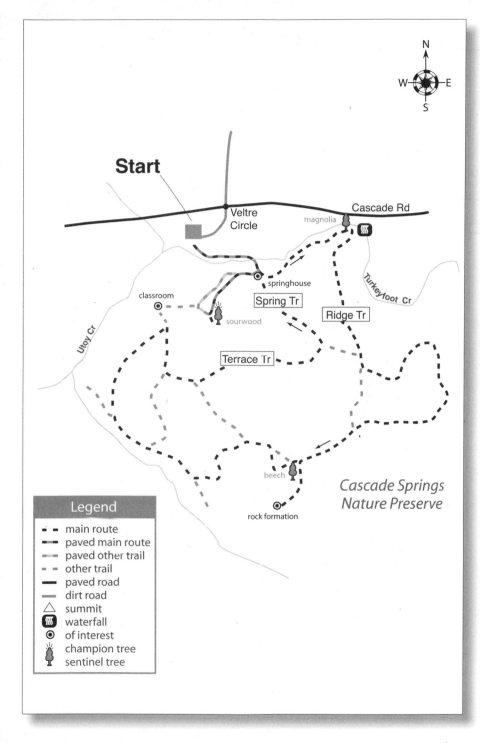

Cascade Springs
Nature Preserve

Legend

- - main route
▬▬ paved main route
━━ paved other trail
- - other trail
▬ paved road
━ dirt road
△ summit
♨ waterfall
◉ of interest
♠ champion tree
♟ sentinel tree

W.D. THOMPSON PARK

Unlike many other forested parks in the Decatur area, W.D. Thompson is not situated in the bottomlands of the South Fork of Peachtree Creek. Instead, this park provides an excellent hike through an area of piedmont forest cut by several small streams. The forest here is older than in some areas of the South Fork of Peachtree Creek, and the terrain will remind you of the Appalachians with its rocky soil and rolling hills.

DISTANCE FROM DOWNTOWN ATLANTA • 8 MILES

BY CAR FROM I-85 Take I-85 to exit 89 for GA 42/North Druid Hills Road. Go east on North Druid Hills and drive for 2 miles, then turn right onto Clairmont Road. In 0.4 mile, turn right onto Mason Mill Road. Drive 0.5 mile and make a right onto Mason Woods Drive. The park entrance and parking area is on your right.

PUBLIC TRANSPORTATION
Take the 19 Clairmont Rd MARTA bus to the corner of Mason Mill Road and Clairmont Road. Walk 0.5 mile west on Mason Mill Road to the park entrance on your right.

PARKING Paved parking area next to tennis courts; GPS N 33° 48.5045, W 84° 19.0152

ADDRESS 955 Mason Woods Drive NE, Atlanta, GA 30329

HIKE DISTANCE
1-mile lollipop loop

Exposed beech roots cover this hillside.

HIKING ATLANTA'S HIDDEN FORESTS

WHY THIS HIKE IS GREAT Unlike nearby city parks which have flat trails, W.D. Thompson provides a beautiful piedmont experience with hardwood trees, undulating paths, and pristine creeks— all nestled in the middle of a residential neighborhood.

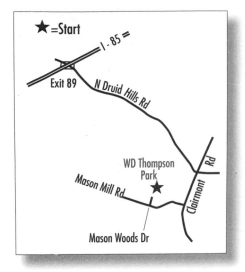

DIFFICULTY

Overall— Easy

Terrain — Well-maintained single-track trails on hard-packed soil; one stream crossing involves rock-hopping

Elevation change — Rolling hills, but no sustained ascents or descents

HOURS 7 am to sunset, year-round

DOGS Leashed dogs permitted

FACILITIES No toilets; playground, tennis courts, basketball goal, and picnic area

FEES & PERMITS None

LAND MANAGER DeKalb County Parks

SENTINEL TREES

State Champion Basswood – GPS N 33° 48.6179, W 84° 19.0440
- 7'2" circumference, 128' tall, 50' crown spread (226 total champion points)
- Basswood is a species often overlooked in piedmont forests. This one grows right beside the trail on the slope of the ravine. Though typically basswoods grow to medium size, individuals (such as this giant) can grow taller than 120 feet. This is one of the largest basswoods in the entire state.

Black Oak – GPS N 33° 48.6780, W 84° 19.0380
- 7'9" circumference
- Look to the trees on the downhill side of the trail. Most of them grow straight up towards the sky, but this particular black oak has some gnarled twists and turns. It could be that throughout its life (probably more than 100 years), it's had to bend around other trees in order to reach for the sunlight it needed to thrive.

Beech roots – GPS N 33° 48.6900, W 84° 19.0199

- As you cross the creek to the left of the small wooden bridge, look at the hillside to the right. Much of the topsoil has eroded away, and you can see a massive collection of roots holding in the remaining soil. These are all roots of the beech trees in front of you. Beech trees are easily identified by their smooth gray bark.

HIKE

From the parking area between the tennis courts and the gated entrance above the basketball court, walk down the hill on the concrete path. There are trail entrances on either side of the basketball goal. Take the path on the right into the woods and up the hill. This is Blue Trail.

This trail winds up and down several small hills, passing a small side trail on the left after 0.15 mile. In another 0.1 mile, you'll come to an intersection marked by orange, blue, and yellow posts. Turn left to take Yellow Trail.

In 0.1 mile, pass a junction on the right that leads down to the creek, then pass a bench overlooking the creek valley. Next to the bench is a small side trail leading up the hill.

Continue straight on Yellow Trail for 0.1 mile, then turn right at a junction with Green Trail. Immediately cross a small wooden bridge and parallel the creek on a hillside covered with English ivy. Pass the state champion basswood, then a bit farther along the sentinel black oak on your right. When the trail dips down to the creek, cross on rocks to continue straight, toward the orange post (not over the footbridge to the right). On the hill to your right (beyond the footbridge) are the sentinel beech roots.

Hike up the hill and turn left at the red post and trail junction. Pass another junction with an unmarked trail and hike down and up the hill before you pass another unmarked trail junction and then Red Trail junction on your right. Continue straight past both side trails until you come to the back gate of the park (which leads to an apartment complex). Turn right to continue on Orange Trail and hike 300 feet to the junction with Yellow and Blue Trails.

Stay left to rejoin Blue Trail, which will take you a third of a mile back to the parking area to end the hike.

HIKING ATLANTA'S HIDDEN FORESTS

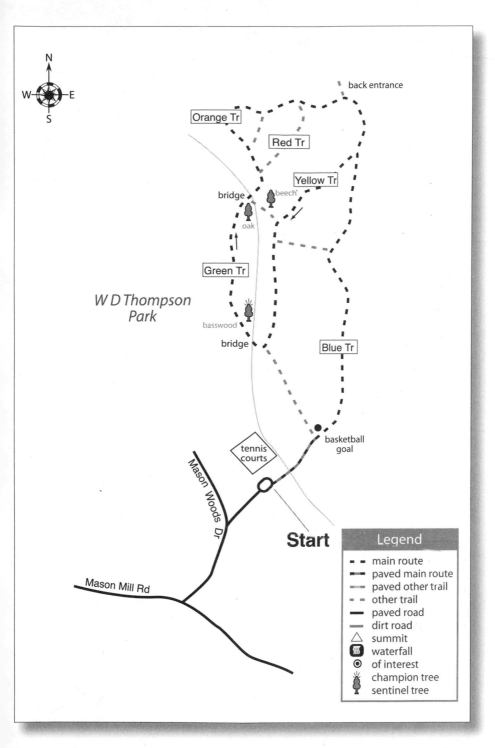

Atlanta Memorial Park

Beloved by Buckhead residents for hiking, jogging, and walking dogs, this park on the site of the Civil War Battle of Peachtree Creek is home to some of the largest and most interesting trees in Atlanta. You'll pass gigantic water oaks and remarkable osage orange, southern catalpa, cottonwood, and river birch. Because the trails here are close to many roads, you'll never forget you're in a city while on this hike, but you'll be awed by Atlanta's natural beauty just the same.

Distance from Downtown Atlanta • 6 miles

By car from I-75 Take exit 252A and go north on Northside Drive for 1.4 mile to reach the intersection with Peachtree Battle Avenue. Street parking is available on Manor Ridge Drive on the right. There is also a large parking lot on the left, but you should not park there without permission from the Ahavath Achim Synagogue.

Public Transportation
Take the MARTA 12 bus to the corner of Howell Mill Road and Peachtree Battle Avenue. This corner is on the actual hike route, so you can begin your hike by walking east on the sidewalk along Peachtree Battle Avenue.

Parking Street parking on Manor Ridge Drive; GPS N 33° 49.4369, W 84° 24.4174

Address 2525 Northside Drive, Atlanta, GA 30305

Hike Distance
2.5-mile loop

Trees of many sizes and shapes make this hike interesting.

WHY THIS HIKE IS GREAT This forested park in the heart of Buckhead has deep roots in Civil War history. If you are excited about visiting incredibly large trees, Atlanta Memorial Park is a perfect destination.

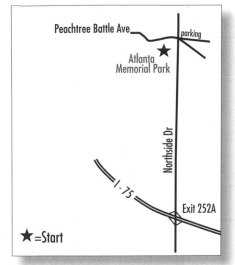

DIFFICULTY

Overall — Easy

Terrain — Paved and hard-packed soil trails with a section on a sidewalk

Elevation change — Little or no elevation loss or gain

HOURS 6 am to 11 pm, year-round

DOGS Leashed dogs permitted

FACILITIES No toilets, benches and a playground

FEES & PERMITS None

LAND MANAGER City of Atlanta Office of Parks

SENTINEL TREES

City Champion Osage Orange – GPS N 33° 49.1642, W 84° 24.5331

- 10' circumference, 90' tall, 70.5' crown spread (227.6 champion points)
- Though not related to the orange — it's in the mulberry family — this species produces an orange-sized fruit that looks a little like a small green brain. Its dense wood withstands rot and has been used for centuries to build tool handles. This huge tree grows near the playground to the left of the trail and has a multitude of trunks; it is the second largest osage orange in Atlanta.

Cottonwood – GPS N 33° 49.2298, W 84° 24.5441

- 15'2" circumference, 100' tall
- This is the largest tree in Atlanta Memorial Park and one of the largest in Atlanta. Growing beside the path near Woodward Way, it feels more impressively large the closer you get to its trunk. How many people would it take to encircle this tree?

City Champion River Birch – GPS N 33° 49.2321, W 84° 24.5180

- 10' circumference, 74' tall, 75' crown spread (213 champion points)
- This river birch is unusual because it stands very straight upright and is very large; most river birches hang diagonally over streambanks. It is also the largest of its species in Atlanta. Find it next to the trail along Woodward Way, just beyond the sentinel cottonwood.

HIKE

Start hiking at the 5-way intersection of Northside Drive, Peachtree Battle Avenue, and Manor Ridge Drive at the beginning of the paved multi-use Peachtree Creek Trail that runs through Haynes Manor Park. Cross two bridges before reaching the corner of Northside Drive and Woodward Way. Cross Northside then Woodward before crossing Peachtree Creek on the sidewalk of the Northside Drive bridge to enter Atlanta Memorial Park.

The route starts with a rubberized composite surface, but at the first junction you'll turn right onto a hard-packed soil trail. Pass a bent southern catalpa tree with an information tag on your left, and look to the left about 100 feet off the trail to find the enormous city champion osage orange tree with multiple trunks near the playground. This tree also has an information tag.

After viewing the osage orange, continue on the trail. Pass the playground on your left and walk 0.15 mile to where the route cuts between two giant water oaks (the one on the left has a 12'7" circumference, the one on the right 14'4"), then passes an interesting dead tree.

Walk another 0.1 mile before the trail meets another dirt track parallel to Wesley Drive. Follow the trail between Wesley Drive and Peachtree Creek for 0.15 mile to reach another large water oak (13'1" circumference). Continue on the trail nearest the creek for 0.2 mile before reaching a junction and a small footbridge. Bear right, cross the bridge, and go 0.1 mile to reach the sidewalk along Howell Mill Road where there are three historical markers about the Civil War battle that was fought here, as well as information about Howell's Mill for which the road was named.

Go right and walk along the Howell Mill Road sidewalk across Peachtree Creek to the corner of Howell Mill and Peachtree Battle Avenue (also the best public transit connection point to this hike). Turn right and follow the Peachtree Battle sidewalk along Peachtree Creek.

In 0.3 mile reach the corner of Woodward Way and Peachtree Battle Avenue and a sign for Atlanta Memorial Park. Bear right onto a hard-packed soil trail between the creek and Woodward Way. Follow this path for 0.4 mile before reaching the largest tree in Memorial Park, the 15'2" sentinel cottonwood tree. No more than 50 feet farther along, dwarfed by the cottonwood, is the city champion river birch.

Reach Northside Drive 0.1 mile after passing the sentinel trees. Cross Woodward Way to the left, then cross Northside Drive to get back on the paved Peachtree Creek Trail which leads 0.2 mile back to where you parked and ends the hike.

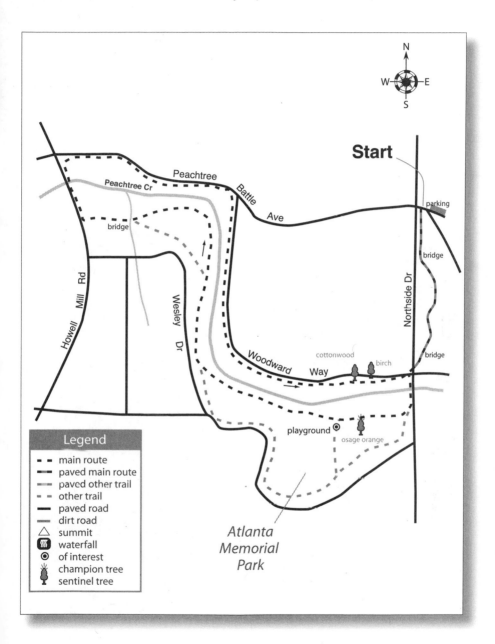

MERCER UNIVERSITY NATURE TRAIL

It's unusual to find an undulating hike route with old-growth timber on a small college campus, and this trail is a pleasant surprise. Used by many runners, college students, and neighbors, the Mercer Nature Trail is unique among intown hikes because it keeps to the ridges and away from creeks and floodplains. The forest is mainly pines and young hardwoods, and the trail passes an old homesite with some interesting historical remains and a grove of large oak trees.

DISTANCE FROM DOWNTOWN ATLANTA • 14 MILES

BY CAR FROM I-85
Take exit 94 toward Chamblee-Tucker Road and go east. In 0.2 mile turn right onto Mercer University Drive. In 0.4 mile turn right onto Mercer Lane, then turn left onto University Circle. Pass the bookstore and gym on your right, then park at the far south end of the parking lot on your right. The trailhead is across University Circle.

PUBLIC TRANSPORTATION
Take the MARTA 126 Chamblee/Northlake bus to the corner of Flowers Road South and University Circle. Walk less than 0.2 mile on University Circle to the trailhead on your right.

PARKING
Paved parking area; GPS N 33° 52.3186, W 84° 15.6258

Go ahead—give that big tree a hug!

ADDRESS On University Circle near 3209 Flowers Road South, Atlanta, GA 30341

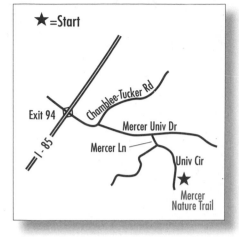

HIKE DISTANCE 1-mile loop

WHY THIS HIKE IS GREAT It's a short, easily accessible hike great for exercise, dog walking, or exploring with children. Several extended uphill climbs lead you to an old homesite, oak grove, and an enormous tulip tree.

DIFFICULTY

Overall — Easy

Terrain — Wide, hard-packed soil trails

Elevation change — Extended ascent at the beginning of the hike; several ascents and descents throughout the rest of the hike

HOURS Dawn to dusk, year-round

DOGS Leashed dogs permitted

FACILITIES None

FEES & PERMITS None

LAND MANAGER Mercer University

SENTINEL TREES

White Oak – GPS N 33° 52.4986, W 84° 15.4417
- 10'11" circumference
- This old homestead tree is one of several large white oaks. It was likely planted here or protected by the family who lived here decades ago. At that time most of the forest you see now would have been meadows or farmland. In recent years, the forest has grown up around these older trees. Some people call trees swallowed up by forest "wolf trees."

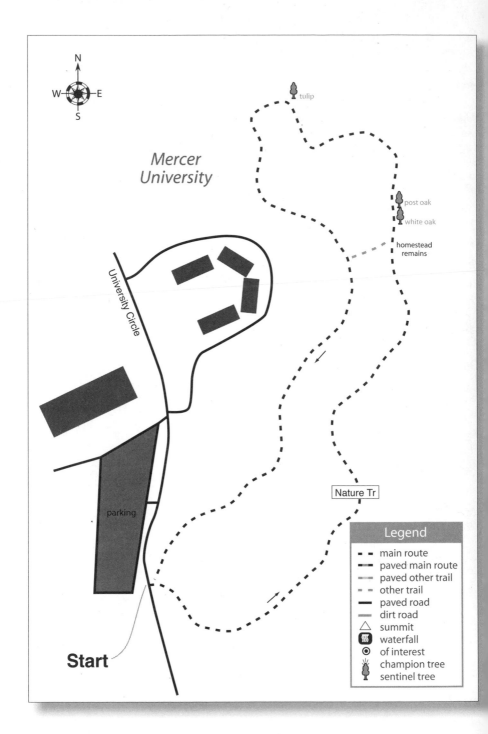

Mercer
University

University Circle

parking

Nature Tr

Start

tulip

post oak
white oak

homestead
remains

Legend

- - - main route
▬ ▬ paved main route
▬ ▬ paved other trail
- - other trail
▬ paved road
▬ dirt road
△ summit
♨ waterfall
◉ of interest
🌳 champion tree
🌲 sentinel tree

Post Oak – GPS N 33° 52.5115, W 84° 15.4457

- 7'1" circumference
- Post oaks are common homestead trees. They can survive nearly all conditions Mother Nature throws at them and sometimes live for centuries. This tree likely provided good shade for the family that lived here many years before this was a university campus. To identify this tree, look for its thick, dark green leaves roughly the shape of a cross.

Tulip Tree – GPS N 33° 52.5854, W 84° 15.5085

- 14'8" circumference, 125' tall
- Tulip trees thrive in the piedmont region of Georgia, and this beauty is a prime example of how large they can get. They are a pioneer species that move into an area after forest has been cut, burned, or otherwise removed from the land. Although they are the first hardwoods to move into old field sites, they can outlive many of the other trees that move in later. Some tulip trees have been known to live for 500 years.

HIKE

Enter the Nature Trail loop across University Drive from the parking lot and cross a small wooden bridge over a drainage ditch. Start your hike on the right fork. The trail winds uphill fairly steeply for about 0.3 mile before it levels off at an old homesite and cutoff trail on your left.

On your right, just before the cutoff trail, are the remains of the homestead. If you explore the area you'll find signs of the buildings that used to dot this area.

Pass the junction with the cutoff trail, then pass two large white oaks on the right; the first is the sentinel. The third, a smaller oak tree on the right, is a sentinel post oak, recognizable by its cross-shaped leaves and less flaky bark.

In 0.15 mile the trail reaches a low point. To your right is a sentinel tulip tree, by far the largest tree in this forest. Walking 50 yards downhill off the trail to visit the tulip tree is definitely worthwhile, but watch out for briars.

Back on the trail, the route ascends and then curves left. In 0.2 mile pass the cutoff trail and continue another 0.3 mile, mostly downhill, to finish the hike at the University Drive trailhead.

N
W **E**
S

West Metro

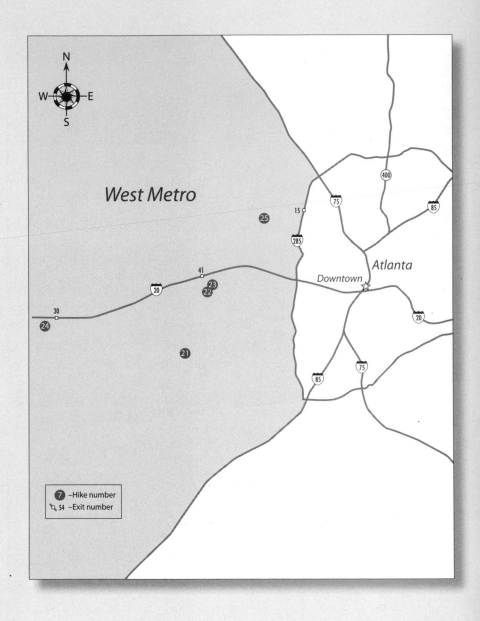

㉑ Boundary Waters Park

Sweetwater Creek State Park

㉒ Red & White Trails

㉓ Yellow Trail

㉔ Clinton Nature Preserve

㉕ Heritage Park

W est Metro Atlanta is home to beautiful Sweetwater Creek Slato Park which offers great photo opportunities, including the historic Manchester Mill ruins. Don't forget to bring your camera!

The slow-flowing Chattahoochee cuts a deep channel through Boundary Waters Park.

BOUNDARY WATERS PARK

Known primarily for its sports complex and aquatic center, Boundary Waters Park is the gem of the Douglas County park system. It contains over 8 miles of trails and is the best way to visit the Chattahoochee River south of Atlanta. Wide, well-marked trails make navigation easy, and the hills on the northern section of the park will get your heart pumping.

DISTANCE FROM DOWNTOWN ATLANTA· 22 MILES

BY CAR FROM I-20 Drive west from Atlanta on I-20 and take exit 41 for Lee Road. Turn left onto Lee and drive 3 miles before turning left onto GA 92S/Fairburn Road. In 2.3 miles, turn right to continue on GA 92S. After 2.6 miles, turn left into Boundary Waters Park. Follow signs for hiking, and turn right at the aquatics center to reach the parking lot behind the building.

PUBLIC TRANSPORTATION *This hike is not easily accessible by public transportation.* The MARTA 72 bus stops 7.7 miles from the park. The Xpress commuter bus service stops in Douglasville, 9.9 miles from the park.

PARKING Paved parking lot behind the Aquatics Center building; GPS N 33° 40.1637, W 84° 39.5386

ADDRESS 5000 GA 154, Douglasville, GA 30135

HIKE DISTANCE 7-mile figure-8 loop

WHY THIS HIKE IS GREAT This relatively strenuous hike is one of the best ways to visit the Chattahoochee River south of Atlanta. The slow-flowing river cuts a deep channel, and the trail winds through healthy piedmont forests.

DIFFICULTY

Overall — Moderate to difficult

Terrain — Wide, well-marked trails, mostly hard-packed soil

Elevation change — Many ascents and descents which are particularly steep on the Chattahoochee Circle section at the north end of the Red Trail

HOURS Weekdays 8 am to 8:30 pm; Saturdays 8 am to 5:30 pm; Sundays 1 to 5:30 pm

DOGS Leashed dogs permitted

FACILITIES Toilets at the Aquatics Center; many benches and several picnic tables on the trail

FEES & PERMITS None

LAND MANAGER Douglas County Parks

SENTINEL TREES

Southern Red Oak (dead) – GPS N 33° 40.1189, W 84° 39.2326
- 19'3" circumference
- Before its demise, this would have been the largest southern red oak in Atlanta. Its massive trunk still stands, dwarfing all other trees in this park, and will stand for many years to come.

Sycamore – GPS N 33° 41.0504, W 84° 39.1910
- 7'6" circumference
- In such a young forest, this small, graceful sycamore specimen (the largest in Atlanta is over 17 feet in circumference) qualifies as a sentinel. Find it on the left at a low point in the trail, where sycamores prefer to grow. Notice how the identifying peeling bark begins higher up on its trunk.

INSIDER TIP

BOUNDARY WATERS PARK IN SMALLER BITES

This 7-mile hike can be split into smaller loops. Depending on your timeframe and stamina, you can do a 1-mile loop on the paved multi-use path, or a 4-mile loop on the Blue & Yellow Trails starting at the Aquatic Center parking area, or a 4.5-mile lollipop loop on the Red Trail if you start at the sports complex parking area.

Water Oak and Cherry –
GPS N 33° 40.5549, W 84° 39.3168

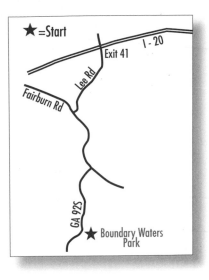

- 4'11" circumference
- Just before the trail begins a gentle ascent, notice the cherry tree growing right out of the trunk of this young water oak. Neither is very large. Originally separate, the fast-growing oak has engulfed the cherry which, instead of dying, is thriving.

Hike

Start hiking at the far corner of the parking lot on the paved sidewalk leading to a circular sidewalk and the beginning of the multi-use path. Walk 0.1 mile to a junction with a hard-packed soil trail on the right. Take the left fork of the two natural-surface trails at this junction and walk 0.15 mile to reach a clearing and trail junction. Ignore the arrow pointing to the left and go to the right across the clearing. Just beyond the clearing, reach a junction with Blue and Yellow Trails.

Go straight on Yellow Trail, passing another spur trail on the left, then following yellow arrows to the left, under power lines. Yellow Trail parallels a farm and horse pasture south of the park for just over 0.5 mile before reaching a junction with a trail on the left. Stay straight and walk another 0.3 mile to a picnic table. Stay right to reach a covered bridge in 100 yards.

You'll come to a clearing 0.15 mile beyond the covered bridge. You can see the Chattahoochee River on the right. Follow the arrows across the clearing as Yellow Trail re-enters the woods.

Stay straight at a junction with a bench on the left in 0.15 mile, then continue another 0.15 mile to arrive at the enormous dead sentinel southern red oak next to a large bench and a hitching post. This tree still dwarfs every other tree in the park and was one of the largest trees in the metro area before its demise.

Continue straight on Yellow Trail for 0.2 mile to reach a junction with a spur on the right that leads to Red Trail. Turn right and hike 0.3 mile, past junction with a trail on the left, to reach a T-junction with a wide trail surrounded by young pine trees. Go right and hike 0.4 mile, past several trails on the left, to reach a bridge.

Cross the bridge and hike uphill for 0.1 mile to reach a large green trail sign and a bench. Turn left here toward Chattahoochee Crossing/Circle. In 0.25 mile, the trail descends and passes a connector trail on your right before crossing a bridge next to a picnic table. Just across the bridge is a 4-way junction and another green trail sign. Continue straight across this junction on the right fork of the route labeled "Continue Red Trail." This is the most strenuous part of the hike. If you want an easier route, make a hard right to skip this section.

In 0.1 mile, come to the first view of the Chattahoochee River on your right. The trail follows the river for another 0.1 mile before turning sharply left at a bench overlooking the river. The trail crosses a bridge near another picnic table and turns right. In 0.1 mile, it turns left and dips to a low point where you'll find the sentinel sycamore tree with a distinct lean. From this point you'll ascend steeply, reaching the hilltop in 0.15 mile. Follow the arrows as the trail then climbs down and up several hills, past another bench, and over a bridge on the right. In 0.4 mile, head uphill, pass a house on your right, and make a sharp left turn up the hill to the highest point in the park.

From there, follow arrows for 0.2 mile downhill to the 4-way junction and green trail sign. Make a soft left and follow the arrow to River Route to Exit. Cross a bridge, pass a bench and connector trail on the right, then walk parallel to the river on a wide trail through a privet thicket. In 0.3 mile, the river becomes visible, and you'll soon pass a bench overlooking the water. A slough from Camp Creek (mostly obscured in the summer) cascades into the river on the opposite bank.

In 0.15 mile, the trail curves sharply to the right and gradually ascends the ridge, providing views of the river from above in winter and spring. In 0.3 mile, the trail dips slightly and then passes the sentinel water oak on the right with the cherry tree growing out of its trunk. After the tree, the trail gently ascends to a bench and T-junction in 0.15 mile. Follow the Exit sign, turn left, and hike downhill.

Cross the bridge at the bottom of the hill and turn left. Follow Red Trail back the way you originally came, until you come to a Y-junction with a spur leading to the left. Stay right on the main trail, pass a junction on the left in 0.1 mile, and hike 0.3 mile farther, following red arrows, to a T-junction and large green trail sign. Go right in the direction the sign labels as "EXIT Red Trail Toward Athletic Complex" and hike 0.15 mile to a junction at the edge of the athletic fields.

Before the information kiosk, turn left and hike 100 yards to reach the paved multi-use path. Turn left and walk 0.75 mile on the multi-use path, past the pond, a gazebo, and several side trails to reach the parking area and end the hike.

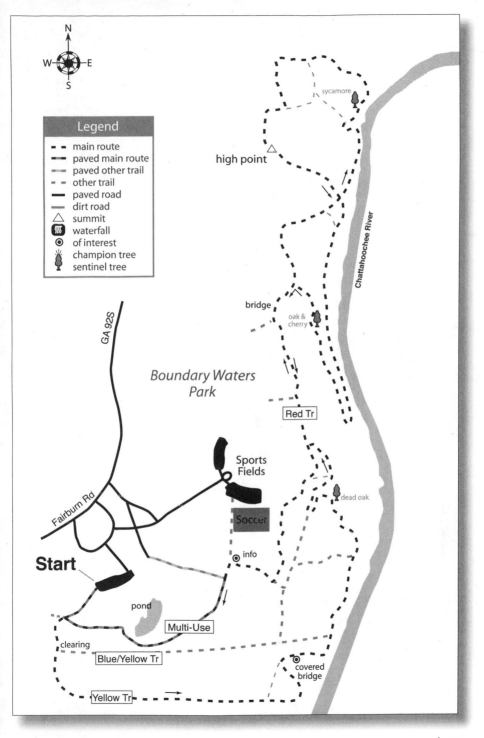

This historic mill was captured and destroyed by the Union Army during the Civil War.

Red & White Trails

Sweetwater Creek State Park

One of the most popular hikes in the Atlanta area, Sweetwater's Red and White Trails provide exercise, history, nature, and a waterfall. Sweetwater Creek State Park includes the site of the Manchester Mill, captured and destroyed by the Union Army during the Civil War, and is one of the most beautiful parks in the state. During times of high water, Sweetwater Creek can seem to rival the Chattahoochee in size. The hike itself covers diverse terrain with wide, flat footbeds, rocky tread, and narrow winding paths through piedmont hills.

DISTANCE FROM DOWNTOWN ATLANTA • 19 MILES

BY CAR FROM I-20 *Although interstate signs suggest using exit 44 to get to Sweetwater State Park, the following directions are recommended.* Take exit 41 toward Lithia Springs and go south on Lee Road. In 1.0 mile turn left onto Cedar Terrace Road. Drive 0.8 mile, pass an entrance sign for the state park, and turn right onto Mt. Vernon Road. In 0.3 mile turn left onto Factory Shoals Road and pass the ranger kiosk, then continue straight for 0.6 mile to the circular parking area at the end of Factory Shoals Road.

PUBLIC TRANSPORTATION *This hike is not easily accessible by public transportation.* The MARTA 73 bus stops 7 miles from the park's main entrance. The park can also be accessed from Factory Shoals Road on the east side of Sweetwater Creek, 4 miles from the bus stop at Camp Creek Parkway and Fulton Industrial Boulevard.

PARKING Paved parking area; GPS N 33° 45.1945, W 84° 37.7140

ADDRESS 1750 Mt. Vernon Road, Lithia Springs, GA 30122

HIKE DISTANCE 3-mile figure-8 loop

WHY THIS HIKE IS GREAT It leads past an impressive mill ruin and a scenic waterfall—the perfect destination for exercise, dog-walking, or a family outing.

DIFFICULTY
Overall— Moderate
Terrain—Very rocky section on Red Trail, other trails well maintained
Elevation change —Generally fairly level with several short ascents and descents

HOURS 7 am to sunset, year-round; visitor center open 9 am to 5 pm

DOGS Leashed dogs permitted

FACILITIES Toilets, visitor center, picnic facilities, other state park amenities

FEES & PERMITS $5 daily or $50 annual parks pass

LAND MANAGER Sweetwater Creek State Park

SENTINEL TREES
Tulip Tree – GPS N 33° 44.9615, W 84° 37.4975
  - 14'4" circumference
  - This gnarly tulip tree is the largest in this area of the park and is worth a short walk off the main path to visit. Its massive bent trunk has been hollowed out by fire and curves dramatically upward.

Tulip Tree – GPS N 33° 44.7333, W 84° 37.5318
  - 4'11" circumference of largest trunk (original fallen trunk was 8' circumference)
  - This tulip tree is not particularly large but it is unusual. When its original trunk fell, it stayed rooted in the soil and produced multiple trunks rising perpendicular to the original.

BIRDS TO LOOK FOR

SWEETWATER CREEK STATE PARK

Spring: great-crested flycatcher, indigo bunting, yellow-breasted chat

GPS N 33° 45.0540, W 84° 37.4847
- 8'11" circumference
- The largest tree in this area of the forest, this oak would have been only a sapling when the New Manchester Company Store (behind the tree) existed at this site.

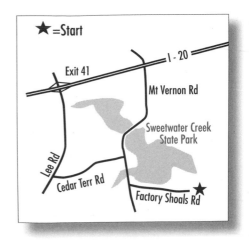

HIKE

Start the hike on White Trail by walking along the paved path toward the main doors of the visitor center. Pass the visitor center and follow the trail as it curves to the right, around the back of the building. Turn left into the woods on White Trail.

Continue for 0.45 mile past several benches and over multiple wooden footbridges. At a junction turn right, following the sign for Factory Ruins.

Just past a bench at the top of the hill in 0.15 mile, look to your left to find the sentinel tulip tree. This thick, bent tree about 200 feet off the trail is by far the largest tree in the forest, and worth an off-trail excursion to see close up.

Continue on White Trail for 0.25 mile, curving right across a small bridge, then left. In another 0.2 mile reach a junction with a sign that indicates you are 1.1 mile from the visitor center. Go left and walk downhill for 0.1 mile to reach a junction with Red Trail at the mill ruins.

Turn right and walk past the overlook platform and benches near the mill ruins. Just past the ruins, turn left down the wooden stairs to continue your hike on Red Trail. This trail along the edge of Sweetwater Creek is very rocky and rugged but only 0.5 mile long.

Cross a bridge in 0.2 mile, then ascend a steep set of stairs to an overlook platform. Descend another set of stairs and continue 0.3 mile to stairs leading up to a rock overlook of the falls.

Just past this overlook, walk up another steep set of stairs to a junction with White Trail. Go right on White Trail, passing several benches with views of the creek below.

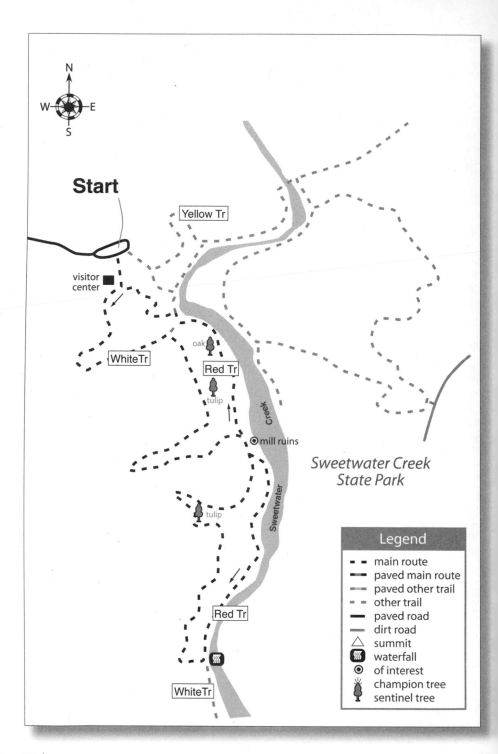

In 0.1 mile, pass the sentinel tulip tree on the right that fell over but continued growing multiple new trunks from its felled trunk. In another 0.1 mile the trail bends right. Continue for 0.25 mile to the junction with Red Trail at the mill ruins.

Stay straight to take Red Trail all the way back to the parking area. To do so, you'll cross a bridge in 100 yards and continue 0.15 mile to a junction on the right. This trail crosses a bridge over the millrace and follows the length of the island on your right. Continue straight for another 100 yards to a sign about the New Manchester Company Store. Across from the sign is the ruined foundation of the old store and the sentinel white oak with a small sign next to it.

In 0.2 mile you'll reach a junction with a sign for the visitor center. If you go straight at this junction, a small connector trail leads to Yellow Trail Loop. To end the hike, turn left and follow Red Trail to reach the visitor center and parking area in less than 0.25 mile.

Yellow Trail leads through lesser-known areas of Sweetwater Creek without the crowds of Red and White Trails.

YELLOW TRAIL

SWEETWATER CREEK STATE PARK

Though it is one of the most popular hiking destinations in the Atlanta area, Sweetwater Creek is full of hidden treasures. Yellow Trail is one such secret. Inaccessible from the main park entrance for several years after flooding washed away a bridge in 2009, Yellow Trail offers a great way to get away from the crowds on Red and White Trails. Winding through the hills on the east side of the creek, this route will surprise you with, among other things, a vantage point from which you can see the Atlanta skyline and a creekside view of the Manchester Mill ruins.

DISTANCE FROM DOWNTOWN ATLANTA • 19 MILES

BY CAR FROM I-20 *Although interstate signs suggest using exit 44 to get to Sweetwater State Park, the following directions are recommended.* Take exit 41 for Lee Road toward Lithia Springs and go south on Lee Road. In 1 mile, turn left onto Cedar Terrace Road. Drive 0.8 mile, pass an entrance sign for the state park, then turn right onto Mt. Vernon Road. Cross the lake, then turn left onto Factory Shoals Road in 0.3 mile. Pass the ranger kiosk, then continue straight for 0.6 mile to the circular parking area at the end of Factory Shoals Road.

PUBLIC TRANSPORTATION *This hike is not easily accessible by public transportation.* The MARTA 73 bus stops 7 miles from the park's main entrance. The park can also be accessed from Factory Shoals Road on the east side of Sweetwater Creek, 4 miles from the bus stop at Camp Creek Parkway and Fulton Industrial Boulevard.

PARKING Paved parking area; GPS N 33° 45.1945, W 84° 37.7140

ADDRESS 1750 Mt. Vernon Road, Lithia Springs, GA 30122

HIKE DISTANCE 3.5-mile lollipop loop

WHY THIS HIKE IS GREAT Yellow Trail leads through lesser known areas of this very popular park, with ascents and descents, quiet forests, and views of the Manchester Mill without the crowds of people on Red and White Trails.

DIFFICULTY

Overall — Moderate

Terrain — Wide, hard-packed soil and gravel trails

Elevation change — Mostly level with one significant ascent and descent

HOURS 7 am to sunset, year-round; visitor center open 9 am to 5 pm

DOGS Leashed dogs permitted

FACILITIES Toilets, visitor center, picnic facilities, other state park amenities

FEES & PERMITS $5 daily or $50 annual parks pass

LAND MANAGER Sweetwater Creek State Park

SENTINEL TREES

Chestnut Oak – GPS N 33° 45.1428, W 84° 37.0531
- 11'1" circumference
- The largest tree in this part of forest, this chestnut oak has siblings to its left and right. But why were these trees not harvested when the rest of the ridge was cut? While we can't know for sure, large trees were often used as property boundaries in times before GPS technology. Perhaps they were saved because they marked a property border on the ridgeline.

Chestnut Oak – GPS N 33° 45.0318, W 84° 37.1590
- 9'11" circumference
- To the right of the trail is another sentinel chestnut oak. Though slightly smaller than the sentinel chestnut oak you passed previously, this one is unique because its branches are growing much closer to the ground than other chestnut oaks.

INSIDER TIP

ALTERNATE ACCESS TO YELLOW TRAIL

You can access Yellow Trail via Factory Shoals Road on the east side of Sweetwater Creek. From Thornton Road, Factory Shoals Road leads to Bullard Road and Douglas Hills Road, both of which take you to the old dirt Factory Shoals Road, on which you can walk to the bridge over Sweetwater Creek. There is no official parking here.

Beech –
GPS N 33° 45.0396, W 84° 37.3249
- 8'3" circumference
- The beech tree to the left of the small bridge is intriguing because its roots have created a small waterfall in the creek. Someday, water and erosion will probably be the end of this tree, but for now it is fun to watch the water cascade through its root system.

HIKE

Along this trail are many posts labeled with numbers. You can pick up an interpretive brochure at the visitor center or download it from the park's website.

Start on the far end of the parking lot at a map and information kiosk. In less than 100 yards, at a junction with a gravel road, go straight to begin the Yellow Trail.

Continue on Yellow Trail for the next 0.3 mile, passing a couple of small side trails on your right. At a junction, go left, cross a bridge, and continue on Yellow Trail as it parallels Sweetwater Creek. You might hear gunshots from the nearby police firing range.

In 0.3 mile, arrive at the main bridge over the creek. Walk up the wooden ramp and cross the bridge. At the end of the bridge, turn right to follow Yellow Trail along the bank of the creek. Do not go straight on the dirt road at the end of the bridge.

In 0.1 mile, turn left at a junction and hike up the steep hill, passing several benches along the way. In 0.4 mile, pass the sentinel chestnut oak on the right next to a post labeled with the number 9.

In 0.25 mile, pass the second sentinel chestnut oak on the right. A smaller tree than the previous one, it has branches significantly lower to the ground. Walk down the stairs next to a chain-link fence on the left that surrounds a radio tower.

In 0.1 mile, reach a junction. To the left is a logging road and a clearcut section of forest. From the logging road on the ridge, you can see views of downtown Atlanta. Continue straight at this junction to stay on Yellow Trail, and hike 0.2 mile before

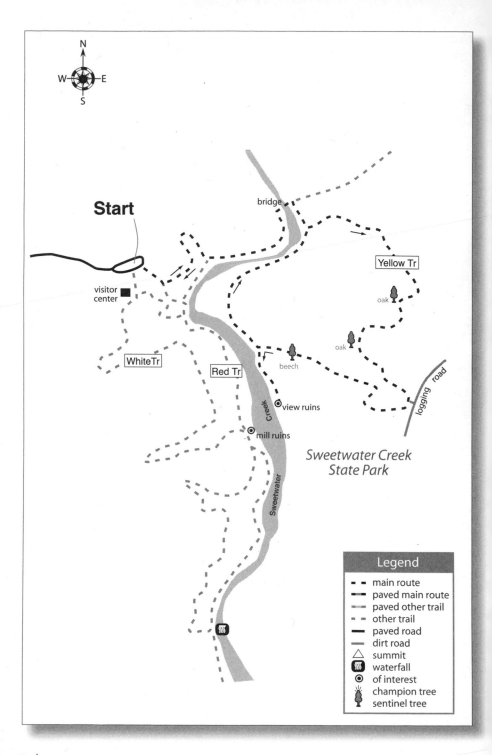

the trail begins to descend along a small stream. On the left across Sweetwater Creek is an overhanging rock where Native American artifacts have been found. Please do not disturb this area.

Cross the stream on stepping-stones, then cross a wooden footbridge labeled with number 15. On the left, the stream runs through the roots of the sentinel beech, creating a small cascade.

In 0.1 mile, reach a junction near Sweetwater Creek. Turn left on a 0.1 mile spur that leads to a nice view of the mill ruins across the creek. Back at the junction, continue on Yellow Trail as it parallels the edge of the creek. In 0.4 mile reach a junction and turn left. This takes you back to the large bridge over the creek.

Cross the bridge and follow the trail back the way you came. In 0.3 mile you'll reach a junction after crossing a small wooden bridge. You can go straight to stay along the edge of Sweetwater Creek and connect with Red Trail to join the Sweetwater *Red & White Trails* hike (p. 129), or go right to follow Yellow Trail back to the parking lot in 0.3 mile.

CLINTON NATURE PRESERVE

This unexpectedly large and scenic greenspace on the west side of town should draw many more hikers than it does. Clinton Nature Preserve offers great trails, a historic cabin, interesting woods and streams, and a unique rock outcrop. The beauty of this preserve demonstrates why settlers first came here in the early 1800s. As you explore, consider the footsteps of those who walked this land before you—Native American, white, and black.

DISTANCE FROM DOWNTOWN ATLANTA • 29 MILES

BY CAR FROM I-20 Take exit 30 and go south on Post Road for 0.9 mile. Turn right on Ephesus Church Road and drive 1.2 mile before turning right into the Clinton Nature Preserve on Clinton Road. Park in the lot on your left before you reach the main buildings on the property.

PUBLIC TRANSPORTATION
This hike is not easily accessible by public transportation. The Xpress 461/462 commuter bus stops in Douglasville, 6 miles from the nature preserve.

PARKING Gravel parking lot; GPS N 33° 42.4407, W 84° 51.8052

ADDRESS 8720 Ephesus Church Road, Villa Rica, GA 30180

HIKE DISTANCE
3.75-mile loop

WHY THIS HIKE IS GREAT
The payoff at the far end of this scenic hiking loop is a historic cabin from the early 1800s.

The nature preserve's historic cabin is a high point of this hike.

DIFFICULTY

Overall — Easy to moderate

Terrain — Hard-packed soil trails with an area of rock outcrop

Elevation change — Several ascents and descents of moderate length

HOURS Dawn to dusk, year-round

DOGS Leashed dogs permitted

FACILITIES Toilets, picnic areas, visitor center, playground

FEES & PERMITS None

LAND MANAGER Douglas County Parks

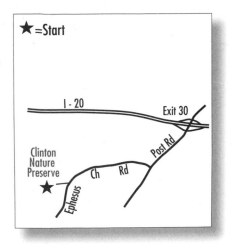

SENTINEL TREES

Chestnut Oak – GPS N 33° 42.4427, W 84° 51.8533
- 9'3" circumference
- This is the first large tree you see after leaving the parking lot. Its roots are fully exposed, and a picnic table has been placed on them. How long will this tree find a way to thrive in this tenuous situation?

Red Cedar – GPS N 33° 42.5528, W 84° 52.2552
- 4'3" circumference
- The Clinton Nature Preserve has a large population of red cedar, perhaps because it's a tree that was commonly planted by homesteaders and/or it thrives in the sandy and rocky soil of the preserve. This specimen is at a major trail junction near the park's granite rock outcrop.

White Oak – GPS N 33° 42.3589, W 84° 52.5242
- 10'11" circumference
- Though off the main loop, this tree's size qualifies it as a sentinel; it was protected from logging by its proximity to a homestead building. There's a lot of poison ivy here, so don't leave the trail; instead go right on a side trail just before the historic cabin. Halfway down the hill, look to the right; the tree is to the left of a collapsed cabin.

HIKE

Begin hiking along the gravel road next to the parking lot, toward the farmhouse with a red barn in the back. You'll see the sentinel chestnut oak. For the most part, this route follows Red Trail. Continue on the main trail for almost 0.5 mile, passing a junction with Blue Trail on your right, the pond on your left, and a junction with Yellow Trail on your left.

At another picnic table and a map sign, turn left onto the granite outcrop. The gravel road continues straight; pay attention as this turn is easy to miss. Also at this turn is the sentinel red cedar tree. In fact, the rock outcrop hosts a whole grove of mature red cedar trees. Take time to explore the outcrop, and be on the lookout for diamorpha, a tiny red plant growing in solution pits there.

From the map sign at the left turn, follow the left edge of the outcrop for a very short distance to two small paths exiting left into the woods. Take the second path, leaving the outcrop and heading into the woods.

Hike downhill for 0.15 mile. Pass a junction on the right and continue descending on a rocky trail to a bridge over a creek. Just beyond the bridge at a picnic table, turn right. The trail you were on continues straight back to the pond, so keep an eye out and don't miss this turn.

Continue 0.75 mile as the route winds and switchbacks through the forest to reach a junction with a map sign near a power line clearing.

Enter the clearing, turn right, and walk under the powerlines, but don't cross the gravel road. Follow several orange metal signs for the cabin. The second of these can be confusing as the silhouette of the cabin looks a little bit like an arrow pointing the wrong direction.

Re-enter the woods and hike downhill on the wide rocky path. Pass the first unmarked junction. At the second junction (also unmarked) look off to the right to see an abandoned building with a metal roof about 150-200 feet off the main path. At the third junction, there is an unmarked path going to the right of the main path (and no path to the left; look again to the right here to find another abandoned building about the same distance from the main path). Take this unmarked path and go about halfway down the hill toward a creek to have a better view of the abandoned building on the right. Look carefully to find the sentinel white oak tree standing tall to the left of the abandoned building. (Note that foliage during the summer makes viewing both of these abandoned buildings difficult.)

Return to the main path and continue downhill for about 0.1 mile to reach a historic cabin dating back to the early 1800s. Look to the left of the cabin to see onions still growing in the yard. There are also many rose bushes in front of the house, visible among other vegetation. Continue on the main trail for a short distance, passing a boxed spring on the left and two more outbuildings before arriving at the powerline clearing once again.

Turn left and walk up the hill through the clearing under the powerlines for 0.3 mile to reach the same junction with a map sign you passed earlier. Once back in the woods, go right on a wide trail that was formerly a dirt road. In about 0.2 mile, turn right at a junction. In just a short distance, follow a sign for Yellow and Red Trails to the right. Continue to another junction and turn right, following a sign for Red Trail.

In 0.35 mile, turn right at a junction near a bench and cross a small creek. Pass another bench and map sign in 0.15 mile, but ignore the map—the You Are Here dot is incorrect. Walk another 0.2 mile to a junction where the main trail turns left. Take the smaller trail to the right and cross a very steep wooden bridge. Beyond the bridge the trail joins a wide path. Go right and continue through a field, passing a covered amphitheater and picnic shelters to reach the farmhouse and parking area and end your hike.

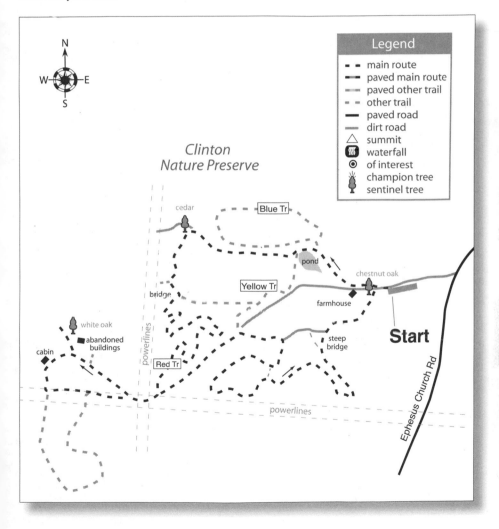

HERITAGE PARK

L ittle known but adjacent to the popular Silver Comet Trail, Heritage Park is a great place to escape into the woods from the crowded pavement. This hike passes the ruins of the historic Concord Woolen Mill on Nickajack Creek, destroyed by Union forces during the Civil War because it produced uniforms for the Confederate Army. The far end of the trail brings you to a nice waterfall near a quiet country lane and covered bridge.

DISTANCE FROM DOWNTOWN ATLANTA • 16 MILES

BY CAR FROM I-285 Take exit 15 for South Cobb Drive towards Smyrna. Go northwest (outside the perimeter) on South Cobb for 1.5 mile. Turn left onto the East-West Connector and continue for 2.4 miles before turning left onto Fontaine Road. The trailhead parking area is on the right in 0.5 mile at the intersection with Nickajack Road.

PUBLIC TRANSPORTATION
This hike is not easily accessible by public transportation. Take Cobb County Transit bus 20 to Emory Adventist Hospital and walk 2.8 miles to the trailhead, or take CCT bus 30 to Floyd Road and Veterans Memorial Highway and walk 2.5 miles to the trailhead. It can also be accessed via the Silver Comet Trail (p. 147).

PARKING Paved parking area; GPS N 33° 50.3372, W 84° 32.5487

ADDRESS 585 Nickajack Road SE, Mableton, GA 30126

Hike to a small waterfall on this little known trail.

HIKE DISTANCE 3.4 miles out & back

WHY THIS HIKE IS GREAT An easy creekside trail that packs several points of interest into one hike: historic mill ruins, a waterfall, a boardwalk through wetlands, and a covered bridge

DIFFICULTY

Overall — Easy

Terrain — Wide gravel and hard-packed soil trails with a section of boardwalk

Elevation change — Only minor elevation change

HOURS 6 am to 11 pm, year-round

DOGS Leashed dogs permitted

FACILITIES Toilets, picnic tables

FEES & PERMITS None

LAND MANAGER Cobb County Parks

SENTINEL TREES

Beech – GPS N 33° 50.3489, W 84° 32.5955
- 11'7" circumference
- Just before beginning the hike, stop to look at this enormous beech tree to the right. This tree's smooth gray bark is relatively unblemished by graffiti, unlike many other older trees of its species.

Red Maple – GPS N 33° 50.4559, W 84° 32.4405
- 8'6" circumference
- This red maple at the end of the footbridge over Nickajack Creek has been around a long time. Covered with moss and lichen, it still shows signs of life in the form of many shoots growing from nodes along its trunk and branches.

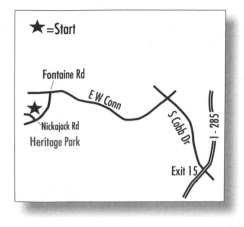

Tulip Tree – GPS N 33° 50.9945, W 84° 33.3829

- 11'1" circumference
- On the left as you walk up the path toward the Silver Comet Trail, this tulip tree has seen quite a few disasters. Its top was lopped off about 25 feet up, and the base of its large trunk is hollow. But the tree has stayed alive for many years, as demonstrated by its girth.

HIKE

Start your hike at the far end of the parking lot along Nickajack Road. Just before entering the trail, pass the sentinel beech tree on the right.

The trail switchbacks down to the floodplain, then reaches a boardwalk in 0.1 mile. Follow the boardwalk for 0.15 mile, cross a bridge over Nickajack Creek, then turn left on the trail parallel to the creek. On your left next to the bridge is the sentinel red maple.

Follow this trail along the creek for 1.15 miles, passing several picnic tables and crossing four small bridges. Go straight at a junction with a gravel access road on the right, then reach the mill ruins in less than 100 yards.

The trail passes between the two mill buildings propped up by steel girders, then comes to a picnic area and trail junction. To the right are two trails that connect to the Silver Comet Trail. Thirty yards up the trail to the left is the sentinel tulip tree.

Continue straight on the main trail for 0.2 mile. Just before reaching the trail's end at the Concord Road covered bridge and a historical marker about the Battle of Ruff's Mill, a narrow and steep trail leads down to a small waterfall. Be very careful if you choose to climb down this trail to the water's edge.

Turn around here and retrace your steps to the mill ruins, then continue back to the bridge over Nickajack Creek and the boardwalk, which leads to the parking area and the hike's end.

BIRDS TO LOOK FOR

HERITAGE PARK

All Year: brown-headed nuthatch, cardinal, Carolina chickadee, robin, tufted titmouse

HIKING ATLANTA'S HIDDEN FORESTS

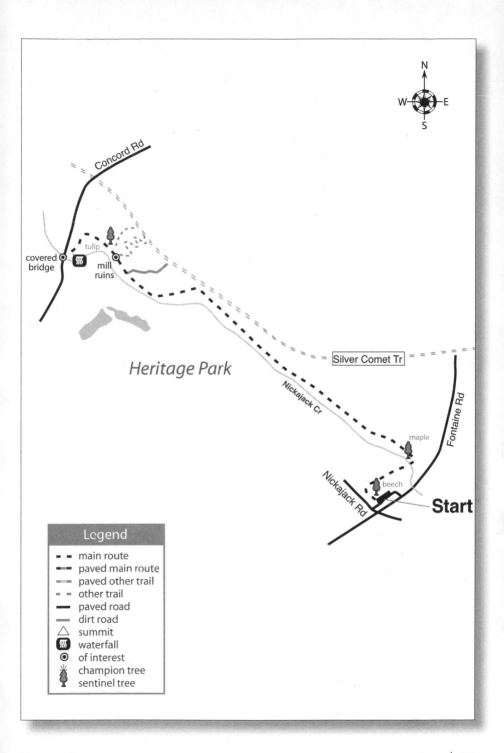

Start

Concord Rd

covered bridge

tulip

mill ruins

Heritage Park

Silver Comet Tr

Nickajack Cr

Fontaine Rd

maple

Nickajack Rd

beech

Legend
- - - main route
▬▬▬ paved main route
▬▬▬ paved other trail
- - other trail
▬▬ paved road
▬▬ dirt road
△ summit
♨ waterfall
⊙ of interest
🌲 champion tree
🌲 sentinel tree

SOUTH METRO

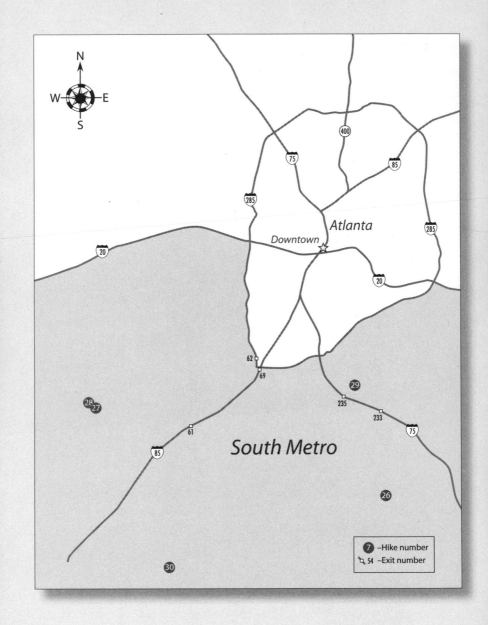

SOUTH METRO

㉖ Melvin L. Newman Wetlands Center

㉗ Cochran Mill Park

㉘ Cochran Mill Nature Center

㉙ Reynolds Nature Preserve

㉚ Line Creek Nature Area

If you love waterfalls, South Metro Atlanta hikes will not disappoint. The Cochran Mill Nature Center trails can lead you on an adventurous trek past four major waterfalls that spill over rock outcrops and old mill dams in beautiful cascades.

This beautiful wetlands center is part of Clayton County's innovative water treatment system.

MELVIN L. NEWMAN WETLANDS CENTER

The Newman Wetlands Center is an exceptional greenspace created by the nationally known Clayton County Water Authority, an industry leader in wastewater treatment. These wetlands are beautiful and provide excellent habitat for many species of animals and plants. They are also a crucial part of Clayton County's innovative water treatment system, which utilizes the natural environment to provide clean and efficient drinking water for its population.

DISTANCE FROM DOWNTOWN ATLANTA • 24 MILES

BY CAR FROM I-75 Take exit 235 toward Tara Boulevard/US 19/US 41/Griffin/ Jonesboro and drive south on Tara Boulevard for 8 miles. Turn left on Freeman Road, one block after the light at South Main Street. Drive 2.5 miles on Freeman Road to the Wetlands Center entrance on the right.

PUBLIC TRANSPORTATION *This hike is not easily accessible by public transportation.* The Xpress commuter bus service provides the closest service (though with very few coaches running each day), with a park-and-ride station in Jonesboro, 5 miles north of the Wetlands Center.

PARKING Gravel lot next to the interpretive building; GPS N 33° 28.3021, W 84° 18.3707

ADDRESS 2755 Freeman Road, Hampton, Georgia 30288

HIKE DISTANCE 0.75 mile loop

WHY THIS HIKE IS GREAT This wetlands is unique in the metro area for its plants and wildlife. The hike is perfect for birders, families with young children, and seniors.

DIFFICULTY

Overall — Easy

Terrain — Trails are crushed gravel and boardwalk; wheelchairs can be accommodated.

Elevation change — With the exception of the 0.1-mile Turkey Ridge spur trail, there is almost no elevation change on this loop.

In 0.1 mile, you'll reach Hammock Overlook Trail, a 50-yard spur that leads to a wetlands view worth exploring.

In another 0.1 mile, pass another hexagonal seating area along the boardwalk, then a covered bridge on the left that is closed to the public.

Hike 0.1 mile to a very short spur on a small dirt trail to an educational sign about habitat and a view of another cypress tree.

In 100 yards the trail closes the loop. Go straight and continue up the hill to return to the parking area and finish the hike.

INSIDER TIP

Water Purification at Melvin L. Newman Wetlands Center

This center is an integral part of the nationally famous Clayton County water treatment infrastructure. Because of its innovative thinking, the county has never been faced with a water shortage–even in the midst of droughts that stretched neighboring counties to the brink. By collecting all waste water in reservoirs and using the wetlands to naturally filter it and begin the purification process, Clayton County has created a sustainable water system for its population and a beautiful greenspace as well.

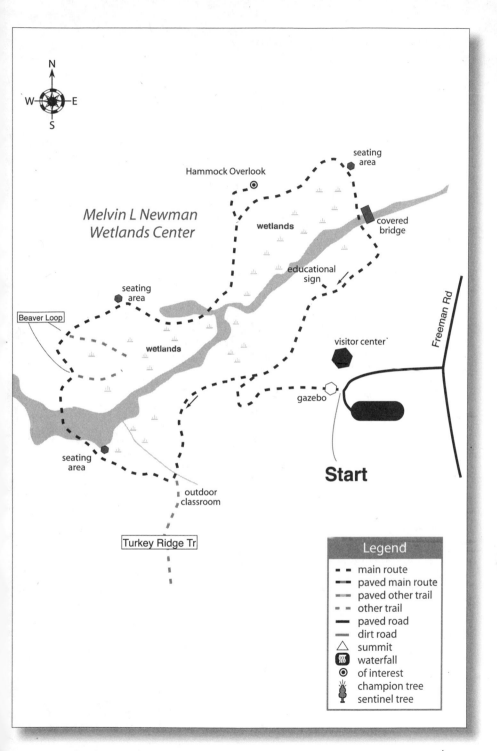

Melvin L Newman
Wetlands Center

Hammock Overlook

seating area

wetlands

covered bridge

educational sign

seating area

Beaver Loop

wetlands

visitor center

gazebo

seating area

Start

Freeman Rd

outdoor classroom

Turkey Ridge Tr

Legend
- - main route
— paved main route
— paved other trail
- - other trail
— paved road
— dirt road
△ summit
🌀 waterfall
◉ of interest
🌱 champion tree
🌱 sentinel tree

COCHRAN MILL PARK

Ready for an adventure? Though improvements are under way, hiking at Cochran Mill Park is still an off-the-beaten-path expedition. Be prepared for misleading signs, a ford that forces you to take off your shoes and wade through a creek, and trails that can be overgrown in the summer. The payoff at the end is a fabulous waterfall and a feeling of accomplishment.

DISTANCE FROM DOWNTOWN ATLANTA • 28 MILES

BY CAR FROM I-85 Take exit 69 to merge onto GA 14 Spur W and continue on South Fulton Parkway for 12.5 miles. Turn right onto Cochran Mill Road. In 0.4 mile make a left into the park entrance. Parking is up the hill on the right.

BY CAR FROM I-285
Take exit 62 to merge onto GA 14 Spur W and continue on South Fulton Parkway for 12.5 miles. Turn right onto Cochran Mill Road. In 0.4 mile make a left into the park entrance. Parking is up the hill on the right.

PUBLIC TRANSPORTATION
This hike is not easily accessible by public transportation. The 180 Palmetto MARTA bus will bring you closest; if you get off at the corner of Main Street and Griffin Drive in Palmetto, it is 5.6 miles to the park.

PARKING Gravel parking area; GPS N 33° 34.3024, W 84° 42.7916

You'll find a fabulous waterfall at the end of the hike.

HIKING ATLANTA'S HIDDEN FORESTS

ADDRESS 6800 Cochran Mill Road, Palmetto, GA 30268

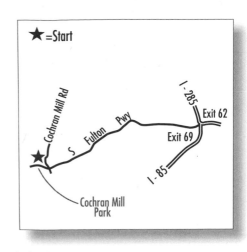

HIKE DISTANCE 5.5 miles out & back

WHY THIS HIKE IS GREAT One of the most adventurous hikes in this book. Getting to the waterfall at the end means navigating some confusing trail junctions and fording a creek—tons of fun and the destination is spectacularly worth it.

DIFFICULTY

Overall— Moderate

Terrain — Hard-packed soil trails and a creek ford

Elevation change — Ascents and descents are few and generally short

HOURS Dawn to dusk, year-round

DOGS Leashed dogs permitted

FACILITIES Toilets seasonally (portable toilet year-round), picnic pavilion, playground

FEES & PERMITS $5 daily parking fee (cash only) or $25 annual pass (available for purchase online); free for residents of Chattahoochee Hills

LAND MANAGER City of Chattahoochee Hills Parks

SENTINEL TREES

Sycamore – GPS N 33° 34.4949, W 84° 43.0253
- 11'2" circumference
- This sycamore stands out as a sentinel giant in a privet thicket near the entrance to a large clearing. Its trunk leans, then bends upwards. Notice the typically flaky bark at the base and smooth white branches at the top.

Water Oak – GPS N 33° 34.4268, W 84° 43.2639
- Five trunks, 19'3" circumference
- Of the many large water oaks along this trail, this one on the right just beyond a creek crossing really stands out. With five large trunks, it is one of the largest living organisms in this area.

Basswood – GPS N 33° 34.7857, W 84° 43.4897
- 8'3" circumference
- Champion-level in size and located a few feet from the creek bank, this tree is not as big as other trees on this hike but is impressively large for its species. Fun fact: basswood is an excellent wood for creating fire by friction.

HIKE

Start the hike on the gravel road adjacent to the entrance to the parking lot (on the same side of the road as the lot). Pass a green metal gate to begin.

In 0.3 mile, reach a ford for vehicles. Cross the creek on a pedestrian bridge to the right, then reach a trail junction. Go right, up the hill. In 0.1 mile, continue straight at a junction with a trail on the left.

In 0.25 mile, just before reaching an open field, pass the leaning sentinel sycamore tree on the right. Enter the field and continue straight toward the opening on the left. Leave the field and follow the old road through an open corridor, passing campsites on the left. In 0.15 mile, when a parking area surrounded by posts comes into view, look to the right for a sign marking the entrance to the H Trail. The sign reads "H".

Turn right onto the H Trail and hike 0.1 mile to the third H sign. The arrow points in an ambiguous direction. Go left and cross the small creek. After crossing the creek, walk down the path and you'll see the huge sentinel water oak with five trunks on your right at the creek's edge.

In 100 yards, pass another H sign pointing the wrong way. Stay on the main path, then go right when the trail splits in 100 feet. These two trails reconnect in 0.2 mile. Continue straight.

After the trails reconnect, walk 0.1 mile to reach a junction and the creek ford. Turn right on the path, take off your shoes, and wade across the creek. Even in rainy weather this ford is crossable as it is sandy and relatively shallow. Once on the other side, turn left to follow the creek downstream. This section of the H Trail can be overgrown and confusing. If you generally follow the creek, you'll make it to Henry Mill Falls at the end.

In 0.25 mile, the trail makes a short descent to a flat path along the creek bank and passes the sentinel basswood tree on the left just as you reach the water.

In 0.2 mile, hop across a small creek and turn left as the trail returns to the side of Bear Creek. Follow the creekside trail for 0.4 mile, then stay left at a junction with a small trail on the right. In 0.1 mile the trail climbs up a small embankment and turns to the left.

In another 0.2 mile, hop across another small creek and turn left.

The trail splits one last time as you approach Henry Mill Falls. Take the right fork and descend in 0.1 mile to a junction near the base of the falls. Turn left on this trail for an excellent view of the falls and good wading opportunities.

Turn back and hike 2.0 miles the way you came in.

At the end of the H Trail go right through the clearing toward the posts surrounding a parking area. Turn left onto the gravel road just beyond the posts and hike 0.3 mile to the vehicle ford. Cross the pedestrian bridge on the left and go left after passing a bench. This trail leads up a steep hill for 0.2 mile and back to the parking area to end the hike.

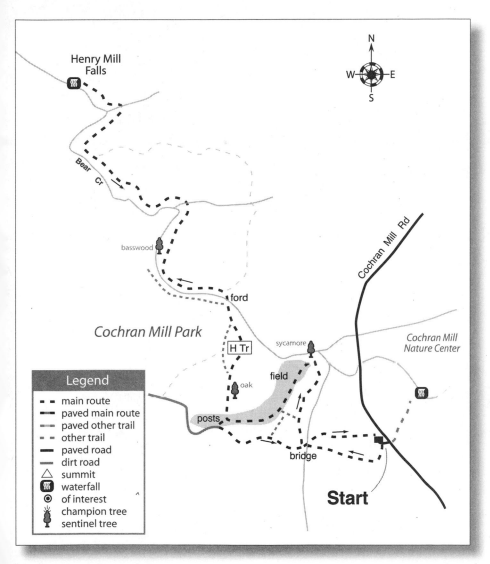

Cochran Mill is the best place
in Atlanta to see waterfalls.

Cochran Mill Nature Center

Especially if you love waterfalls, the trails of the Cochran Mill Nature Center provide some of the best hiking in metro Atlanta. Bear Creek and Little Bear Creek spill over rock outcrops and old mill dams in beautiful cascades. The trail leads you along the creeks, through rolling piedmont hills, and past four major waterfalls. And don't forget another major attraction: the Nature Center's reptile exhibit and birds of prey compound.

Distance from Downtown Atlanta • 28 miles

By car from I-85 Take exit 69 to merge onto GA 14 Spur W and continue on South Fulton Parkway for 10.5 miles. Turn right on Rivertown Road. After 2.3 miles turn left onto Cochran Mill Road. Make a left in 0.2 mile into the Nature Center driveway.

By car from I-285 Take exit 62 to merge onto GA 14 Spur W and continue on South Fulton Parkway for 10.5 miles. Turn right on Rivertown Road. After 2.3 miles turn left onto Cochran Mill Road. Make a left in 0.2 mile into the Nature Center driveway.

Public Transportation *This hike is not easily accessible by public transportation.* The 180 Palmetto MARTA bus will take you closest; if you get off at Main Street and Griffin Drive in Palmetto, it's 6.1 miles to the Nature Center.

Parking Gravel parking area; GPS N 33° 34.8604, W 84° 42.4619

Address 6300 Cochran Mill Road, Palmetto, GA 30268

Hike Distance 3.75-mile figure-8 loop

Why this hike is great Waterfalls! Cochran Mill is the best place in the Atlanta area to see waterfalls, and this trail leads you to four of them.

Difficulty
Overall — Moderate

Terrain — Hard-packed soil trails with a few rock outcrops that can be slippery in wet weather

Elevation change — Two steep uphill climbs; otherwise rolling hills and steady ascents

HOURS Monday through Saturday, 9 am to 5 pm. If you plan on hiking past 5 pm, alternate trailheads (noted on map) along Cochran Mill Road can be used. You can also park at Cochran Mill Park if you're willing to wade across Little Bear Creek at the start of your hike.

DOGS Leashed dogs permitted

FACILITIES Toilets, picnic area, nature center with reptile exhibit, birds of prey compound

FEES & PERMITS $3 per adult, $2 per child (ages 3-12)

LAND MANAGER Fulton County Parks & Recreation

SENTINEL TREES
White Oaks – GPS N 33° 34.6206, W 84° 42.4094
- Two white oaks with a circumference greater than 10'
- Near the mill dam ruin stand two ancient white oaks in their last stages of life; they are relics of a piedmont forest of bygone days. Resurrection ferns — so called because they look dead in dry weather but lush and green after a rain — growing on their branches are a sign of the trees' age.

Water Oak – GPS N 33° 34.5401, W 84° 42.8233
- 10'8" circumference
- This tree, 200 yards down a side trail to the right, stands sentinel over a much younger forest. The rounded shape of its crown demonstrates that it was the only tree growing in this area when the land was under cultivation.

INSIDER TIP

COCHRAN MILL NATURE CENTER AFTER HOURS

Planning on being on the trails after the Nature Center closes for the evening? You can park at Cochran Mill Park, cross Cochran Mill Road, and ford the creek below the closed iron bridge. This connects you to the trail near the Little Bear Creek waterfall. Hiking is allowed during daylight hours only. Fun fact: Scenes from the television show *The Walking Dead* were filmed near the waterfalls along Bear Creek.

Hike

Start your hike at the trailhead kiosk between the Nature Center and the bird compound.

Hike past the Station #1 signpost and uphill on Old Still Trail. In 0.2 mile cross a small footbridge, then pass an old bench and the Station #2 signpost before heading uphill for 0.3 mile to a bench next to the Station #3 signpost. Then the trail descends sharply to the edge of a wetlands area.

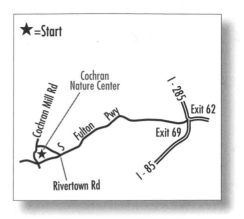

In 0.3 mile pass the Station #4 signpost, then cross a rock outcrop next to a dam and major waterfall. Walk downhill on the rock outcrop, keeping the creek on your left, to where the trail appears again. In another 0.1 mile, come to the Station #5 signpost, a waterfall, and the sentinel white oak with crooked branches on your right. Continue parallel to the creek and pass the second sentinel white oak on your left, near the overlook at the historic dam and waterfall.

After passing the sentinel trees, continue on the pine-straw-covered trail that leads to another rock outcrop. Continue straight across the outcrop and down to a trail along the edge of the creek. Mill Road Trail turns right here and leads back to the parking lot. Stay left and walk downhill to the creek's edge where you'll find the trail to continue this hike.

On this trail, walk next to the creek, crossing a small footbridge after 0.1 mile and a small but steep rock outcrop next to a smaller waterfall after another 0.1 mile. Not long after, reach a set of stairs below the first of two iron bridges. Walk up to the bench at the top, turn left, and cross the bridge. At the junction on the other side turn right and hike 0.15 mile on this wide trail to a junction with another wide trail. To visit the sentinel water oak, turn right and walk about 200 yards. The sentinel tree is about 50 feet off the trail on the right. Back at the junction, continue straight for 0.2 mile to reach the waterfall you can see in the distance.

You'll find a picnic table next to the waterfall and a closed iron bridge spanning Little Bear Creek. You can ford the creek below the bridge to reach the Cochran Mill Park parking area.

Just as you enter a clearing, you'll pass a small trail on the left. The route continues away from the waterfall and into the woods on this trail that ascends steeply for 250 yards. Pass a bench at the crest of the hill. Just after the bench, a small trail leads down to a waterfall overlook where you can examine the mill ruins more closely.

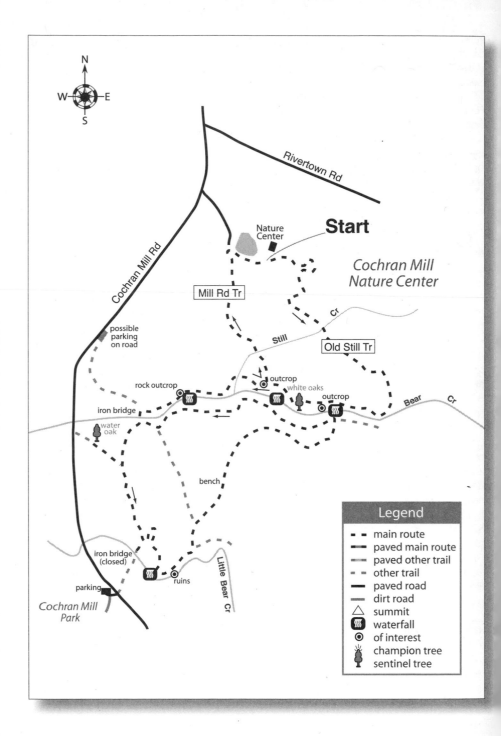

Follow this trail to the left from the ruins to merge with the main trail.

In 0.15 mile, bear left away from the creek at a junction with a small trail that stays right along the creek's edge. At the next junction, take the right fork. Around you on the ground is running cedar, a delicate evergreen plant.

In 0.1 mile at a bench, look to your left and you'll see old farming terraces. In 0.35 mile, the trail arrives at the old dam and rock outcrop you saw from the opposite side of Bear Creek at the beginning of the hike. Turn left, following the trail that parallels the creek for 0.5 mile to the first iron bridge. On the way, pass two benches and several junctions, staying right at each.

Cross the iron bridge, turn right, walk down the stairs, and follow the trail for 0.3 mile across the footbridge and small rock outcrop to the large outcrop next to the dam. When you reach the top of the outcrop, continue up and to the left where you'll find the wide Mill Road Trail that leads you 0.4 mile back to the parking area. On the way, pass the Station #6 signpost. When the trail meets the gravel road, turn right past the gate and follow the edge of the pond back to the parking area to end the hike.

.... a hidden gem where you can walk for miles without seeing other hikers.

Reynolds Nature Preserve

Reynolds Nature Preserve contains miles of trails that curve through stands of old-growth piedmont forest along the edge of ponds and creeks. Well-maintained and loved by locals, this preserve is still a hidden gem where you can walk for miles without seeing other hikers. Or you can stay near the entrance and visit the butterfly garden, native azaleas, and nature center. Either way, it offers an excellent outing opportunity for families and individuals.

DISTANCE FROM DOWNTOWN ATLANTA • 14 MILES

BY CAR FROM I-75 Take exit 233 for GA 54 and go north on Jonesboro Road. Drive 0.9 mile then make a left onto Reynolds Road. Reynolds Nature Preserve is on your left in 1.2 mile.

PUBLIC TRANSPORTATION *This hike is not easily accessible by public transportation.* Take the MARTA 55 bus to the corner of Conley Road and Jonesboro Road, which is 3.8 miles from the Nature Preserve.

PARKING Gravel parking area; GPS N 33° 36.0623, W 84° 20.8261

ADDRESS 5665 Reynolds Road, Morrow, GA 30260

HIKE DISTANCE 2.25-mile loop

WHY THIS HIKE IS GREAT Passionate park staff and a team of dedicated volunteers keep the trails in this park in great shape, allowing hikers to enjoy the miles of walking paths, trees, streams, ponds, and hills in pristine condition.

DIFFICULTY

Overall — Easy

Terrain — Wide and well-maintained trails, mostly hard-packed soil or mulched, with some bridges and boardwalks

Elevation change — Significant but short climbs on Back Mountain, High Springs, and Hickory Stump trails

HOURS 8 am to dusk, year-round; nature center open 9 am to 5 pm, Monday through Friday

DOGS Leashed dogs permitted

FACILITIES Toilets in two locations, nature center, picnic tables, outdoor classroom

FEES & PERMITS None

LAND MANAGER Clayton County Parks & Recreation

SENTINEL TREES
White Oak – GPS N 33° 35.9608, W 84° 20.8955
- 11'10" circumference
- The first large tree you come to on Crooked Creek Trail, this white oak is significantly larger than any tree you've passed on the route so far. The oak and tulip trees in this grove are fast-growing but are still by far the oldest specimens in this park.

Tulip Tree – GPS N 33° 35.9520, W 84° 20.9257
- 11'10" circumference
- This tree is memorable both for its size and for the young red maple growing out of its root system. Behind it is a thicket of rhododendron, a common evergreen plant in the Appalachian Mountains but rarer in the metro area.

Tulip Tree – GPS N 33° 36.0874, W 84° 20.9610
- 14'4" circumference
- The prize tree of Reynolds Nature Preserve, this bending tulip tree next to the footbridge is one of the larger of its kind in the Atlanta area. Its beautiful shape makes it even more impressive.

BIRDS TO LOOK FOR

REYNOLDS NATURE PRESERVE

All Year: American goldfinch, barred owl, Carolina wren, pileated woodpecker, white-breasted nuthatch

HIKE

Begin your hike at the map kiosk next to the parking lot and walk straight on the paved path toward the nature center. Turn left in front of the building. Just past a gazebo on your right go left at the sign for Crooked Creek and Brookside Trails.

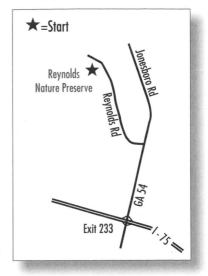

Continue for 0.3 mile on Brookside Trail, passing two junctions with smaller trails on the right. After passing a third junction (this time with a closed trail) on your right, continue straight for another 0.1 mile past a mulch yard and closed parking lot on your left, until you reach the Big Pond pier on your right. This is a great place to view turtles, ducks, geese, and other wildlife — but as the sign says, No Swimming! (not that Big Pond is that enticing for swimmers).

Continue on Brookside Trail, turning right at the end of the pond onto Back Mountain Trail which crosses the dam. After the dam the trail climbs uphill for 0.1 mile until you reach the junction with High Springs Trail.

Turn right. High Springs Trail winds along the slope above the ponds. On your right after 0.1 mile you'll see an area covered with pine straw that might be a nice place to sit and look at the pond.

The trail then climbs uphill again past another junction with a closed trail. In another 0.1 mile make a hard left turn onto Hickory Stump Trail (there is no sign at this junction, but there is a bench) and hike uphill.

After 0.2 mile you'll reach a junction (again, no sign post) with Back Mountain Trail. Turn right and hike another 0.2 mile. This area of the preserve brings you closest to the surrounding neighborhood on Phillips Drive. At a chain-link gate Back Mountain Trail turns right and becomes Crooked Creek Trail. Immediately after this sign, turn right onto Burstin' Heart Trail.

Walk up the ridge on Burstin' Heart Trail, then downhill, past a junction with Oak Ridge Trail on your left. Just after this junction you'll begin to see large tulip and oak trees on the left that make up Poplar Park (a section of older-growth forest along Crooked Creek). One-tenth of a mile beyond Oak Ridge Trail, turn left onto Crooked Creek Trail. You'll immediately pass the sentinel white oak on your left. In 50 yards pass a large tulip tree on your right. Marvel at this tree and then turn around. Fifty feet up the hill you'll see the Back Bend Oak, a white oak that looks like it's doing a back bend.

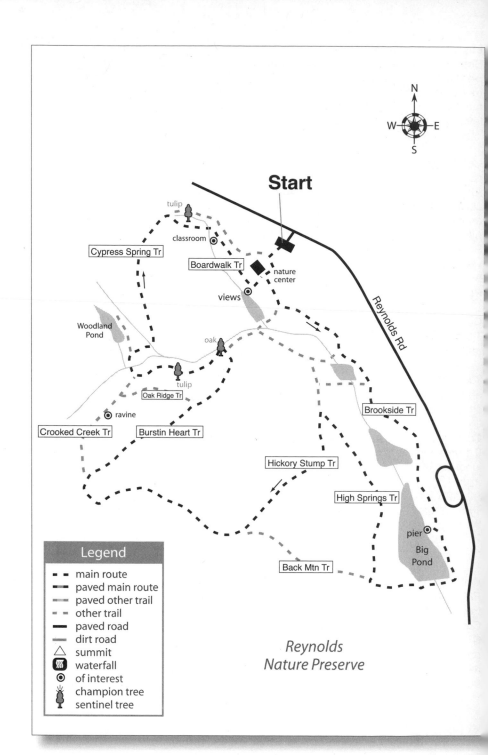

Start

tulip

classroom

Cypress Spring Tr

Boardwalk Tr

nature center

views

Woodland Pond

oak

tulip

Oak Ridge Tr

ravine

Crooked Creek Tr

Burstin Heart Tr

Brookside Tr

Hickory Stump Tr

High Springs Tr

Back Mtn Tr

pier

Big Pond

Reynolds Rd

N
W — E
S

Legend

- – – main route
- – – paved main route
- ~~~ paved other trail
- – – other trail
- —— paved road
- —— dirt road
- △ summit
- 🌊 waterfall
- ◉ of interest
- 🌲 champion tree
- 🌲 sentinel tree

Reynolds
Nature Preserve

Continue on the trail, pass a small stone wall, and you'll come to the sentinel tulip tree on your left with the young red maple growing out of its massive root system.

In another 100 yards leave Poplar Park and turn right onto Cypress Spring Trail. There's no sign here, but the trail is obvious. Cross a small footbridge, pass the junction with Woodland Pond Trail, cross another small footbridge, then hike uphill through a forest of oak trees. After 0.1 mile and a bench, the trail descends to meet Boardwalk Trail in 0.1 mile. At the bottom of the hill, pass a small cutoff trail on the right and walk 25 yards farther to reach the official junction and sign for Boardwalk Trail.

Turn right onto Boardwalk Trail and cross a bridge between a boxed spring on the right and an enormous leaning sentinel tulip tree on the left. Then hike left along the boardwalk until you come to an outdoor classroom and old barn. Turn right after the outdoor classroom and head into the woods. (To reach toilets and a picnic area, go up the small hill to the gravel path and turn right.)

The path through the woods on the right leads you 0.1 mile to the back of the nature center and two viewing platforms above a small pond on the right. After passing the nature center turn left across from the second viewing platform and walk up the stairs to the left, circling back to the front of the building on the brick path. The paved path in front of the nature center leads left back to the parking area to end the hike.

Line Creek Nature Area

Once you set foot in the Line Creek Nature Area you'll forget it is sandwiched between several housing and commercial developments. The trail along Line Creek (which creates the "line" between Coweta and Fayette Counties) is fabulously beautiful with native azalea, wild blueberry, and other flowering shrubs—a great walking route for any group. On weekend afternoons you'll see families and people of all ages. For a more strenuous hike you can continue your trek along the shore of the newly built reservoir.

Distance from Downtown Atlanta • 32 miles

By car from I-85 Take exit 61 toward Fairburn/ Peachtree City and go south on GA 74/Senoia Road for 11 miles. Turn right onto GA 54. In 0.8 mile, make a U-turn at the light at McDuff Parkway, then an immediate right into the Line Creek Nature Area driveway. The parking area is at the end of this gravel drive in 0.2 mile.

Public Transportation *This hike is not easily accessible by public transportation.* The Xpress 450 and 451 commuter buses stop in Newnan, 7.5 miles from the trailhead.

Parking Gravel parking area; GPS N 33° 23.6000, W 84° 36.2456

The trail along Line Creek is fabulously beautiful.

ADDRESS 2010 Highway 54,
Peachtree City, GA 30269

HIKE DISTANCE 2.65-mile lollipop loop

WHY THIS HIKE IS GREAT The scenery
along Line Creek is unbeatable on a sunny
afternoon. The fast-moving creek bubbles
over rock outcrops and through thickets of
laurel, azalea, and blueberry.

DIFFICULTY

Overall — Easy

Terrain — Hard-packed soil trails with areas
of exposed granite that can be slippery

Elevation change — Only minor elevation
change

HOURS Dawn to dusk, year-round

DOGS Leashed dogs permitted

FACILITIES Portable toilet, several picnic areas

FEES & PERMITS None

LAND MANAGER Southern Conservation Trust

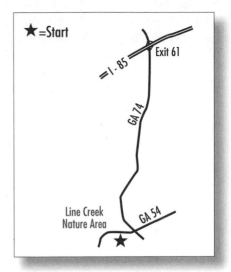

SENTINEL TREES AND PLANTS

Native Azalea – GPS N 33° 23.7004, W 84° 36.3986

- Masses of these native flowering bushes grow along the banks of Line Creek;
  it's worth making a pilgrimage each year to see their early spring blooms.
  To identify them without their orange and yellow flowers, look for slender,
  crooked, woody stalks 4 to 8 feet high, with small teardrop-shaped leaves.

Wild Blueberry – GPS N 33° 23.5055, W 84° 36.3250

- Though not as prodigious in fruit production as their cultivated cousins, the
  wild blueberry bushes to the left of the trail just beyond the Creek Trail sign
  are impressive for their size. They have crooked trunks with rough, peeling
  bark and small oval leaves.

Yucca – GPS N 33° 23.2875, W 84° 36.0612

- Yucca is not a tree but is an important native plant to know—and easy to spot along Line Creek. Similar in look to both cactus and palmetto, its succulent, waxy fronds grow from a single base in the ground. Its root can be made into soap, and its flowers are edible. The fibers in its leaves are the strongest of any fiber that grows naturally in Georgia.

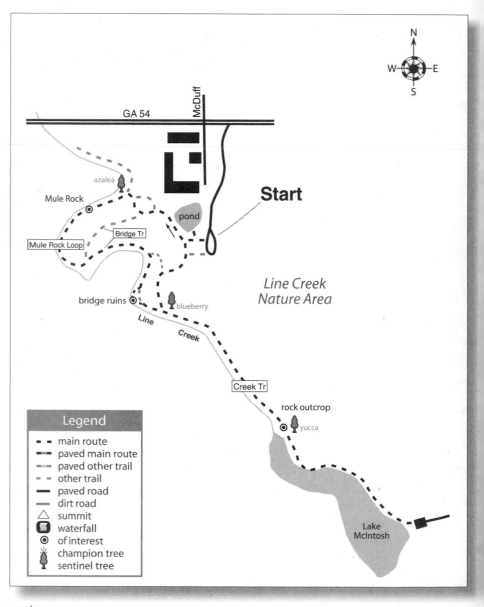

HIKE

Start on the trail that begins at three short posts near the start of the parking lot and walk to the right toward the gazebo and pond. After taking some time to admire the pond, turn back to the main path and go right at the map and information kiosk.

At the junction with Bridge and Creek Trails, go right on Bridge Trail along the edge of the pond, passing two benches. At a junction at the end of the pond, go left then right onto Mule Rock Loop. Hike downhill for 0.1 mile and turn left at the next two junctions. Once you are alongside Line Creek—where sentinel native azalea grow *en masse*—hike 100 yards, then cross Mule Rock (just after crossing the rock, turn around to see the carving of a mule in the rock) and continue straight for 0.15 mile to reach a junction with the Bridge Trail.

Turn right and hike 0.15 mile. Cross a bridge and carefully walk across exposed rock along the creek. Where the trail splits, bear left toward a bench up the hill from the creek, pass the bench, then come to a sign for Bridge Trail and an arrow pointing left. Turn right here on a side trail that leads down to the creek. You'll cross the foundation of a Civil War-era bridge before meeting back up with Bridge Trail. Continue straight at this junction for 100 yards, parallel to the creek, to reach a junction with Creek Trail.

Stay straight along a portion of the creek with beautiful views. Just after passing the Creek Trail sign, pass the grove of large sentinel wild blueberries on your left.

From here the trail becomes more rocky. After hiking 0.4 mile and crossing several small bridges, reach a rock outcrop where the trail continues up and to the left. Just past the rock, sentinel yucca plants grow on either side of the trail. These evergreen plants are more obvious in the winter when they are the main greenery along the trail. In summer you'll have to pay attention to find the yucca among all the lush growth.

Follow the main trail another 0.4 mile along the banks of Lake McIntosh to reach the south entry to the park. Turn back, retracing your steps for 0.8 mile to a junction with a several trail signs. Go right and uphill on Trail to Pond. In 0.1 mile go right, following another Trail to Pond sign.

At the next junction go left and hike 100 yards farther to a junction at the edge of the pond. Turn right to return to the parking area.

EAST METRO

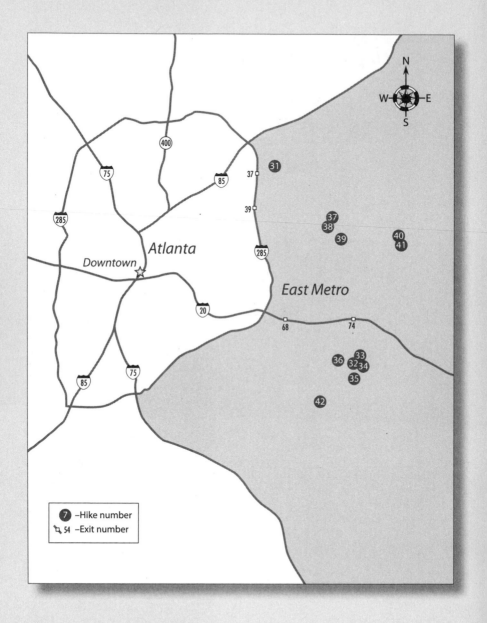

EAST METRO

㉛ Henderson Park

Davidson–Arabia Mountain Nature Preserve
㉜ Mountaintop Trail
㉝ Forest & Mile Rock Trails
㉞ Mountain View Trail
㉟ Laurel Creek Trail
㊱ Cascade & Wilburn Farm Trails

Stone Mountain Park
㊲ Walk-Up Trail
㊳ Cherokee Trail
㊴ Songbird Habitat Trails

Yellow River Park
㊵ North Loop
㊶ South Loop

㊷ Panola Mountain State Park

Come to East Metro for its three monadnocks (granite mountains). If you have time to hike only one, choose Arabia Mountain, the oldest and least famous of the three—more accessible than Panola Mountain and without the crowds of Stone Mountain. Arabia is a place where many nature-lovers have fallen in love with Atlanta!

The trails and impressively large trees will be what you remember from your visit here.

HENDERSON PARK

Most people know Henderson Park for its soccer fields, but the trail system in this community park is extensive and diverse. This route will take you through coves of wildflowers, along the banks of Lake Erin, past wetlands, streams, and waterfalls. Stop to feed the ducks or play on the playground if you like, but the trails and impressively large hardwood trees will be what you remember from your visit here.

DISTANCE FROM DOWNTOWN • 15 MILES

BY CAR FROM I-285 Take exit 37 and drive east (outside the perimeter) on Lavista Road toward Tucker. In 1.8 miles, turn left on Henderson Road. Continue 0.8 miles to turn right into the Henderson Park Community Garden parking lot.

PUBLIC TRANSPORTATION Take the 124 Pleasantdale-Chamblee-Tucker bus to the intersection of Brown Road and Chamblee Tucker Road. Walk west on Brown Road for 0.3 miles, turn left, and walk 0.3 miles on Tipperary Road. Then turn right on Henderson Road and walk 0.3 miles to the Henderson Park Community Garden parking lot.

PARKING Paved parking lot at Henderson Park Community Garden; GPS N 33° 51.825, W 84° 13.927

ADDRESS 2723 Henderson Road, Tucker, GA 30084

HIKE DISTANCE 2.5-mile lollipop loop

WHY THIS HIKE IS GREAT This is one of the more hidden trail systems in the metro area, where you can watch the sunset over Lake Erin, marvel at massive oaks, and photograph wildflowers.

DIFFICULTY

Overall — Easy

Terrain — Mostly hard-packed soil with some bridges, stone stairs, and asphalt

Elevation change — Regularly undulating trails; no extended uphill climbs

HOURS 7 am to sunset, year-round

DOGS Leashed dogs permitted

FACILITIES Toilets sometimes available near the soccer fields on the east and west sides of the park; playground near Lake Erin, gazebos and picnic tables near the community garden parking lot

FEES & PERMITS None

LAND MANAGER DeKalb County Parks & Recreation

SENTINEL TREES

"Praise God" Beech – GPS N 33° 52.0330, W 84° 13.6800
- 7' circumference
- This beech with "Praise God" carved into its trunk grows near a well-traveled trail junction next to a gully and is intertwined with a tulip tree. Beeches have smooth gray bark and produce small nuts encased in a spiky shell. Early settlers in America used beech nuts to produce a coffee substitute.

White Oak – GPS N 33° 52.0990, W 84° 13.6390
- 13' circumference, 123' tall
- Just downslope on the right of the trail, this is without question the largest oak (and possibly largest tree) in all of Henderson Park, and it's a beauty. Both big and tall, this tree commands attention. Someone nailed a ladder into the back of the trunk. White oak acorns contain less tannic acid than other native oaks and were an important food source for Native Americans in the region for many years. Don't try to crack one open and eat it, though; the taste is quite bitter and will upset your stomach. The native people washed acorns clean in local creeks before cooking and consuming them.

Northern Red Oak – GPS N 33° 51.9260, W 84° 13.5820
- 11'2" circumference, 120' tall
- This very large specimen is rooted quite precariously on a steep slope above a trail junction at the edge of the park boundary. View this tree from the trail; the slope is slippery, and any foot travel would likely cause hillside erosion damage.

Hike

From the parking lot, walk away from your vehicle along the dark asphalt path toward the gazebo. Walk around the gazebo, keeping it on your left. The path enters the woods and switchbacks down the hill. After 0.2 mile, at the bottom of the switchbacks, look for stone steps on your right and walk down onto a dirt trail that leads farther down the hill.

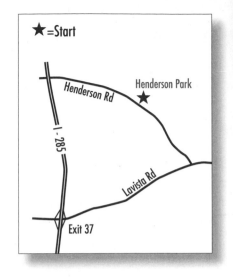

Once on the trail stay right at the retaining wall, then continue straight past a drainage area on your right. This section of the park is feathered with various side trails; stay on the main trail unless otherwise directed. Hike toward the lake (which will become visible through the trees shortly) past several trail junctions until you reach a junction near the water's edge marked with a post that identifies White and Blue trails. Turn left onto White Trail to parallel the lakeshore. In 100 yards, turn right and follow the trail across the dam.

At the end of the dam walk right to follow the lakeshore. A playground and picnic shelter are on your left. Just past a platform on the water's edge you'll join a paved sidewalk leading to a map kiosk that was an Eagle Scout project. The trails on the map are unlabeled, but this map can give you a general idea of the park's trail system. Follow the paved trail leading into the woods. In 100 yards you'll reach a gully on your right. At the edge of the gully is the sentinel "Praise God" beech. Look for the old carving on its bark that gives the tree its name, then continue straight along the edge of the gully (not down the hill) to stay on White Trail. Look for a white blaze if you need guidance.

The trail climbs up a hill, and the gully on your right becomes a cove replete with bloodroot, ferns, and pawpaw. In 0.1 mile you'll see a sentinel white oak on your right about 20 feet off the trail. This tree is hard to miss because it is so much larger than the others around it.

Just past the white oak turn right and head down the hill, following white blazes on the trees. Stay on White Trail until you reach the soccer field entrance and junction with Red Trail. There is often a portable toilet located near this trailhead.

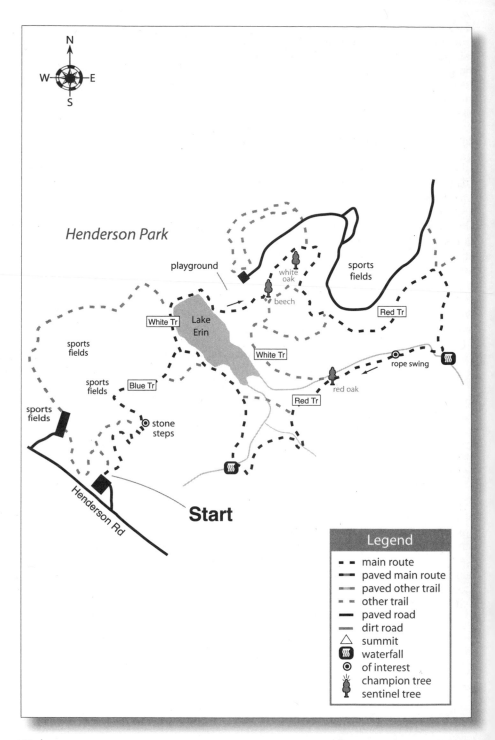

Henderson Park

playground

white
oak

beech

sports
fields

Red Tr

White Tr

Lake
Erin

White Tr

rope swing

sports
fields

sports
fields

Blue Tr

red oak

Red Tr

sports
fields

stone
steps

Start

Henderson Rd

Legend

- - - main route
— paved main route
— paved other trail
- - other trail
— paved road
— dirt road
△ summit
🌊 waterfall
◉ of interest
🌲 champion tree
🌲 sentinel tree

Stay straight to begin Red Trail, and walk downhill past large rocks on your left. You will pass many side trails but stay on Red Trail, following red blazes, for 0.2 miles. At a 4-way junction turn right and continue to follow the red blazes. In another 0.2 miles you'll cross a small waterfall and climb up and around tree roots to continue on Red Trail, which follows the creek downhill. In the cove at the bottom of the hill you'll see many umbrella magnolia trees around you. These trees have the largest leaves in the forest, so they are easy to identify.

The trail soon levels out and follows the creek. Look for a rope swing on a bough of one of the several beech trees on the hill to your left. When you reach the post marking the trail junction of Red and White Trails, look up the hill to your left to find the sentinel northern red oak. Continue straight on; do not cross the creek on the right.

Continue hiking on the Red Trail, following the red blazes and passing several more trails leading back toward the lake. Soon you'll head down a steep embankment to cross the creek below a large two-tiered waterfall. Enjoy viewing the waterfall, but don't explore beyond it, as that area is private property.

After crossing the creek, continue on this trail for 0.2 mile, when you'll come to a small canyon on your left and a trail junction on your right. There are also park boundary signs here. Continue straight and hike uphill. Bear right and follow the lakeshore (which is now on your right). Hike another 0.1 mile, cross a wooden bridge, and turn left on Blue Trail at the post identifying the junction of White and Blue Trails.

From here retrace your steps along this trail, past the drainage area, left at the concrete retaining wall, up the stone steps, and left on the asphalt path to reach the Henderson Park Community Garden parking lot where the hike began.

MOUNTAINTOP TRAIL

DAVIDSON–ARABIA MOUNTAIN NATURE PRESERVE

A rabia Mountain is the oldest and least famous of the three monadnocks (granite mountains) in the Atlanta area; its summit and surrounding land are spectacularly beautiful, pristine, and peaceful. More accessible than Panola Mountain and without the crowds and development of Stone Mountain, Arabia is a place where many nature-lovers have fallen in love with Atlanta. If you have time to hike only one trail in this book, choose this one.

DISTANCE FROM DOWNTOWN ATLANTA • 20 MILES

BY CAR FROM I-20 Take exit 74 toward Evans Mill Road. Continue straight on the access road for 1.1 mile, past an intersection with Lithonia Industrial Boulevard, and take the right exit for Evans Mill Road East. Turn left onto Evans Mill Road, then right at the light onto Woodrow Drive. In 0.8 mile, turn right onto Klondike Road. Just beyond the traffic circle at Rockland Road in 1.2 mile, pass the visitor center on the right, then drive 1 mile farther to a small parking area on the left, just past North Goddard Road on the right. The parking area is marked with an AWARE animal rescue center sign.

PUBLIC TRANSPORTATION
This hike is not easily accessible by public transportation. Take the MARTA 111 or 116 bus to the Mall at Stonecrest. You can pick up the PATH Foundation's Arabia Mountain Trail (a paved multi-use trail) at the corner of Mall Parkway and

If you only have time for one hike in Atlanta, this is it.

Klondike Road. From there, it is 3 miles to the parking area and trailhead just beyond North Goddard Road.

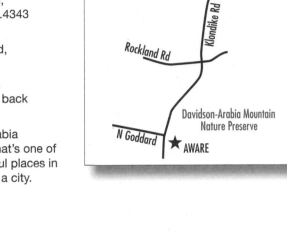

PARKING Small gravel parking area with overflow parking at the visitor center 1 mile north on Klondike Road; GPS N 33° 39.5904, W 84° 07.4343

ADDRESS 4158 Klondike Road, Lithonia, GA 30038

HIKE DISTANCE 1-mile out & back

WHY THIS HIKE IS GREAT Arabia Mountain, a unique location that's one of the most inspiring and peaceful places in Atlanta, doesn't feel like it's in a city.

DIFFICULTY

Overall — Easy to moderate

Terrain — Granite trail surface

Elevation change — Short but steep ascent and descent from the summit

HOURS Dawn to dusk, year-round

DOGS Leashed dogs permitted

FACILITIES Portable toilet

FEES & PERMITS None

LAND MANAGER Arabia Mountain National Heritage Area

Sentinel Trees and Plants

Diamorpha – GPS N 33° 39.7234, W 84° 07.1797

- "What's the red stuff?" This sign marks the beginning of the Arabia Mountain summit ascent and is a perfect place to begin looking for diamorpha. Though not a tree, diamorpha is one of the most important plants in the park. The solution pits of Georgia monadnocks are the primary habitat of this small red plant which puts on an amazing show each year. In late winter and early spring only its succulent red stems are visible; in the summer the plants become dry and brittle. But when its white flowers bloom in late spring, it is one of the most spectacular sights in the state.

Stunted Red Cedar – GPS N 33° 39.8012, W 84° 07.1806

- Just to the left of the third cairn (stone trail marker) past the diamorpha sign you'll find this stunted red cedar growing more like a bush than like a tree, with multiple trunks in the shallow soil of a mountainside solution pit. Red cedars can grow to over 75 feet, but the marginal ecology of Arabia Mountain has stunted its growth.

Loblolly Pines – GPS N 33° 39.9060, W 84° 7.0660

- From the top of the mountain, look around at the plant growth. Though there are a few stunted red cedars and some bushes, the primary trees surviving on this "moonscape" are fast-growing loblolly pines. They find larger pockets of soil for their roots and are still able to grow 20 to 30 feet tall. They represent the final stage of primary plant succession on this monadnock.

Hike

Begin at the information pavilion to the left of the AWARE entrance. Enter the rock outcrop and follow cairns on the otherwise unmarked trail. Take care not to step in the solution pits where delicate flowers and plants flourish.

After 0.3 mile, pass a cairn with a blue blaze, several blue blazes on the rock, and one on a tree. This is the junction with Mountain View Trail. Stay left and follow the cairns to the base of the mountain past an interpretive sign about diamorpha. Continue to follow the cairns up the mountain.

The sentinel stunted red cedar is near the third cairn as you ascend.

Reach the last cairn after 0.2 mile and continue hiking another 100 yards to the top of the mountain, where you will see the sentinel loblolly pines.

From the top of the mountain, look around. To the west on a clear day you can see the Atlanta skyline. To the southwest is Panola Mountain, another monadnock. To the northeast is the second peak of Arabia Mountain. It has been quarried and is not as pristine as the one you are standing on.

Though there are no trails leading to the second peak, it is a great place to explore if you are feeling adventurous. You can make your way down the slope of this peak to reach the other. To return, just find your way back to the first peak, pick up the trail of cairns, and follow them back to your vehicle to end your hike.

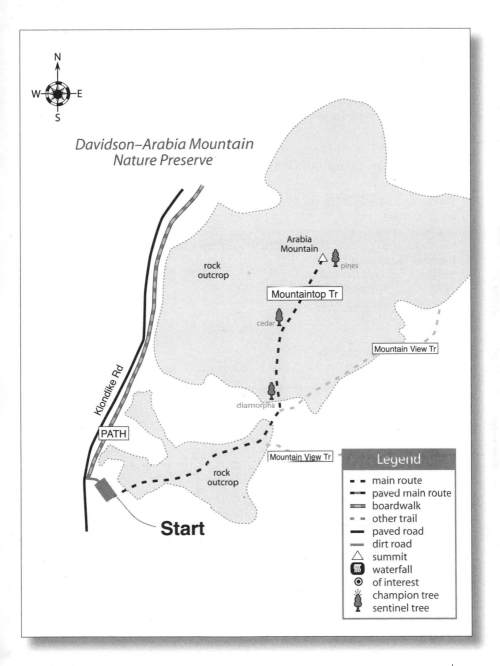

FOREST & MILE ROCK TRAILS

DAVIDSON–ARABIA MOUNTAIN NATURE PRESERVE

Though not the iconic summit hike, this route is perhaps the most interesting in the whole preserve. Leading through forests, past the scenic Arabia Lake, and across a semi-quarried rock outcrop, this trail provides many places that will make you stop and say, "Wow!" With colorful foliage reflected on the lake in the fall; yellow, red, and blue flowers in spring; and croaking frogs in the summer, this loop hike is exciting in all seasons. The random polished slab of granite, the drill holes, and ruined quarry buildings give you a glimpse of the history of the place.

DISTANCE FROM DOWNTOWN ATLANTA • 20 MILES

BY CAR FROM I-20 Take exit 74 toward Evans Mill Road. Continue straight on the access road for 1.1 mile, past an intersection with Lithonia Industrial Boulevard, and take the right exit for Evans Mill Road East. Turn left onto Evans Mill Road, then go right at the light onto Woodrow Drive. In 0.8 mile turn right onto Klondike Road. Just beyond the traffic circle at Rockland Road in 1.2 mile, park in the visitor center parking lot on the right.

PUBLIC TRANSPORTATION *This hike is not easily accessible by public transportation.* Take the MARTA 111 or 116 bus to the Mall at Stonecrest. You can pick up the PATH Foundation's Arabia Mountain Trail (a paved multi-use trail) at the corner of Mall Parkway and Klondike Road. From there, it is just over 2 miles to the visitor center and trailhead.

PARKING Gravel parking area near visitor center; GPS N 33° 40.3311, W 84° 06.9650

The solution pits on Arabia Mountain are full of life.

ADDRESS 3787 Klondike Road, Lithonia, GA 30038

HIKE DISTANCE 2-mile loop

WHY THIS HIKE IS GREAT It's one of the most diverse trails in this park. With a minimum of elevation change you can see a scenic lake, rock outcrops with solution pits full of flowers, quiet forests, and historic buildings.

DIFFICULTY

Overall — Easy

Terrain — Hard-packed soil and granite trails with a short section of pavement

Elevation change — Little to no elevation change

HOURS Dawn to dusk, year-round

DOGS Leashed dogs permitted

FACILITIES Visitor center with flush toilet, portable toilet, picnic tables, access to multi-use path, water fountain

FEES & PERMITS None

LAND MANAGER Arabia Mountain National Heritage Area

SENTINEL TREES

Loblolly Pine – GPS N 33° 40.4410, W 84° 07.3111
- 9'8" circumference
- Loblolly pines larger than 10 feet in circumference in the Atlanta area are rare, but this tree on the right side of the trail is close to that mark. Its trunk splits about 20 feet off the ground; the right trunk is now dead.

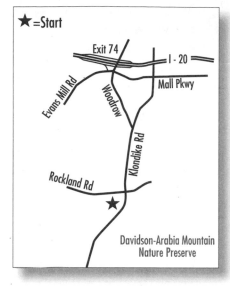

Loblolly Pine – GPS N 33° 40.4182, W 84° 07.3388

- 6'9" circumference
- Like many pines in this area of the forest, this loblolly on the right side of the trail sustained damage years ago that split its trunk. It has continued growing in a fashion that looks like two arms circling upwards.

Red Cedar – GPS N 33° 40.0997, W 84° 07.4032

- 2'7" circumference
- Just beyond the fourth cairn (a stack of rocks used as a trail marker) after the frog pond, these two specimens on the right are growing so close together they look like one tree. Red cedars are common on granite outcrops like this one, and these are flourishing in the solution pit despite the minimal amount of soil there.

HIKE

Begin the hike at an information kiosk in front of the visitor center and go right on a boardwalk following yellow-blazed Forest Trail. In 0.15 mile, stay straight at a junction and arrive at the paved multi-use path.

Cross the paved path and re-enter the woods, following a sign for the lake. Parallel the paved path for a few yards, then turn left at the next junction. When the trail splits in 0.2 mile, bear right to pass the sentinel loblolly pine on the right. After the trails reconnect, pass the second sentinel loblolly pine on the right.

Just past the sentinel tree, stay straight at a junction, then hike 0.2 mile to reach a second junction. Stay left and follow a sign for Arabia Lake. Then stay left at a third junction. Pass an old metal culvert and follow the lakeshore for 0.2 mile. Native azalea grows along the right side of the trail.

At the end of the lake go left on the rock outcrop toward the pavilion. Follow a sign for Mile Rock Trail. At the pavilion, look across the rock and hike toward the cairns. Be careful to not step in the many solution pits where delicate plants flourish in the rain water they collect. In 0.25 mile, the trail curves left. At the sixth cairn, go left at the junction toward subsequent cairns on the rock outcrop.

BIRDS TO LOOK FOR

DAVIDSON–ARABIA MOUNTAIN PRESERVE

Winter: brown creeper, dark-eyed junco, downy woodpecker, hermit thrush, song sparrow

The next cairn is near an old quarry building and an access trail for the multi-use path. Stay left and slightly uphill to follow the cairns across the rock outcrop. Between the fourth and fifth cairns beyond a frog pond, pass the sentinel red cedar on the right. Continue following the cairns across the outcrop, then down into a lower quarried area. In 0.2 mile pass another old quarry building and re-enter the woods.

At the first junction in the forest follow a sign for the nature center to the left (going right leads to the multi-use path). In 0.15 mile, reach a junction with the paved multi-use path near the visitor center. Go right, then left over the bridge to reach the parking area and finish the hike.

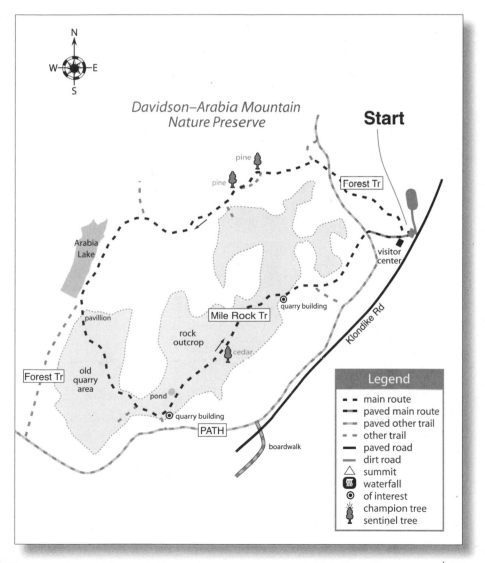

MOUNTAIN VIEW TRAIL

DAVIDSON–ARABIA MOUNTAIN NATURE PRESERVE

Mountain View Trail is the newest trail in the Davidson–Arabia Preserve, built on an area of land acquired by the county in 2012. This scenic route skirting the base of the mountain and circling the lake is one of the most beautiful in the park and can be combined with the *Mountaintop Trail* hike (p. 188) and other off-trail explorations for a full day of forest and granite outcrop adventures.

DISTANCE FROM DOWNTOWN ATLANTA • 20 MILES

BY CAR FROM I-20 Take exit 74. Continue straight on the access road for 1.1 mile, past an intersection with Lithonia Industrial Boulevard. Take the right exit and turn left onto Evans Mill Road, then go right at the light onto Woodrow Drive and turn right onto Klondike Road in 0.8 mile. Just beyond the traffic circle at Rockland Road in 1.2 mile, pass the visitor center on the right, then drive 1 mile farther to a small parking area on the left, just past North Goddard Road on the right. The parking area is marked with an AWARE animal rescue center sign.

PUBLIC TRANSPORTATION

This hike is not easily accessible by public transportation. Take the MARTA 111 or 116 bus to the Mall at Stonecrest. You can pick up the PATH Foundation's Arabia Mountain Trail (a paved multi-use trail) at the corner of Mall Parkway and Klondike Road. From there, it is 3 miles to the parking area and trailhead just beyond North Goddard Road.

The route circling the lake is one of the most beautiful in this park.

PARKING Small gravel parking area with overflow parking at the visitor center 1 mile north on Klondike Road; GPS N 33° 39.5904, W 84° 07.4343

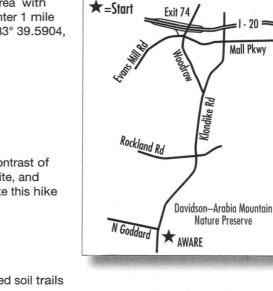

ADDRESS 4158 Klondike Road, Lithonia, GA 30038

HIKE DISTANCE 2.5-mile loop

WHY THIS HIKE IS GREAT The contrast of blue skies, green trees, gray granite, and shimmering water in the lake make this hike incredibly scenic.

DIFFICULTY

Overall — Easy to moderate

Terrain — Granite and hard-packed soil trails

Elevation change — Fairly level with a few minor ascents and descents

HOURS Dawn to dusk, year-round

DOGS Leashed dogs permitted

FACILITIES Portable toilet

FEES & PERMITS None

LAND MANAGER Arabia Mountain National Heritage Area

SENTINEL TREES AND PLANTS

Red Maple – GPS N 33° 39.9757, W 84° 06.6566
- 5'2" circumference (tree on the right)
- Notice the sizable red maples growing on either side of the trail, a transition area between granite outcrop and piedmont forest. They lean out over the rock to seek more sunlight and avoid competition from other trees.

Mountain Laurel – GPS N 33° 39.9600, W 84° 06.6550
- Though relatively rare in the Atlanta metro area, mountain laurel thrives at Arabia Mountain. Identify these woody shrubs by their evergreen, tear-drop-shaped leaves and peeling bark. Laurels usually bloom around Mother's Day, so take your mom hiking on the Mountain View Trail to celebrate.

Red Cedar – GPS N 33° 39.7124, W 84° 06.7141
- 4'5" circumference
- This cedar can be seen from across the lake, growing prominently next to an old cabin. Red cedars thrive in rocky soils and are common in this park; this one has no competition and therefore has a straight trunk and full boughs.

HIKE

Begin your hike under the information pavilion to the left of the AWARE entrance. Enter the rock outcrop and follow cairns (stacks of rocks used as trail markers) along the same route as for Mountaintop Trail. Be careful not to step in the many solution pits which catch rain water and where delicate flowers and plants flourish. Use caution because the rock can be slippery when wet.

In 0.25 mile, between the 11th and 12th cairns, look for three blue blazes painted on the rock. This is where the trail reconnects at the end of the loop. Continue forward toward the 13th cairn, then go right toward a blue blaze painted on a tree.

Follow blazes painted on the rock and on trees. The trail skirts the edge of the forest at the base of the mountain for 0.2 mile before turning right into the woods. After 0.1 mile in the forest where the trail passes large mountain laurels, it re-emerges onto the granite outcrop and continues above the forest.

Pass a viewpoint at the edge of the lake in 0.1 mile. Beyond this viewpoint the trail continues to skirt the lake but a little higher on the mountain. The blue blazes painted on the rock are a little harder to find, so pay attention. In 0.2 mile, the trail descends to the right and enters the forest. As you enter the woods, the two largest trees on either side of the trail are the sentinel red maples. Just beyond is the sentinel mountain laurel.

The trail follows an intermittent stream and then the edge of the lake, making a slight turn inland in 0.2 mile to avoid an area of mucky ground. You will soon reach a grove of pines with a bed of pine straw on the ground that makes a good picnic spot. Follow blazes on trees and cross an old woods road to continue on the trail. Blue-blazed trees are at the crossing.

In 0.2 mile cross a small stream, then hike uphill to an old roadbed. Turn right and walk 0.1 mile to an old hunting cabin with the sentinel red cedar next to it.

Just past the tree, before you reach the cabin, turn right and walk down a set of stairs, then go left on an old roadbed leading across the dam.

At the far side of the dam turn left and hike downhill. Follow blazes across a rock outcrop. The trail crosses an intermittent stream on the rock at the edge of the woods. Bear left uphill into the woods; the path merges onto a woods road. Follow blue blazes uphill another 100 yards to a field. The trail skirts the right side of the field past oak and cherry trees and re-enters the woods in 0.1 mile.

In just over 100 yards, re-emerge onto the rock outcrop to meet up with the cairns of Mountaintop Trail. Just before you step onto the rock, pass yucca plants on the left. Walk out onto the rock toward the cairns, turn left, and follow the cairns 0.25 mile back to the parking area to end the hike.

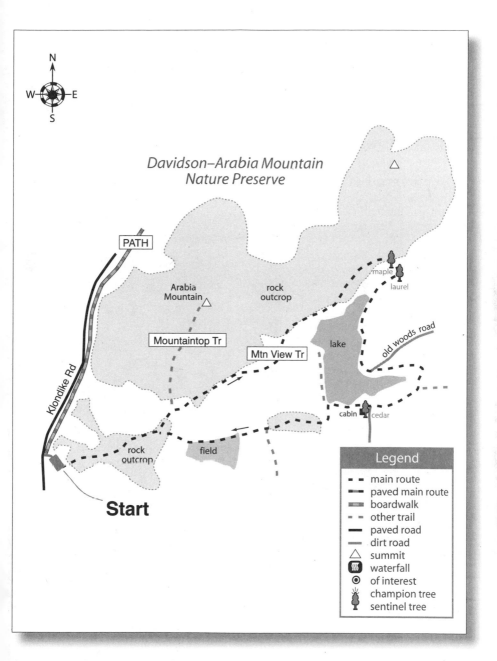

Laurel Creek Trail

DAVIDSON–ARABIA MOUNTAIN NATURE PRESERVE

The least-hiked trail at Davidson–Arabia Preserve is also one of its prettiest. Mountain laurel evokes images of fast-flowing creeks and craggy peaks, and this hike lives up to that image. After the route crests, it follows a quiet, forested ridge to meet up with a bubbling creek with two cascades, mountain laurel, and the feeling of exploring a forgotten hollow in the Appalachian Mountains. Then, just like that, you're back on a paved path next to an elementary school—it's like magic!

DISTANCE FROM DOWNTOWN ATLANTA • 20 MILES

BY CAR FROM I-20 Take exit 74 toward Evans Mill Road. Continue straight on the access road for 1.1 mile, past an intersection with Lithonia Industrial Boulevard, and take the right exit for Evans Mill. Turn left onto Evans Mill Road, then right at the light onto Woodrow Drive. In 0.8 mile, turn right onto Klondike Road. In 1.2 mile, just beyond the traffic circle at Rockland Road, pass the visitor center on the right, then drive almost 2 miles farther to Murphey Candler Elementary School. Turn right on South Goddard Road (across from the abandoned Oak Grove Junction Convenience Store). Continue on South Goddard just past the school to the entrance to the Arabia Mountain multi-use path.

PUBLIC TRANSPORTATION
This hike is not easily accessible by public transportation. Take the MARTA 111 or 116 bus to the Mall at Stonecrest. You

Mountain laurel blooms along the trail in spring.

can pick up the PATH Foundation's Arabia Mountain Trail (a paved multi-use trail) at the corner of Mall Parkway and Klondike Road. From there, it is just over 4.6 miles on the multi-use trail to the spur trail that leads to the Laurel Creek Trail and 3.7 miles to the parking area next to Murphey Candler Elementary School.

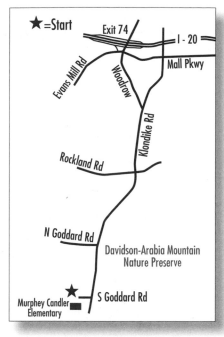

PARKING On evenings and weekends park along South Goddard Road next to Murphey Candler Elementary School near the Arabia Mountain Trail PATH entrance (At other times access is via the multi-use Arabia Mountain Trail from the visitor center 2 miles north on Klondike Road or the parking area on Evans Mill Road); GPS N 33° 39.1070, W 84° 07.7090

ADDRESS 6775 South Goddard Road, Lithonia, GA 30038

HIKE DISTANCE 2.5-mile loop

WHY THIS HIKE IS GREAT In contrast to other hikes in this park, this route has no rock outcrops—you are instead treated to cascading streams and quiet forests.

DIFFICULTY

Overall — Easy to moderate

Terrain — Hard-packed soil trails and paved multi-use path

Elevation change — Several extended ascents and descents

HOURS Dawn to dusk, year-round

DOGS Leashed dogs permitted

FACILITIES None

FEES & PERMITS None

LAND MANAGER Arabia Mountain National Heritage Area

SENTINEL TREES AND PLANTS

Dogwood–GPS N 33° 39.4918, W 84° 07.8082
- This forest is replete with dogwood trees; look for this one on the right just before the trail descends from the ridge. Notice its bark's geometric-shaped plates and its bent, craggy branches. This tree did not die when it fell. Instead, it now has three trunks growing from the original.

Mountain Laurel–GPS N 33° 39.5413, W 84° 07.6623
- Across the creek from the trail junction, a thicket of mountain laurel serves both as a sentinel and the trail namesake. Mountain laurel prefers to grow in rocky alpine soil, and the area surrounding the Arabia monadnock provides similar terrain. Its spring-blooming flowers are beautiful, but beware—laurel is one of the most poisonous plants in the forest if ingested.

Tulip Tree–GPS N 33° 39.5869, W 84° 07.8782
- 11'2" circumference
- This tulip tree on the far bank of the creek is a giant in this new-growth forest. Tulip trees grow fast and tall, but this one is definitely older than the surrounding trees. There is no easy way to get across the creek to see this tree up close, but if you're creative you probably can find a way.

HIKE

Begin hiking downhill on the paved multi-use path. Continue 0.1 mile before reaching the junction with white-blazed Laurel Creek Trail on the right.

Follow Laurel Creek Trail up a steep hill for 0.25 mile. When you reach a picnic table at the top, go right and hike 0.2 mile before the trail descends. Just before going downhill, pass the remarkable sentinel dogwood tree on the right with three new trunks growing from the old fallen trunk.

Hike 0.3 mile to a junction near the creek. Across the creek is the sentinel stand of mountain laurel. To the right a short spur trail leads to a small cascade. Turn left and continue 0.25 mile along the creek to a junction with a sign that reads Rapids.

To your right across the creek is the sentinel tulip tree. Go straight through a laurel thicket to reach the rapids (another small cascade) in about 100 yards. Returning to the trail junction, turn right and hike uphill, away from the creek.

In 0.2 mile, reach a junction. The right trail leads to the paved multi-use path. Turn left, cross a bridge after 0.1 mile, and continue uphill to the junction with a picnic table at the top of the hill.

Take the wide trail to the right and hike downhill for 0.25 mile, back to the multi-use path. Turn left to return to the parking area and end the hike.

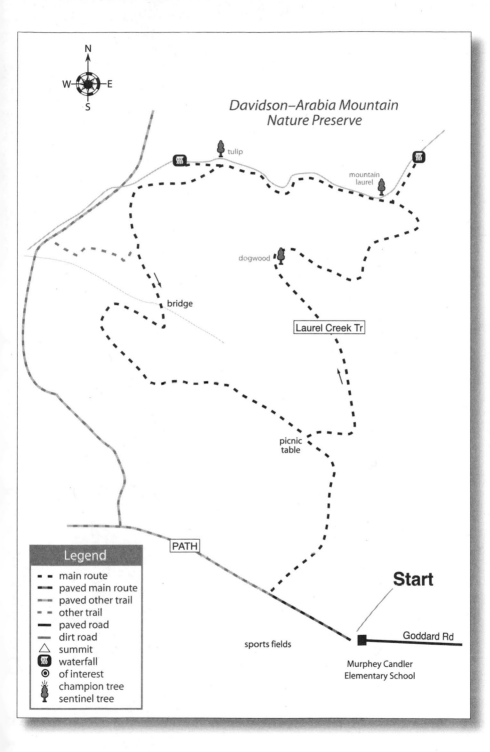

Cascade & Wilburn Farm Trails

Davidson–Arabia Mountain Nature Preserve

The Cascade-Wilburn Farm loop is easily accessible but known by few because Wilburn Farm Trail only opened in 2010. Though many people use the paved Arabia Mountain Trail, the true beauty of this area lies on Cascade and Wilburn Farm trails. The loop leads you past cascading rapids running over a smooth granite rock outcrop, then up onto a ridge above the farm where you can see a view of Arabia Mountain. The farm itself is intriguing because of its sentinel trees, the collapsed ruins of a farmhouse, a horse barn, and a scenic pond. You'll end with a relaxing walk down the paved multi-use path. It's a hike with something for everyone.

DISTANCE FROM DOWNTOWN ATLANTA • 18 MILES

BY CAR FROM I-20 Take exit 74 toward Evans Mill Road. Continue straight on the access road for 1.1 mile, past an intersection with Lithonia Industrial Boulevard, and take the right exit for Evans Mill Road East. Turn right onto Evans Mill Road and drive 2.9 miles to reach a parking area on the left at the beginning of the Flat Rock Spur of the Arabia Mountain multi-use path.

PUBLIC TRANSPORTATION *This hike is not easily accessible by public transportation.* Take the MARTA 86 or 111 bus to the corner of Evans Mill, Woodrow Drive, and Mall Parkway. The MARTA 115 and 116 buses also stop nearby. From this intersection, it is 2.9 miles on Evans Mill Road to the parking area.

PARKING Paved parking area; GPS N 33° 40.1168, W 84° 09.0131

ADDRESS 4028 Evans Mill Road, Lithonia, GA 30038

An old barn still stands at the Wilburn Farm.

HIKE DISTANCE 3.5-mile figure-8 loop

WHY THIS HIKE IS GREAT Cascading rapids, old farmstead, pond, views of Arabia Mountain, and lush forests.

DIFFICULTY

Overall — Moderate

Terrain — Hard-packed soil trails and paved multi-use path

Elevation change — Several extended ascents and descents

HOURS Dawn to dusk, year-round

DOGS Leashed dogs permitted

FACILITIES None

FEES & PERMITS None

LAND MANAGER Arabia Mountain National Heritage Area

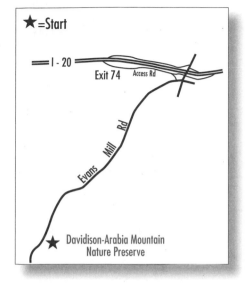

SENTINEL TREES

Sycamore – GPS N 33° 40.1030, W 84° 09.0396
- 8'6" circumference
- Sycamores usually grow close to water, so it's no surprise to find this one near the creek. This tree was topped about 10 feet up but continued growing two large limbs that make it look like a candelabra.

Pear – GPS N 33° 40.0854, W 84° 08.3069
- These two old pear trees have seen significant damage; one even has a hole all the way through its trunk. Amazingly, both are thriving and still produce fruit each year. Several other varieties of pear have recently been planted nearby.

Red Cedar – GPS N 33° 40.0681, W 84° 08.3134
- 8' circumference
- This red cedar is a giant among its species. Planted by the family that once occupied the now-collapsed farmhouse, its size demonstrates how long this land has been settled and under cultivation.

HIKE

Before beginning the hike, take a short walk on the spur trail just before the paved multi-use path begins. This spur leads to a picnic area near the site of historic Evans Mill and a sentinel sycamore tree on the right next to an interpretive sign. Remains of the old dam can be seen at the edge of the creek.

Back at the beginning of the multi-use path, walk for 50 feet to where the parking lot ends, and turn right on Cascade Trail next to a bicycle-shaped bike rack.

Cross an old wooden bridge to reach the cascades for which the trail is named. Continue hiking as the trail leaves the creek and ascends the ridge in 0.2 mile. In another 0.4 mile, reach a junction with the multi-use path. Cross the pavement and go straight to begin on Wilburn Farm Trail.

After a 0.4-mile steady uphill climb, reach a junction with an old farm road. Turn right to reach a junction at the top of a large, sloping field. From here you can see the peak of Arabia Mountain to the east. There are two paths through the field below which can be somewhat overgrown in the summer, depending on how recently they've been mowed and mulched. Hike down the hill on the path on the right side of the field and reach a junction in 0.15 mile. Go straight, then left to walk toward the barn.

When you reach the barn and a swing attached to a limb of a nearby water oak, look across the field to a collapsed farmhouse. Follow the trail toward the farmhouse for just over 100 yards to reach the two sentinel pear trees on the right at the next junction, next to the farmhouse. You can take a photo of your face through the hole in one of these trees.

Continue straight, passing the sentinel red cedar on the left across from the farmhouse. Fifty yards beyond the farmhouse, as the trail begins to descend, there is an old boxed spring about 30 feet off the trail to the right if you care to explore and find it.

In another 0.1 mile past the farmhouse you'll reach a pond fed by the spring. Hop across a small rivulet, and follow the trail across the dam. The trail then winds through a lush piedmont forest for 0.6 mile to a junction with Boomerang Trail.

INSIDER TIP

CONNECTING WILBURN FARM TRAIL AND LAUREL CREEK TRAIL

To connect Laurel Creek and Wilburn Farm Trails, use the paved multi-use path and Boomerang Trail. From the junction of Wilburn Farm and Boomerang Trails, go left and continue for 0.4 mile to reach the multi-use path. Turn right. After crossing a bridge over Laurel Creek, turn left onto a spur trail that leads to Laurel Creek Trail.

If you go left you can connect with the multi-use trail, from which you can reach a spur trail that leads to Laurel Creek Trail. To continue this loop, turn right on Boomerang Trail.

In 0.1 mile you'll reach a junction with the multi-use path. Go right and walk 1 mile back to the parking area to end the hike.

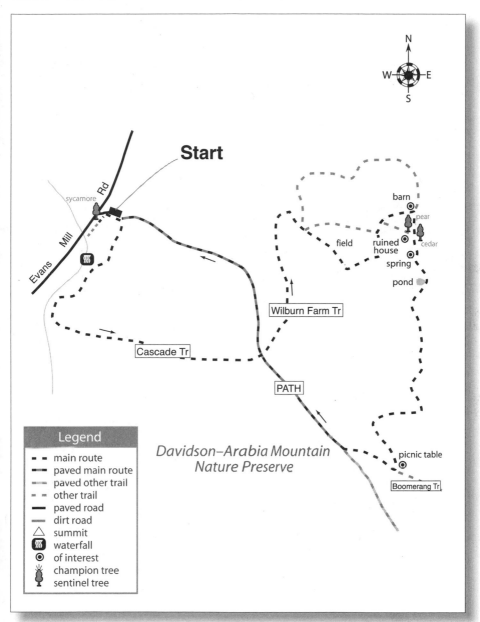

Start

N
W–E
S

sycamore
Evans Mill Rd

barn
pear
field
ruined house
cedar
spring
pond

Wilburn Farm Tr

Cascade Tr

PATH

Legend
- – – main route
- ▬▬ paved main route
- ~~~ paved other trail
- – – other trail
- — paved road
- — dirt road
- △ summit
- ♨ waterfall
- ◉ of interest
- 🌲 champion tree
- 🌲 sentinel tree

Davidson–Arabia Mountain Nature Preserve

picnic table

Boomerang Tr

WALK-UP TRAIL

STONE MOUNTAIN PARK

Stone Mountain is one of the icons of Atlanta, and its Walk-Up Trail is the most-used—and most spectacular—trail in the metro area. Once a meeting site for the Ku Klux Klan, the mountain now draws an incredibly diverse cross section of people from all over America and the world. Though it is a strenuous route, you will see elders and toddlers hiking to the top. It will make you sweat, but on a clear day the views make it all worthwhile—you can see as far as the Appalachian Mountains in north Georgia.

DISTANCE FROM DOWNTOWN ATLANTA • 18 MILES

BY CAR FROM I-285 Take exit 39B to merge onto US 78E toward Snellville/Athens. Travel 8 miles, then take exit 8 toward the Stone Mountain Park entrance. Merge onto Jefferson Davis Drive, pay the entrance fee, and drive 1.0 mile to Robert E. Lee Boulevard. Bear right onto Robert E. Lee and drive 1.0 to the parking area near Confederate Hall.

PUBLIC TRANSPORTATION Take the 121 Memorial Dr MARTA bus to the corner of Main Street and West Mountain Street in Stone Mountain. Then walk east on East Mountain Street for 0.5 mile to reach the parking area for Walk-Up Trail.

PARKING Paved parking area near Confederate Hall; GPS N 33° 48.6378, W 84° 09.7327

Atlanta's iconic hike is up Stone Mountain.

Address 1000 Robert E. Lee Boulevard, Stone Mountain, GA 30083

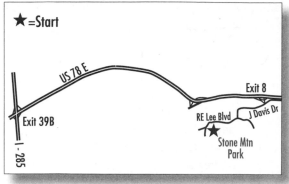

Hike Distance
2-mile out & back

Why this hike is great
This is the iconic Atlanta hike. Besides good exercise and spectacular views, you'll be hiking alongside thousands of people from all over the world—a true Atlanta experience.

Difficulty

Overall — Moderate to strenuous

Terrain — Granite surface with many roots and rocks

Elevation change — Very steep the whole way up and the whole way down

Hours Dawn to dusk, year-round

Dogs No dogs permitted

Facilities Toilets and water fountains at the bottom and top of the mountain, seasonal snack bar at the top

Fees & Permits $10 one-day parking fee or $35 annual parking pass

Land Manager Stone Mountain Park

Sentinel Trees
Georgia Oak – GPS N 33° 48.5027, W 84° 09.1468
- Georgia oaks grow only on rock mountains (monadnocks) like Stone Mountain, Arabia Mountain, and Panola Mountain. Evolved to thrive on granite with very little soil, these trees look more like bushes—but with telltale oak-shaped leaves. You'll see many Georgia oaks here; this sentinel to the left of the path has multiple thick, gnarled trunks.

Stunted Sweetgum – GPS N 33° 48.4273, W 84° 08.9647
- 4'10" circumference
- Environment can turn even the largest and most majestic species into small stunted trees. To the left of the trail between several large boulders you will find one of the highest-growing deciduous trees on the mountainside. This sweetgum is probably old enough to have grown to a circumference of more than 11 feet in a different location, but exposure to the elements and lack of good soil have stunted its growth.

Stunted Loblolly Pine – GPS N 33° 48.3729, W 84° 08.8413
- This tree, alone on the granite mountainside to the right of the trail, is as close to a naturally created bonsai tree as you'll find in the metro area. Typically straight-trunked loblolly pines regularly attain 80 to 100 feet and were once used for ships' masts. This one is bent by the winds and stunted by the lack of soil, yet it continues to grow in this marginal ecotone.

HIKE
Start your hike near the restrooms. Cross the railroad tracks and walk across the rock toward the flags.

Pass the flags on your right in 0.1 mile, then cross a service road. Stay straight for another 0.1 mile to reach a junction with Cherokee Trail. Continue straight at this junction, then pass two poles covered with bubble gum (gross!).

In 0.25 mile, just before reaching call box #3, you'll come to a Georgia oak in the middle of the trail. The larger sentinel Georgia oak is on your left.

Pass the call box and cross a gravel road, continuing uphill for another 100 yards to reach Halfway House, a pavilion with benches that is a good place for a break.

In 0.1 mile, reach the steepest section of the hike where railings have been installed. Where the railings end, look to the left to find the sentinel sweetgum tree—the only deciduous tree among the boulders, about 50 feet from the trail.

Continue uphill and you'll see the sentinel loblolly pine on your right, stunted and standing alone on the rock.

In another 0.1 mile you'll reach the top of the mountain and the Top of the Mountain facility, which includes the Skyride gondola entrance, a snack bar, and some interpretive signs explaining geological and ecological information about the mountain.

On a clear day you will be able to see the skyscrapers of downtown, midtown, and Buckhead; Kennesaw Mountain to the northwest; and possibly the Appalachian Mountains to the north.

After taking in the view, return the way you came to finish your hike at the parking lot.

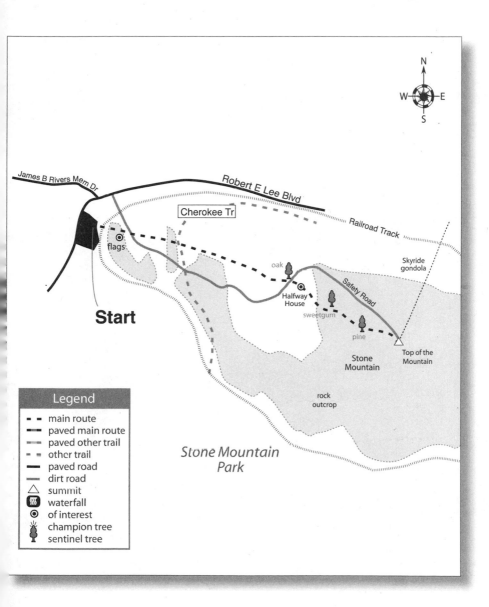

Confederate generals race across the mountainside above you as you hike.

CHEROKEE TRAIL

STONE MOUNTAIN PARK

Cherokee Trail is a perfect way to tour Stone Mountain Park. Leaving behind the crowds of the Walk-Up Trail, it winds through hardwood forests, past a spectacular lakeside view of the stone face, and up and over the mountain itself. Though this is one of the most visited parks in the state, spending time on Cherokee Trail can make you feel like you own the place. The trail has something for everyone: forests, water, a historic mill, and views of the mountainside. Even if you've been to Stone Mountain before, go back and try this route for a change.

DISTANCE FROM DOWNTOWN ATLANTA • 18 MILES

BY CAR FROM I-285 Take exit 39B to merge onto US 78E toward Snellville/ Athens. Travel 8 miles, then take exit 8 toward the Stone Mountain Park entrance. Merge onto Jefferson Davis Drive, pay the entrance fee, and drive 1.0 mile to Robert E. Lee Boulevard. Bear right onto Robert E. Lee and pass the parking area near Confederate Hall in 1.0 mile. The nature garden parking lot is on your right in 0.75 mile.

PUBLIC TRANSPORTATION *This hike is not easily accessible by public transportation.* Take the MARTA 121 bus to the corner of Main Street and West Mountain Street in Stone Mountain. Walk south 0.2 mile on Main Street to the Stone Mountain Visitor Center (at the red trolley) and follow the PATH Foundation multi-use path to Robert E. Lee Boulevard (1.0 mile). You can turn right to reach the trailhead or cross the street and take the orange-blazed Connector Trail 0.5 mile to reach the trailhead at the nature garden.

PARKING Paved parking lot across Robert E. Lee Boulevard from the Harold Cox Nature Garden; GPS N 33° 48.2852, W 84° 09.5498

ADDRESS 1000 Robert E. Lee Boulevard, Stone Mountain, GA 30083

HIKE DISTANCE 6-mile loop

WHY THIS HIKE IS GREAT Though not as famous as the Walk-Up Trail, the Cherokee Trail is hands down the best way to experience Stone Mountain Park. Its route through mature hardwood forests, along the lakeshore, and across the mountain's ridge is peaceful and spectacular.

Difficulty

Overall — Moderate to strenuous

Terrain — Well maintained and graded hard-packed soil trails; mountainside section can be slippery

Elevation change — Mostly level grade except very steep section on the mountainside

Hours Dawn to dusk, year-round

Dogs Leashed dogs permitted

Facilities Toilets, water fountains

Fees & Permits $10 daily parking fee or $35 annual parking pass

Land Manager Stone Mountain Park

Sentinel Trees

Sweetgum – GPS N 33° 48.4889, W 84° 08.2225
- 11'3" circumference
- There are a couple of large sweetgum trees in this grove, the largest standing 20 feet from the path on the left. Sweetgums can be identified in the summer by their star-shaped leaves. In the winter look for their round, spiky seed pods on the ground.

Tulip Tree – GPS N 33° 48.5296, W 84° 08.5557
- 11'1" circumference
- On the northern side of the mountain, the trees are older and thicker. However, this tulip tree dwarfs all around it and serves as a reminder of old-growth forests that stood on this land when it was a sacred site of the Cherokee people.

INSIDER TIP

Free Admission to Stone Mountain Park Trails

Admission to Stone Mountain Park trails is free for people who enter by bicycle or on foot. There is a pedestrian entrance on East Mountain Street, but the easiest way to walk or bicycle in is via the paved multi-use path from the Stone Mountain Visitor Center on Main Street. Check the Public Transportation directions above for more information; there is even free parking at the visitor center.

Beech & Tulip Tree –
GPS N 33° 48.3633,
W 84° 09.5372

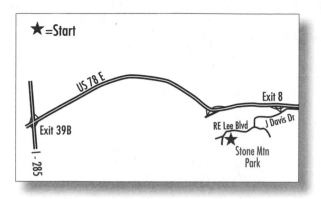

- 10'9" circumference and 13'2" circumference, respectively
- Two sentinel trees flank the trail on the back half of the Nature Garden Trail loop. The tulip tree in particular is memorable because of its hollow base and its top, which was damaged by a storm years ago.

Hike

From the parking lot across the street from the Harold Cox Nature Garden, cross the road and begin your hike at the covered information kiosk in the Nature Garden. Turn right onto Nature Garden Trail, cross a bridge over the creek, then walk 0.1 mile to another creek. Cross this creek to the right on a slab of granite that creates a small cascade.

In 100 yards, come to a junction with the orange-blazed Connector Trail. Turn right, then right again on the white-blazed Cherokee Trail. Pass the chimney of an old building standing alone on a hill and follow an arrow left.

The trail winds through the woods, parallel to the road, for 0.4 mile before crossing the road to the right near a playground. The trail parallels the playground's fence line. At the back corner of the fence, pass a large white oak on the right, then the trail turns left and crosses the dam. At the far side of the dam, cross a small bridge and then follow the trail left.

Cross another bridge in 100 yards, then continue 0.2 mile to Stonewall Jackson Drive. After crossing the road the trail skirts the lakeshore, providing excellent views of the mountain. In 0.4 mile cross a creek on a granite slab, then hike another 0.4 mile to a bridge. Cross the bridge to the left and hike across the dam to another trail junction.

Turn right at the junction to stay on the Cherokee Trail, and continue 0.6 mile along the edge of the lake before crossing a sizable granite outcrop. Follow blazes on trees and on the rock to stay on the trail.

In 0.15 mile, reach a covered bridge but do not cross it. Follow the Cherokee Trail across the road, where it continues between the road and lake. The trail becomes narrow and is paved with granite stones for a short stretch. Look for heart-shaped stones.

In 0.3 mile, reach the mill where the trail makes quite a few well-marked turns. Turn right on the wooden walkway attached to the mill, then left, then right. The trail continues alongside the millrace. In 0.2 mile where the millrace begins, follow blazes as the trail turns left, then right, then left, then crosses the road.

Barely 0.1 mile beyond the road crossing, pass the sentinel sweetgum on the left. In another 0.1 mile, follow blazes to the left at a junction with an unmarked trail, then cross the railroad tracks.

Hike 0.2 mile, parallel to a sheer wall of granite on your left, past a nature garden created by the Atlanta Branch of the National League of American Pen Women (an organization of artists, composers, and writers). Then, just before reaching a gravel maintenance road, pass the sentinel tulip tree on your left.

The gravel road begins a short section of trail through the most developed area of the park. Turn right onto the gravel road, and follow blazes and signs to navigate. Turn left onto a second gravel road, then left onto a stone path that leads you past a small pond with fountains beneath the Confederate Generals carving on the mountainside. At the far side of the pond, turn right then immediately left, back into the woods.

In 0.2 mile, stay straight at a junction with the Connector Trail. After another 0.5 mile, reach another Connector Trail junction. This time turn left, up the mountain. Ascend steeply on granite for 0.2 mile before reaching a junction with Walk-Up Trail. Cross under the power lines and continue straight on the white-blazed Cherokee Trail. In another 0.1 mile, cross a gravel maintenance road and follow white blazes out onto the rock.

Turn right at a warning sign telling you that the trail is slippery and hazardous in some areas and to use extreme care. Please heed this sign, especially after a rain. Even agile, experienced hikers have slipped and fallen on this section of trail.

Follow the white blazes on the rock as the trail descends steeply for 0.2 mile before re-entering the woods. Parallel the railroad tracks for 0.1 mile, then cross the tracks to meet a junction with the Connector Trail. Turn right, then right again onto the green-blazed Nature Garden Trail.

On this section of the route, you'll pass many benches and interpretive signs about geology, forests, and stream ecology. At the first such sign (Our Forests), take a look at the old tulip tree (with an almost 12-foot circumference) next to it. Then, in 0.2 mile, bear left at a junction with the Connector Trail, following the green arrow. Soon you will hike between the sentinel beech and the sentinel tulip tree. The trail winds along the creek for another 0.1 mile, crosses a bridge (passing a hemlock grove), and reaches a junction with Connector Trail. Go straight to stay on the Nature Garden Trail that leads you back to the Nature Garden kiosk. Go right to cross the road and reach the parking area.

To exit the park, you will have to continue on the one-way Robert E. Lee Boulevard to circle the mountain and return to the main park gate.

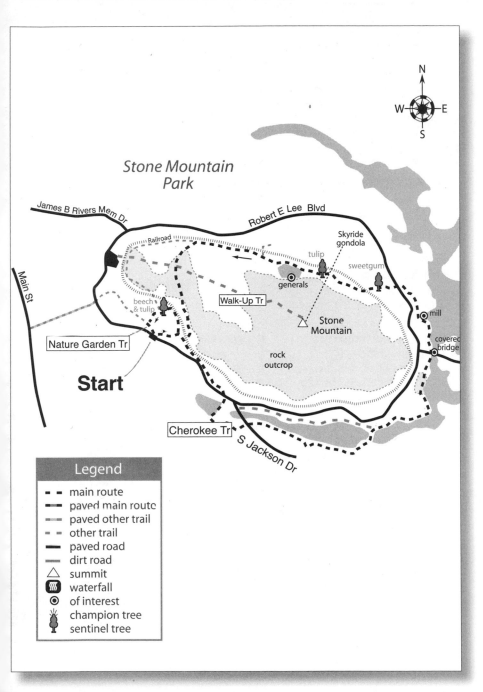

Stone Mountain Park

James B Rivers Mem Dr

Robert E Lee Blvd

Railroad

Main St

Skyride gondola

tulip

sweetgum

generals

Walk-Up Tr

beech & tulip

Stone Mountain

mill

Nature Garden Tr

covered bridge

Start

rock outcrop

Cherokee Tr

S Jackson Dr

Legend

- – main route
- paved main route
- paved other trail
- – other trail
- paved road
- dirt road
- △ summit
- waterfall
- ⊙ of interest
- champion tree
- sentinel tree

SONGBIRD HABITAT TRAILS

STONE MOUNTAIN PARK

This beautiful hike within Stone Mountain Park is a great way to escape the crowds and connect with nature. The Songbird Trails wind through open meadows, young pine forest, and mature hardwood forest. Though few people know about this loop, it is one of the gems of Stone Mountain Park, perfect for birding or just a quiet walk in the woods—and it provides excellent views of the mountain itself.

DISTANCE FROM DOWNTOWN ATLANTA • 18 MILES

BY CAR FROM I-285 Take exit 39B to merge onto US 78E toward Snellville/Athens. Travel 8 miles, then take exit 8 toward the Stone Mountain Park entrance. Merge onto Jefferson Davis Drive, pay the entrance fee, and drive 1.0 mile to Robert E. Lee Boulevard. Bear right onto Robert E. Lee and drive 2.4 miles before turning right onto Stonewall Jackson Drive. Continue 0.5 mile up a very steep hill to reach the turn for the Songbird Trails parking area. Turn right and park in the circular drive near the trailhead.

PUBLIC TRANSPORTATION
This hike is not easily accessible by public transportation. Take the 121 Memorial Dr. MARTA bus to the corner of Main Street and West Mountain Street in Stone Mountain. Walk south 0.2 mile on Main Street to the Stone Mountain Visitor Center (at the red trolley) and follow the PATH Foundation multi-use path 0.4 mile to Robert E. Lee Boulevard. From here you can either turn right to walk Robert E. Lee Boulevard to Stonewall Jackson Drive (1 mile) or take the orange-blazed Connector Trail (across the street) to the Cherokee Trail, which intersects with Stonewall Jackson Drive about 0.5 mile from the Songbird Trails parking area.

Granite stepping-stones lead to a trail junction.

PARKING Paved parking area; GPS N 33° 47.5869, W 84° 08.7891

ADDRESS 1000 Robert E. Lee Boulevard, Stone Mountain, GA 30083

HIKE DISTANCE 1.5-mile figure-8 loop

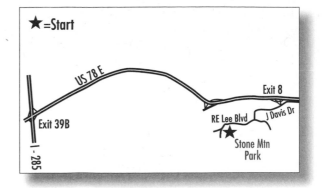

WHY THIS HIKE IS GREAT

After—or instead of—the strenuous and busy hike up Stone Mountain, this trail is the place to cool down and escape the crowds.

DIFFICULTY

Overall — Easy

Terrain — Grass and hard-packed soil trails; several bridges and a flight of stairs

Elevation change — Minimal

HOURS Dawn to dusk, year-round

DOGS No dogs permitted

FACILITIES Portable toilet, plenty of benches along the trail

FEES & PERMITS $10 daily parking fee or $35 annual parking pass

LAND MANAGER Stone Mountain Park

SENTINEL TREES

Tulip Tree – GPS N 33° 47.7268, W 84° 09.0351
- 11'1" circumference
- The largest in this area of forest, this tulip tree is in remarkably good condition for its age. In leaf-free winter you can locate older trees by looking up into the canopy and searching for thick upper limbs similar to the ones on this tree.

Tulip Tree – GPS N 33° 47.7585, W 84° 09.0456
- 8'8" circumference
- This tulip tree is significantly smaller than the sentinel just up the hill, and without counting the age rings on both trees it is hard to know if the smaller size is due to age or just different growing conditions.

Tulip Tree – GPS N 33° 47.6955, W 84° 08.9111
- 12'11" circumference
- This tulip tree is unique because of its size, and also because of its hollow interior and the unusual burl growing at its base. Before there was a fence here, this tree and the large tulip tree just beyond the fence might have been used by surveyors to indicate property boundaries.

HIKE

Start your hike next to the map and information kiosk; take the trail on the right to begin the loop.

The trail takes a hard right almost immediately after the first bench. Walk 0.2 mile along the edge of the meadow until you arrive at a junction with the Woodland Trail; there are views of Stone Mountain from here. Go up the stairs and turn left along the ridge.

Follow the fenceline past an overlook platform with nice views of the meadow and walk 0.1 mile to a trail junction. Follow the arrow straight ahead and cross a footbridge.

Less than 100 yards past a second bridge, pass the sentinel tulip tree on your right. The trail then curves right and descends for another 100 yards before passing the smaller sentinel tulip tree on your right.

Walk another 0.2 mile to return to the previous trail junction. Go straight, through the gate in the fence, and cross some granite stepping-stones to reach another junction

Woodland Trail continues to the right. Before leaving this junction, look to the left next to the fence for the other sentinel tulip tree. Then go right (on the left is a social trail, a shortcut back to Meadow Trail) and follow the fenceline.

BIRDS TO LOOK FOR

SONGBIRD HABITAT TRAILS

All Year: field sparrow
Spring: blue grosbeak, common yellowthroat, indigo bunting, summer tanager, yellow-breasted chat

The trail curves left away from the fence in 0.1 mile, then crosses an old rock wall on a set of four granite steps. The trail reaches another fenceline in 0.2 mile. Notice how the forest changes beyond the fence—hardwoods on this side, young loblolly pine on the other.

In 0.1 mile, turn right at a junction and walk through an opening in the fence to arrive at a junction with Meadow Trail. Turn right onto Meadow Trail and pass a covered bench. The trail winds along the edge of the meadow. Proceed quietly, keeping your eye out for wildlife. There are also nice views of Stone Mountain on this section. In 0.3 mile, the trail loops back to the parking lot where the hike ends.

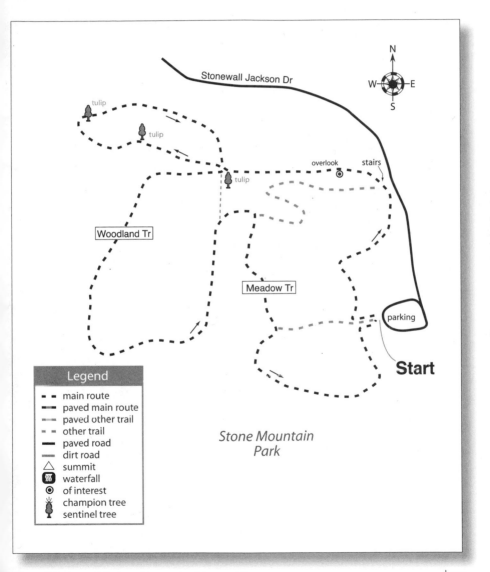

North Loop

Yellow River Park

The north portion of Yellow River Park is used by fewer bicyclists than the southern section, making this hike more solitary and offering an even better feel for the forest. The three-quarter-mile walk on the park's paved multi-use path along the river is a nice warm-up for this loop through an area of beautiful piedmont forest. Deer, wildflowers, and interesting trees abound on this well-maintained trail.

Distance from Downtown Atlanta • 22 miles

By car from I-285 Take exit 39B to merge onto US 78E/Stone Mountain Highway toward Snellville/Athens. After 9 miles turn right onto East Park Place Boulevard, then turn right onto Rockbridge Road. Stay left in 1.3 miles to continue on Annistown Road. In 1.2 miles turn right onto Juhan Road. The parking area is on the left in 0.8 mile.

Public Transportation
This hike is not easily accessible by public transportation. The MARTA 110 bus stops 7 miles from the park.

Parking Paved parking area; GPS N 33° 47.4794, W 84° 04.3140

Address 3232 Juhan Road, Stone Mountain, GA 30087

Hike Distance 4.25-mile figure-8 loop

At Yellow River, the forest is slowly reclaiming the land.

WHY THIS HIKE IS GREAT The forests surrounding Yellow River demonstrate the area's history as farmland—terraces and young trees sprinkled with relic trees. These healthy forests are reclaiming the piedmont terrain after years of being tilled.

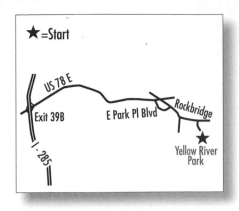

DIFFICULTY

Overall—Easy to moderate

Terrain—Mostly hard-packed soil trails with a stretch of paved multi-use path at the beginning and end of the hike

Elevation change—Mostly level with a few short ascents, including one particularly steep 100-yard descent

HOURS Dawn to dusk, year-round

DOGS Leashed dogs permitted

FACILITIES Toilets, picnic pavilion, playground

FEES & PERMITS None

LAND MANAGER Gwinnett County Parks

SENTINEL TREES

White Oak – GPS N 33° 47.5565, W 84° 04.2033
- 13'10" circumference
- This white oak is one of the larger trees you'll find in the Atlanta area—a relic that has probably seen many clearcuttings of the forest around it.

Tulip Tree – GPS N 33° 47.8411, W 84° 04.8410
- 10'5" circumference
- The largest tree in the small grove surrounding the bridge, this interesting specimen has branches that reach into the sky like arms.

White Oak – GPS N 33° 47.7245, W 84° 04.4951
- 9'4" circumference
- Another relic tree left to grow old by farmers who once plowed this land, this white oak is significantly larger than any tree near it, making it stand out both in size and for the way its branches curve and, like the sentinel tulip, reach skyward.

Hike

Start on the paved multi-use path at the south end of the parking lot and turn right toward the woods and the 0.93 mile marker. Then turn left to continue on the paved path (don't cross the bridge).

After 0.2 mile, pass the very large sentinel white oak on your right. Continue past many benches, some picnic tables, and the 0.25- and 0.50-mile markers, and come to a junction in 0.3 mile. Turn right at the junction and reach the overlook platform where you can get a nice view of the river. Take the trail to the left, across from the overlook, up the hill to Juhan Road.

Cross the road at the crosswalk and cross the field to a cluster of trail signs. Do not enter the woods here. Turn right and walk down the hill along the edge of the field to a trail entering the woods on the left along the bank of a creek.

Once in the woods pass a trail on your left, then turn right at the next junction and cross a bridge. Hike uphill along the creek past several cascading waterfalls. In 0.25 mile, the trail turns left and crosses another bridge. Just after the bridge, pass the sentinel tulip tree on your right.

Pass a small trail on the left in about 100 yards, then make a hard right toward a red blaze at the next junction with a pedestrian trail signpost. In 0.1 mile turn right onto an orange horse trail, and stay straight at a junction with a smaller trail.

In 0.5 mile make a hard right at a junction to stay on the main trail. Pass a small pond and retaining wall on your right. After the pond, go straight at a junction with an orange horse trail toward the 0.3 miles to trailhead sign.

In 0.15 mile, reach the junction labeled #1 and go left on the wide, flat trail. In 0.1 mile, stay left at the junction (not toward the road) and follow orange blazes. Cross a bridge after 0.2 mile, then go straight through the next junction.

In another 0.2 mile, reach the edge of a clearing. You can either go straight (a steep descent and ascent through the clearing) or left (on a relatively level path around the clearing) to reach the other side. At the junction at the far end of the clearing, look down the hill and to your right to find the sentinel white oak.

Continue straight at the next junction (toward the 1.2 miles to trailhead sign), then go straight through the next two junctions (labeled #4 and #3). Right after the junction labeled #3, turn right onto the purple pedestrian trail and hike downhill on a very steep but short trail. Turn right at the bottom of the hill.

In 0.15 mile you'll reach the clearing near the road. Cross Juhan Road at the crosswalk. Descend to the overlook platform and turn right onto the multi-use path. Stay right at the junction, then pass picnic tables and the 0.75-mile marker. Pass a gravel road leading to the gravel parking area and continue 0.2 miles around the playground area before finally making a right just before the 0.93-mile marker to reach the parking lot and complete the hike.

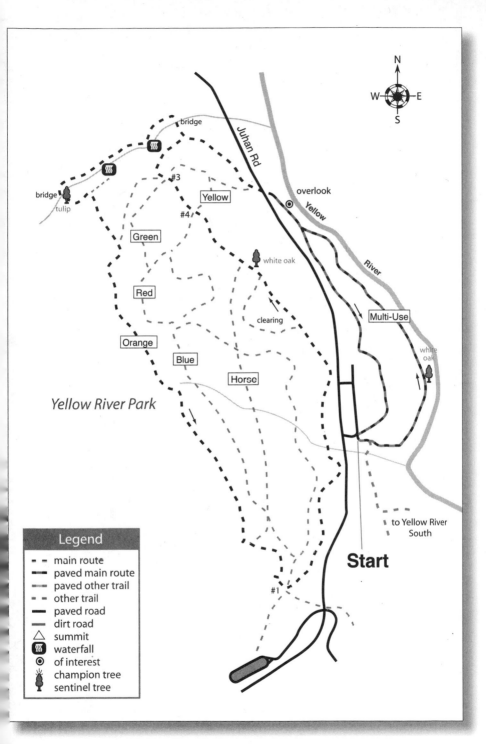

South Loop

Yellow River Park

Though Yellow River is known as a mountain bike park, hikers are welcome on all trails, and walking there is highly recommended. The slower pace of hiking will allow you to more fully take in the beauty of the river and its surrounding forest. The park trails are well marked and extensive. Watch out for bikers and horses on weekends, but on most days you'll have these trails to yourself.

DISTANCE FROM DOWNTOWN ATLANTA • 22 MILES

BY CAR FROM I-285 Take exit 39B to merge onto US 78 E / Stone Mountain Highway toward Snellville/Athens. After 9 miles turn right onto East Park Place Boulevard, then turn right onto Rockbridge Road. Stay left to continue on Annistown Road in 1.3 mile. In 1.2 mile turn right onto Juhan Road. The parking area is on the left in 0.8 mile.

PUBLIC TRANSPORTATION *This hike is not easily accessible by public transportation.* The MARTA 110 bus stops 7 miles from the park.

PARKING Paved parking area; GPS N 33° 47.4794, W 84° 04.3140

ADDRESS 3232 Juhan Road, Stone Mountain, GA 30087

HIKE DISTANCE 2.75-mile loop

Exposed root system of a young sentinel beech.

WHY THIS HIKE IS GREAT Miles of walking along the scenic river's edge make this a fun and relaxing excursion.

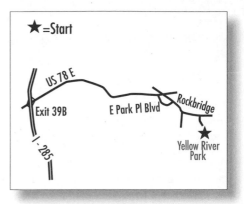

DIFFICULTY

Overall — Easy to moderate

Terrain — Mostly hard-packed soil trails with a short stretch of paved multi-use path at the beginning and end of the hike

Elevation change — Mostly level with a few short but steep ascents

HOURS Dawn to dusk, year-round

DOGS Leashed dogs permitted

FACILITIES Toilets, picnic pavilion, playground

FEES & PERMITS None

LAND MANAGER Gwinnett County Parks

SENTINEL TREES

Beech – GPS N 33° 47.4189, W 84° 04.2236

- This young beech growing on a rock is particularly interesting because the river's power of erosion has fully exposed its roots, demonstrating the extent of a tree system that is usually hidden below ground.

White Oak – GPS N 33° 47.4178, W 84° 04.2229

- 9'4" circumference
- Located at the edge of a short cliff above the river, this red oak is the largest and oldest tree in this area of the forest.

Post Oak – GPS N 33° 47.0669, W 84° 04.1819

- 7'7" circumference
- Though this tree's circumference is not particularly large, its position in the forest makes it noteworthy. It is surrounded by younger trees in an area of former farmland that has only recently begun to be reforested. With no competition for light for most of its life, its branches extend in all directions to create a wide and impressive crown.

HIKE

Start on the paved multi-use path on the south end of the parking lot and turn right toward the woods and the 0.93 mile marker. Then bear right and cross the bridge.

Go left at a junction to visit the overlook platform next to the river. From the platform you can view the sentinel beech tree with exposed roots on the right. Return to the junction and follow the fork labeled for bikes. In 100 yards cross another bridge and come to a junction of many trails. Turn left, then left again to follow a trail signed for horses. The trail immediately forks again; go left to continue on the trail along the river's edge.

The trails in this area regularly split and reconnect, but if you stay on the trail closest to the river's edge you won't go wrong. In less than 75 yards you'll pass the sentinel red oak on the left. Then stay left at each junction for the next 0.6 mile to arrive at a junction where a creek enters the river.

Cross the creek and continue to follow the riverbank. In 0.15 mile the trail turns away from the river and meets the horse trail. Turn left.

In 0.2 mile the river and trail both turn sharply north. Continue staying left to follow the river. At the next junction, bear left as the trail now leaves the river behind. Climb the hill and in 0.3 mile you'll reach a junction labeled #1. Continue straight on the orange horse trail.

Cross a bridge in 75 yards, then go left at a junction. (To detour and visit the sentinel red oak, go straight at this junction and hike 0.15 mile, then return to this junction and go right.) Pass a parking lot on the left and continue straight on, crossing a gravel road. At a junction just after the gravel road make a hard right and hike 0.1 mile before reaching a clearing for the group campground. Follow the trail as it skirts the left edge of the clearing.

After the trail reenters the woods, hike 0.1 mile to reach the junction labeled #6. Go straight here, then continue past an orange horse trail spur on the left. Finally, you'll reach a major junction next to a bridge to close the loop. You were here before, early in the hike. Go straight, cross the bridge, pass the side trail to the overlook on your right, and cross another bridge. Turn left onto the paved path and take another left after the 0.93 mile marker to return to the parking lot and complete the hike.

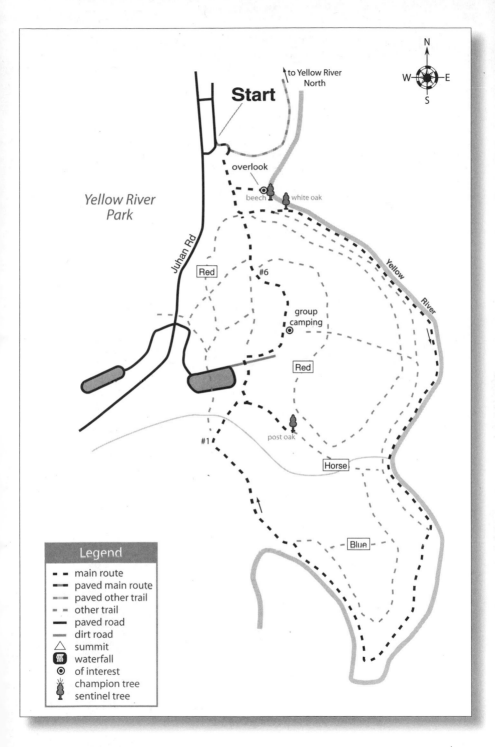

PANOLA MOUNTAIN STATE PARK

One of the three ancient granite outcrop mountains (monadnocks) in the Atlanta area, Panola Mountain is the most well-preserved. Though the mountain itself is only accessible on ranger-led hikes, the state park provides other excellent hiking opportunities. Trails here lead to one of the best views in Atlanta—both Stone Mountain and Panola Mountain are visible—as well as a tour of a piedmont forest watershed.

DISTANCE FROM DOWNTOWN ATLANTA • 19 MILES

BY CAR FROM I-20 Take exit 68 for Wesley Chapel and turn right onto Wesley Chapel Road, immediately getting in the left lane to turn left onto Snapfinger Road. Drive 7 miles (during which Snapfinger Road becomes GA 155), then turn left into the park entrance. Parking is near the nature center.

PUBLIC TRANSPORTATION *This hike is not easily accessible by public transportation.* The MARTA 15 bus stops on Linecrest Road, 6 miles from the park.

PARKING Paved parking area near the nature center; GPS N 33° 37.4967, W 84° 10.2646

ADDRESS 2600 Highway 155, Stockbridge, GA 30281

HIKE DISTANCE 2-mile figure-8 loop

An ancient tulip tree's roots grab whatever soil they can.

WHY THIS HIKE IS GREAT Spectacular view of both Panola Mountain and Stone Mountain

DIFFICULTY

Overall — Easy

Terrain — Wide, well-maintained hard-packed soil trails, boardwalks, and bridges

Elevation change — Rolling hills throughout, with several sustained ascents or descents

HOURS 7 am to sunset, year-round; nature center open 8:30 am to 5 pm (closed Tuesday and Wednesday in winter)

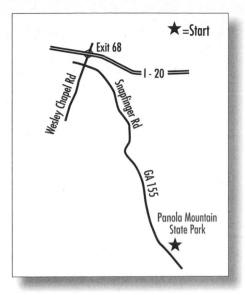

DOGS Dogs not permitted

FACILITIES Toilets, nature center, picnic facilities, playground, other state park amenities

FEES & PERMITS $5 daily or $50 annual parks pass

LAND MANAGER Panola Mountain State Park

SENTINEL TREES

Georgia Oak – GPS N 33° 37.6597, W 84° 10.4456

- 1' circumference
- Georgia oak is a rare species. Sometimes called Stone Mountain Oak, it grows mostly on monadnocks such as Panola, Arabia, and Stone Mountain, seldom growing larger than a bush. Its leaves have the tell-tale oak shape. Find it right next to the boardwalk, just after the Q marker.

Tulip Tree – GPS N 33° 37.5614, W 84° 10.3592

- Four trunks; the largest has a 5'4" circumference
- A sign in front of this unique four-trunked tulip tree can give you a little information about this species. Originally four distinct trees that have fused at their bases, this young tree might someday have four trunks as large as the sentinel tulip tree (below) on Watershed Trail.

Tulip Tree – GPS N 33° 37.4046, W 84° 10.1410

- 10'11" circumference
- This ancient tulip tree can be found to the right of the observation platform, growing precariously on the edge of a steep ravine. Many of its large roots are exposed; it is the largest tree in this area of the forest.

HIKE

Start from the circular drive in front of the nature center and walk the paved path toward the building. Inside the nature center you can pick up brochures that provide information at stations along both Rock Outcrop and Watershed Trails.

Follow the trail around the left side of the nature center to reach the trail information kiosk. Facing the sign, go left onto Rock Outcrop Trail, follow white blazes to the right at a fork, then stay left at the Nature Preserve Mountain Trail junction on the right that is labeled for Guided Hikes Only.

In 0.15 mile reach a junction next to red fences. Go right and downhill, passing a spur trail on your right, just before the D marker. In 0.1 mile, just past a Please Stay on Trail sign, more red fences line the right side of the trail.

Pass an overlook with an Outcrop Geology sign, then come to a larger overlook with views of Panola and Stone Mountains to the northwest.

After the overlook pass the sentinel Georgia oak on the right, just after the Q marker. Go right at a junction at the end of the boardwalk and hike downhill for almost 0.1 mile before crossing a bridge and passing the sentinel four-trunk tulip tree with an information sign on the left. In 100 yards reach the junction next to the information kiosk and continue your hike on red-blazed Watershed Trail that begins to the right as you face the kiosk.

Cross a service road and in 0.1 mile go left at a junction (toward a Microwatershed sign). In another 0.1 mile go right at a junction to begin the second loop, then descend to the side of a ravine.

In 0.1 mile come to another junction. To the left is an overlook and the sentinel tulip tree. After visiting the sentinel tree, cross the bridge and hike downhill some more.

BIRDS TO LOOK FOR

PANOLA MOUNTAIN STATE PARK

Summer: blue grosbeak, indigo bunting, scarlet tanager, summer tanager, wood thrush, yellow-breasted chat
Fall: goldfinch, palm warbler, song sparrow

At a junction and bridge in 0.1 mile, go left and cross the bridge (the right-hand path leads to a fitness trail; you can also connect with the paved multi-use path here). Continuing on Watershed Trail pass a watershed viewing platform with benches, then follow the trail over another bridge.

The trail ascends steeply for 0.2 mile before passing a raised outdoor classroom and trail marked Park Staff Only on the right. Stay left, then go right at the next two junctions and left at the kiosk to return to the nature center in 0.25 mile to end the hike.

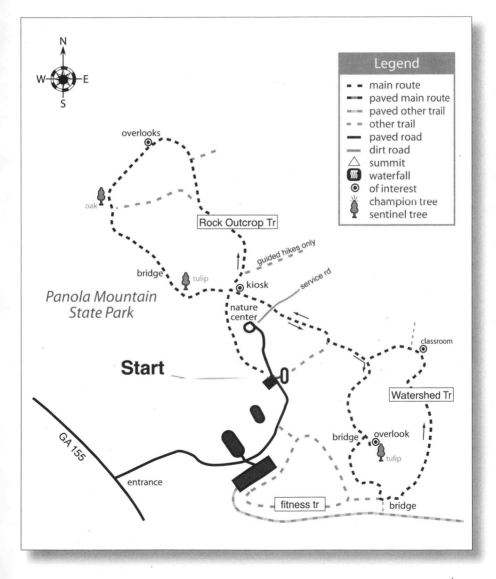

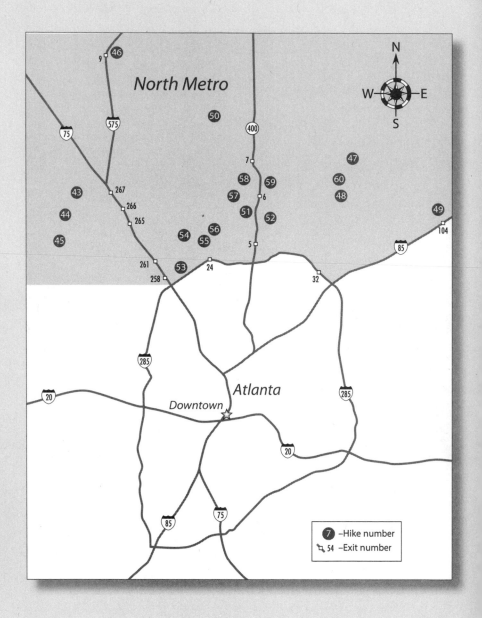

North Metro

Atlanta

Downtown

7 –Hike number
54 –Exit number

North Metro

Kennesaw Mountain National Battlefield Park

㊸ Summit Loop
㊹ Cheatham Hill Loop
㊺ Kolb Farm Loop

㊻ Olde Rope Mill Park
㊼ Autrey Mill Nature Preserve & Heritage Center
㊽ Simpsonwood Conference & Retreat Center
㊾ McDaniel Farm Park
㊿ Leita Thompson Memorial Park
(51) Big Trees Forest Preserve
(52) Dunwoody Nature Center

Chattahoochee River National Recreation Area

(53) Cochran Shoals
(54) Sope Creek
(55) Johnson Ferry South
(56) Johnson Ferry North
(57) Gold Branch
(58) Vickery Creek
(59) Island Ford
(60) Jones Bridge

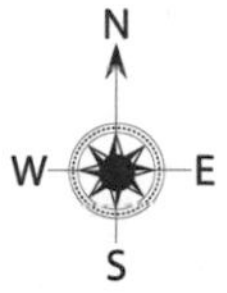

Love history? North Metro Atlanta hikes will delight you with Civil War-era earthworks and battlefield sites, sentinel trees dating from the 1800s, replica Native American structures, and a restored 1930s farmstead—all providing some temporal perspective to the heritage of this area.

The Atlanta skyline is visible from the summit of Kennesaw Mountain.

Summit Loop

Kennesaw Mountain National Battlefield Park

This route follows one of the best-known and well-used trails in the Atlanta area. On warm weekends thousands of people walk up and down the mountain for exercise and to see the view from the top. But most of the trails on this 6-mile loop are used significantly less than the first-mile stretch to the summit. This means you can enjoy the company of other hikers at the beginning and finish your hike in solitude and quiet.

DISTANCE FROM DOWNTOWN • 24 MILES

BY CAR FROM I-75 Take exit 267B toward US 41/GA 5S/Marietta and merge onto Canton Road Connector/GA 5. Take the very first exit for US-41/GA 5/GA 3 and turn right onto Cobb Parkway. In 0.5 mile, turn left onto Bells Ferry Road. In less than 0.2 mile, turn right onto Old US 41. Drive 1.2 mile to the light at Stilesboro Road. You can turn left and park in front of the visitor center or continue beyond the light to an overflow parking area on the left.

PUBLIC TRANSPORTATION *This hike is not easily accessible by public transportation.* The Cobb County Transit 45 Barrett Parkway bus can take you to the intersection of Bells Ferry Road and Cobb Parkway, from which it is 1.5 mile to the visitor center on Stilesboro Road.

PARKING Park in front of the visitor center or at the Old US 41 parking area, just north of Stilesboro on Old US 41 (both lots are paved and can be crowded on weekends); Visitor center parking: GPS N 33° 58.9840, W 84° 34.6938; Old US 41 Parking: GPS N 33° 59.1328, W 84° 34.9240

ADDRESS 901 Stilesboro Road NW, Kennesaw, GA 30152

HIKE DISTANCE 6-mile loop

WHY THIS HIKE IS GREAT This is one of the signature hikes in Atlanta for its views, history, and steep, strenuous first mile. Beyond the crowded beginning, expect quiet solitude.

DIFFICULTY
Overall — Strenuous
Terrain — Wide, well-maintained trails, rocky in places

Elevation change— With two of the steepest ascents in the Atlanta area, expect over 1500 ft. of elevation gain between the two peaks.

Hours 7:30 am to 6 pm (Standard Time); 7:30 am to 8 pm (Daylight Savings Time); visitor center open daily 8:30 am to 5:30 pm except Thanksgiving, Christmas Day, and New Year's Day

Dogs Leashed dogs permitted

Facilities Visitor center, toilets, water fountains

Fees & Permits—None

Land Manager Kennesaw Mountain National Battlefield Park

Sentinel Trees

White Oaks – GPS N 33° 59.0521, W 84° 34.7393
- One oak's circumference measures 13'10", the other 13'4".
- Across Stilesboro Road from the visitor center, the two largest white oaks in the middle of the field are at least as old as the Civil War battle of Kennesaw Mountain. Their size is best appreciated when seen up close.

Chestnut Oak – GPS N 33° 58.1414, W 84° 35.1561
- 12'5" circumference
- This specimen just to the left of the trail is particularly gnarly. Its age is unknown, but it probably also saw the battle of Kennesaw Mountain.

"Gnome Tree" – GPS N 33° 57.9267, W 84° 35.3931
- This chestnut oak at the peak of Pigeon Hill has been used as a sitting and climbing tree by hikers for many years. Its branches stretch in all directions, and the hole in the center could be an excellent gnome home.

BIRDS TO LOOK FOR

Kennesaw Mountain

Spring: American redstart, black-and-white warbler, blackburnian warbler, black-throated green warbler, cerulean warbler, ovenbird, rose-breasted grosbeak, scarlet tanager

Hiking Atlanta's Hidden Forests

Hike

Before you begin, take a look at the enormous sentinel white oaks across Stilesboro Road from the visitor center. These trees date from the time of the battle fought here during the Civil War and help give some temporal perspective to the history of this location.

Start your hike at the visitor center and follow the paved path to the right of the building toward the woods beyond the building and road. Cross the road and enter the woods.

★ =Start

Stilesboro Rd

I-75

Old US 41

Balls Ferry

Exit 267B

GA 5

Kennesaw Mtn
Nat Battlefield Pk

Cobb Pkwy

The trail curves left and ascends Kennesaw Mountain steeply. In total, you'll climb for 1 mile to get to the top. This section of the trail is very busy (especially on weekends), and you can generally follow the crowds to the top of the mountain. At the first junction after crossing the road, take the trail on the right, uphill. In another 0.2 mile at a junction with a wider trail, go right. After another 0.2 mile of ascent, bear right and climb a set of steps. You'll pass several overlooks on the left that make good places to take a breather. After a final 0.4 mile, walk up a flight of stairs to the summit parking area. Stop for a view of the city (on clear days, you can see Stone Mountain, Buckhead, Midtown, and Downtown), then head up another flight of stairs to an observation platform. The trail continues 0.15 mile to the top of the mountain past replica Civil War cannons.

From the peak continue on the main trail down the other side of the mountain; the descent is steep. Cross the road after 0.15 mile and descend another 0.1 mile to a saddle between Kennesaw Mountain and Little Kennesaw Mountain. In the next 0.1 mile the trail crests a rise and then descends to another saddle before Little Kennesaw peak. Beyond this saddle, hike 0.3 mile steeply up to the peak, labeled with a sign that reads Fort McBride.

Just beyond the Little Kennesaw summit look for the trail to veer off to the right. Bear right at two junctions, passing several old windblown red cedars growing on boulders to the left. Descend for 0.5 mile and you'll pass the sentinel chestnut oak with gnarly, crooked limbs. Continue downhill for another 0.2 mile to a trail junction. The descent is very rocky and can be treacherous in bad weather.

At this junction turn left to continue to the visitor center. For an interesting detour go straight to hike the 0.2 mile spur to the top of Pigeon Hill, where you'll find the sentinel Gnome Tree—a chestnut oak with low limbs (perfect for climbing) and a hole in the middle where gnomes might live. This tree and the interesting boulders make for a nice out-and-back diversion from the loop hike. After visiting Pigeon Hill, return to the junction and follow the sign for the visitor center.

In 0.25 mile, turn left onto a trail that follows an old road bed (again following the sign that points you toward the visitor center). After 0.8 mile, pass houses on the right as the trail parallels a privacy fence. Reach the site of Camp Brumby, a Depression-era Civilian Conservation Corps camp from the 1940s in another 0.6 mile. The 0.3-mile loop around the camp area provides an interesting historical tour. Turn left to take the loop. When you reach the main trail, turn left to continue toward the visitor center.

In 0.15 mile turn off the wide roadbed onto a smaller trail with a sign that says the visitor center is 0.7 mile away. When you come to another junction in 0.15 mile, go right (downhill) on the slightly smaller trail.

Enter a field near the visitor center in 0.3 mile. The trail skirts the field, parallels the road, turns right into the woods behind the visitor center, and emerges near the water fountain. Turn right to reach the visitor center and end your hike.

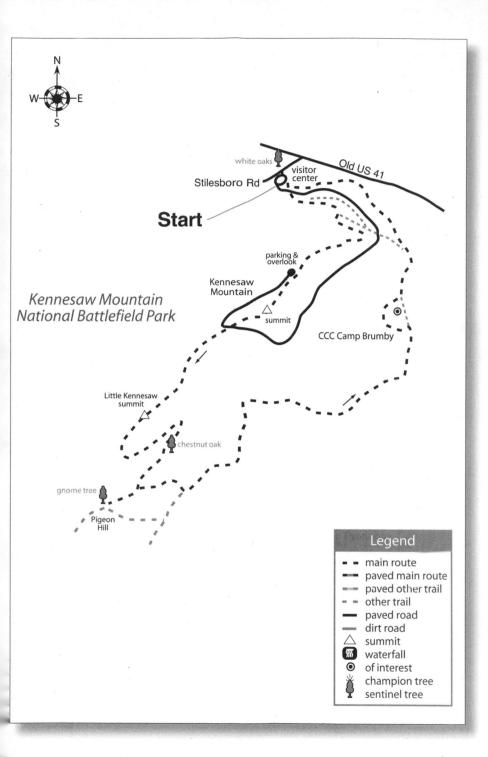

CHEATHAM HILL LOOP

KENNESAW MOUNTAIN NATIONAL BATTLEFIELD PARK

An excellent hike for those wanting to escape the crowds of Summit Loop. The route is split into two sections, West Trail and Noses Creek Trail. You'll begin on a wide gravel roadbed that turns onto a narrow footpath winding through some of the nicest piedmont forest in the Kennesaw Mountain Battlefield Park. As you pass several creeks near Civil War–era earthworks, West Trail offers peace and solitude. The second half of the loop is on a wide gravel roadbed with an easy grade where hikers can walk abreast and chat while cooling down from the more challenging West Trail.

DISTANCE FROM DOWNTOWN ATLANTA • 23 MILES

BY CAR FROM I-75 Take exit 265 and go west on North Marietta Parkway for 2.1 miles. Turn right onto Polk Street and travel 1.6 mile before taking another right onto Burnt Hickory Road. The parking area is on the left in 1.1 mile.

PUBLIC TRANSPORTATION
This hike is not easily accessible by public transportation. The Cobb Community Transit 15 bus can take you to Marietta Square (Roswell Street and Atlanta Street), from which it is 2.9 miles to the trailhead on Burnt Hickory Road.

PARKING
Paved parking area on Burnt Hickory Road; GPS N 33° 57.7955, W 84° 35.6644

ADDRESS
1520 Burnt Hickory Rd NW, Marietta, GA 30064

Escape the crowds to peace and solitude.

HIKE DISTANCE 3.75-mile figure-8 loop

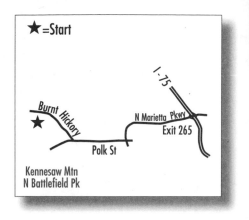

WHY THIS HIKE IS GREAT This loop has significantly less foot traffic than the Kennesaw Summit loop. Instead of views of skyscrapers, peaceful rolling hills and bubbling streams make you feel far away from the city.

DIFFICULTY

Overall — Moderate

Terrain — Gravel and hard-packed soil trails are wide and well maintained with a few rooty and rocky sections

Elevation change — Trails ascend and descend constantly; climbs are steep but not sustained.

HOURS 8 am to 5:30 pm (Standard Time); 8 am to 7:30 pm (Daylight Savings Time)

DOGS Leashed dogs permitted

FACILITIES No toilets; water fountain at trailhead

FEES & PERMITS None

LAND MANAGER Kennesaw Mountain National Battlefield Park

SENTINEL TREES

Four-Trunk Tulip Tree – GPS N 33° 57.2353, W 84° 35.9314
- Look for this unusual tree on your right after the trail descends and turns left; it is made up of four separate trees that have fused together. At the seams where the trunks meet, the wood has grown outward very slowly over many years.

Chestnut Oak – GPS N 33° 56.7494, W 84° 35.8137
- 10'8" circumference
- A relic of the Civil War era, this is one of two trees of its age and size in this area of the park and one of the largest chestnut oaks in Atlanta. Its small-lobed leaves resemble those of the American chestnut, hence its name.

White Oak – GPS N 33° 56.7976, W 84° 35.8104

- 11' circumference
- Down a short hill on the left of the trail is a white oak of similar age to the nearby sentinel chestnut oak. White oaks are more common to Atlanta and are identified by extremely flaky bark on their upper limbs.

HIKE

Start your hike near the information kiosk and water fountain adjacent to the parking lot. Hike through the field on the wide gravel trail, and enter the woods after 0.1 mile.

At the bottom of the hill cross a small creek and then hike up a steep grade, past a small trail leading through a field on your left. After cresting the hill turn right onto West Trail.

In 0.25 mile stay straight at a junction, then hike 0.65 mile. After the trail descends and turns left you'll pass the sentinel tulip tree with four trunks on your right. Beyond the sentinel tree 0.15 mile, reach Noses Creek at a makeshift ford where other hikers have put precarious stepping-stones in the water. The creek is a great place for kids (or adults) to play.

Instead of crossing here, follow the trail left along the bank of the creek to intersect with Noses Creek Trail near a large bridge. Turn right, cross the bridge, and immediately turn right again onto West Trail. Walk along the creek, then follow the trail as it curves uphill to the left—do not take the small side trail along the creek's bank.

As you hike uphill you'll pass old Civil War–era earthworks on your left. A half-mile after leaving the creek, pass a bench next to a small creek in a hollow with some large oak trees. After crossing the creek the trail switchbacks up the hill; in 0.5 mile you'll reach a junction with Noses Creek Trail at Dallas Highway. The trail curves sharply left past a metal gate and onto the wide gravel trail.

Immediately on your right is the sentinel chestnut oak. In less than 100 yards, look below the trail on your left for the second sentinel white oak.

Hike 0.5 mile to reach the bridge over Noses Creek. Cross and continue straight on for 0.4 mile to reach a junction with East Trail. Stay left on the main trail, pass a small side trail that leads across a field on the left, and hike 0.1 mile farther to the junction with West Trail on the left.

Continue straight and hike 0.4 mile back to the parking lot to finish the hike.

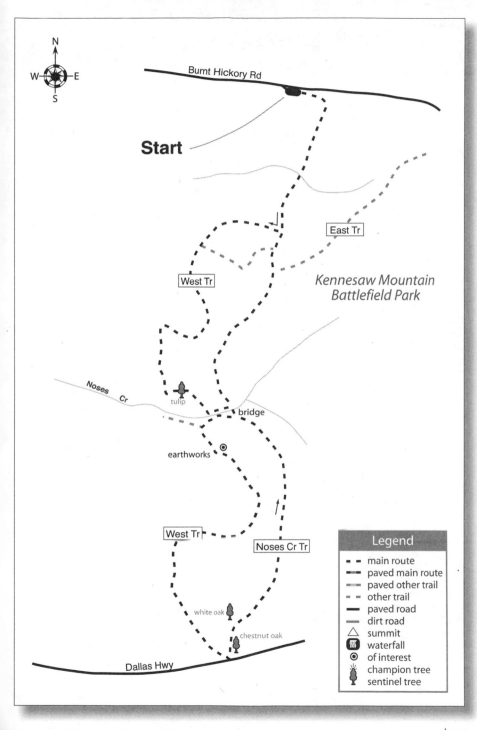

This massive post oak, damaged long ago by a lightning strike, is just off the trail.

KOLB FARM LOOP

KENNESAW MOUNTAIN NATIONAL BATTLEFIELD PARK

Because it is does not have a mountain peak, the Kolb Farm section of the Kennesaw Mountain Battlefield Park is less well known than the Summit Loop, but its 6-mile hike provides similar natural beauty and challenge with a fraction of the foot traffic. This is where Sherman's troops eventually outmaneuvered Johnston's to win the explosive Battle of Kennesaw Mountain during the Civil War. Today the peaceful forests and meandering streams of this park offer respite from the noise and bustle of the surrounding city. This route is shared with horses, so watch your step.

DISTANCE FROM DOWNTOWN ATLANTA • 23 MILES

BY CAR FROM I-75 Take exit 263 toward Southern Polytechnic State University. At the fork follow signs for GA 120 Loop W/Marietta/Southern Poly and merge onto South Marietta Parkway SE. In 3.4 miles turn right onto South Marietta Parkway SW/Powder Springs Street. In 0.4 mile, turn left onto Whitlock Avenue and continue 2.7 miles before turning left, just after a large cemetery, onto Cheatham Hill Drive, at a Dead End sign. Park at the end of Cheatham Hill Drive in 0.6 mile.

PUBLIC TRANSPORTATION *This hike is not easily accessible by public transportation.* The Cobb County Transit 15 Windy Hill Road bus can take you to Marietta Square (Roswell Street and Atlanta Street), from which it is 3.5 miles to the trailhead on Cheatham Hill Drive.

PARKING Paved parking area at the end of Cheatham Hill Drive; GPS N 33° 56.1992, W 84° 35.8239

ADDRESS 1544 Whitlock Avenue NW, Marietta, GA 30064

HIKE DISTANCE 6-mile loop

WHY THIS HIKE IS GREAT To experience the beauty and peacefulness of Kennesaw Mountain Battlefield Park without the crowds who visit the mountain each week, the Kolb Farm loop is perfect alternative to the Summit Loop.

DIFFICULTY

Overall — Moderate

Terrain — Wide, well maintained gravel and hard-packed soil trails; several wooden bridges

Elevation change — Most of the trails are easily graded; expect short ascents and descents constantly, including an extended ascent at the very end of the route.

HOURS 8 am to 5:30 pm (Standard Time); 8 am to 7:30 pm (Daylight Savings Time)

DOGS Leashed dogs permitted

FACILITIES No toilets; water fountain

FEES & PERMITS None

LAND MANAGER Kennesaw Mountain National Battlefield Park

SENTINEL TREES

Black Oak – GPS N 33° 55.8908, W 84° 36.2772
- 11'5" circumference
- This tree dwarfs all others around it. Only a sapling during the Civil War era, it is now a true sentinel. Find it on the left just past the Cheatham Hill Road parking lot.

Post Oak – GPS N 33° 54.5634, W 84° 36.0020
- 13" circumference
- This relic of the Civil War era is one of the largest of its species in Atlanta. Notice the deep gash down its side from a lightning strike long ago. Its cross-shaped leaves identify it as a post oak.

BIRDS TO LOOK FOR

KENNESAW MOUNTAIN

Spring: American redstart, black-and-white warbler, blackburnian warbler, black-throated green warbler, cerulean warbler, ovenbird, rose-breasted grosbeak, scarlet tanager

Double-trunk Tulip Tree –
GPS N 33° 55.4229, W 84° 35.3354

- 11'9" circumference (larger trunk)
- This massive tree with two trunks was two separate trees until the two grew so large they merged at the base. It is the largest tree in this area of the forest, but keep your eye out for mature white oak and beech trees as well.

HIKE

Start the hike at the end of the parking lot near the water fountain and Civil War–era earthworks and follow a sign pointing right, toward the Illinois Monument.

In 0.2 mile you'll reach the Illinois Monument. Go right, hiking downhill on a trail on the right side of the open field below the monument. This trail is steep and curves to the left at the bottom of the hill.

Upon entering the woods cross a creek on a wooden bridge, then turn left. Follow the edge of the creek for 0.15 mile through a grove of ironwood trees before crossing the creek on logs. Reach a junction with the main trail in less than 100 yards after crossing the creek. Turn right, following the arrows on a signpost.

In 0.2 mile go right at a junction, following the sign for Kolb Farm. Pass a line of large tulip trees on the right of the trail and hike 0.25 mile to Cheatham Hill Road. Cross the road and continue straight on the main trail (not toward the parking lot on the right), past a metal gate with a Kolb Farm Loop Trail sign.

On your left just beyond the metal gate is the sentinel black oak. After 0.5 mile, the trail skirts an open field for 0.2 mile before re-entering the woods. In 0.4 mile continue straight at a junction, then follow an elevated path through a swampy area, cross a sewer right-of-way, and cross a bridge over John Ward Creek.

The trail becomes a wide gravel roadbed and passes through an area with young pine trees on the left and bamboo on the right. After crossing a small creek, hike 0.7 mile on the roadbed trail. The trail splits and reconnects several times. You will pass at least one small trail on the left, but stay on the roadbed until it curves left to parallel Powder Springs Road.

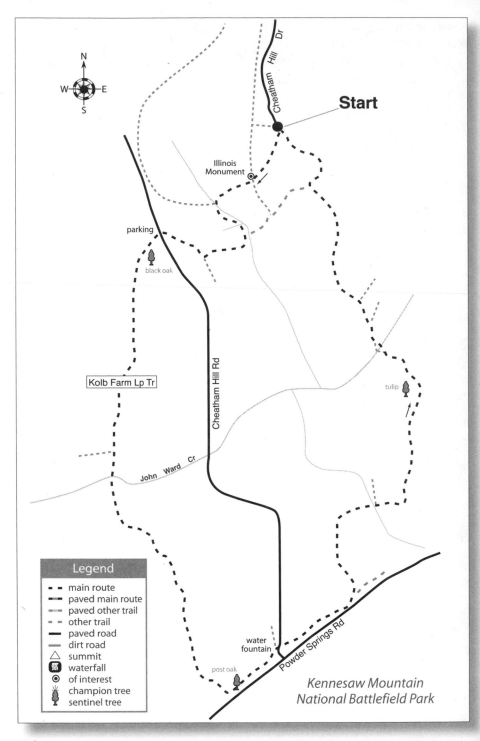

Start

Cheatham Hill Dr

N
W — E
S

Illinois
Monument

parking

black oak

Kolb Farm Lp Tr

Cheatham Hill Rd

tulip

John Ward Cr

water
fountain

Powder Springs Rd

post oak

*Kennesaw Mountain
National Battlefield Park*

Just before passing a metal gate on your right, pass the sentinel post oak with a large split caused by a lightning strike. Continue on the trail, passing a water fountain and a view of the Kolb Farm cabin across the road to the right. Hike 0.2 mile to reach a junction on the left. Go straight, cross Cheatham Hill Road, and hike another 0.3 mile parallel to Powder Springs Road before turning left at a junction near a metal gate. Follow the sign for Cheatham Hill.

For the next 0.5 mile, the trail winds through a forest adjacent to a subdivision. After passing the houses you'll come to a bench on your right, cross a creek, and follow arrows to turn right (uphill) at a junction.

After another 0.5 mile, the trail splits near the sentinel double-trunk tulip tree on your left. Take either fork; the trails reconnect in 50 yards. The trail follows the path of a small creek through a mature forest of white oak, tulip tree, and beech. In 0.2 mile turn right, following a hiker sign, and cross two bridges (the trail to the left of the bridges is a creek ford for horses). Cross a sewer right-of-way, then stay left at a junction following arrows on a post. Stay left, again following signs, at another junction in 0.1 mile and continue for 0.6 mile, past one small trail on your right, until you reach a major junction. Follow the Cheatham Hill–Visitor Center sign to the right and continue steadily uphill for 0.3 mile to return to the parking lot and finish your hike.

OLDE ROPE MILL PARK

This park is well known to mountain bikers and to locals in Cherokee County, Georgia, but it should be known to all Atlantans. A cotton mill that spun fibers into rope stood on this site along the Little River until 1950, and its ruins are still visible. Along with the historical point of interest, this park has an extensive trail system for hikers and bikers. Some trails are designated for both users, so pay special attention when using those.

DISTANCE FROM DOWNTOWN ATLANTA • 31 MILES

BY CAR FROM I-75 Take I-75 to I-575 and drive for 9 miles to exit 9. After exiting go east onto Ridge Walk Parkway. Make an immediate left onto Rope Mill Road and drive 0.7 mile to the Olde Rope Mill parking lot.

PUBLIC TRANSPORTATION
This hike is not easily accessible by public transportation. The 490 and 491 Xpress commuter bus lines stop at the His Hands Church Park & Ride in Woodstock, 5 miles from the park.

PARKING Paved parking area; GPS N 34° 07.8860, W 84° 31.4057

ADDRESS 690 Rope Mill Road, Woodstock, GA 30188

HIKE DISTANCE 12.5 miles total, including 1-mile, 2-mile, 3.5-mile, and 6-mile routes

The Little River bridge accesses the historic mill.

WHY THIS HIKE IS GREAT Options, options, options! Olde Rope Mill has a hike for everyone in the family. You can spend a whole day hiking all the trails, or you can pick and choose the route that's best for your group on a given day. Every trail is beautiful!

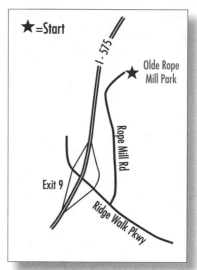

DIFFICULTY

Overall — Easy to strenuous

Terrain — Most trails are hard-packed soil, with a section of paved trail and a short stretch of gravel road; mountain bike trails can be muddy and rutted.

Elevation change — The first two sections have no elevation change, but Explorer and Avalanche Trails have constant, short ascents and descents.

HOURS 7 am to 11 pm, year-round

DOGS Leashed dogs permitted

FACILITIES Portable toilet, picnic tables, large pavilion

FEES & PERMITS None

LAND MANAGER City of Woodstock

SENTINEL TREES

White Oak – GPS N 34° 07.5270, W 84° 31.0522
- 8'11" circumference
- In such a young forest, a tree like this white oak really stands out. Though small for its species—white oaks in the metro area can grow twice this size—this mature specimen shows the forest is recovering from years of clearcutting.

Tulip Tree – GPS N 34° 07.5461, W 84° 30.8637
- 8'11" circumference
- This tree stands tall and straight on the hillside to the left of the trail. The bark at its base is just beginning to show signs of maturity with the exterior flaking off, leaving a smoother bark below. Tulip trees are among the first to grow very large in a young forest.

Ironwood Tree – GPS N 34° 07.7944, W 84° 31.1690
- 1'9" circumference
- With its smooth gray bark, an ironwood tree can be hard to differentiate from a beech. Look closely at the crooked ironwood in the middle of the trail and its triple-trunked sibling to the right—you will see faint ridges on its bark that set it apart from a beech. Another tell-tale sign is its location on the riverbank, where ironwoods thrive.

HIKE

The 12 miles of trail in Olde Rope Mill Park can provide a long day of walking for a seasoned hiker or can be split into shorter routes for those wanting a less strenuous outing. Each trail section begins and ends at the central parking area, so you can easily piece together the appropriate length for your hike.

Section 1 – Trestle Rock Multi-Use Trail (1 mile)
A paved path follows the Little River for 0.5 mile before ending at a short trail that connects with Avalanche Trail. For an easy 1-mile hike, follow this path out and back.

Section 2 – Historic Mill Trail (2 miles)
From the parking area cross the Little River Bridge, then turn right onto the trail where the pavement ends. The route passes through what was once the foundation of the Rope Mill and then follows the path of the millrace for 0.1 mile before reaching the site of the old dam.

Continue on the trail beyond the dam for 0.1 mile to reach a small creek. Cross the creek and continue hiking along the riverbank. In about 100 feet you'll find the sentinel ironwood tree with a bent trunk growing in the middle of the path. The triple-trunk ironwood is on your right.

In 0.25 mile, the trail merges with a sewer right-of-way and continues 0.3 miles farther to a railroad trestle. Stay off the trestle and embankment! From here, turn around and retrace your steps to the parking area.

INSIDER TIP

OLDE ROPE MILL PARK TRAIL ETIQUETTE

Though all trails are multi-use, this park is a favorite of mountain bikers. On Avalanche and Explorer Trails, always follow the posted guidelines for which direction hikers should walk. Use special caution when hiking uphill to avoid bikers racing downhill at high speeds. Correct trail etiquette is for hikers to step aside to let bikers pass. If you have a dog with you, keep it close so the leash does not trip a biker.

Section 3 – Explorer Trail (3 loops; 3.5 miles)

Facing the river, follow the gravel road leading out of the parking area on the left. This road passes under the I-575 bridge and immediately reaches the trailhead for Explorer Trail. This is a mountain bike trail, so be aware and courteous to bicyclists when hiking this route. Be sure to hike OPPOSITE the direction bikers are directed to ride on the trailhead sign. These instructions are based on Saturday directions: bikers ride counterclockwise (right) and hikers walk clockwise (left). Pay special attention while hiking uphill because bikes may be coming downhill toward you at fast speeds. Always keep your eyes open and listen while hiking on trails shared with mountain bikers.

Take Green Trail (loop 1) on the left and pass a junction with a connector trail on the right. Cross a bridge in 0.1 mile, then reach a junction with Explorer Blue Trail (loop 2). You have the option to turn right, cross a bridge, and return to the parking lot from here. To continue your hike, turn left to begin Explorer Blue Trail.

Blue Trail winds through the hills above the Little River. Pass a bench on your left in 0.6 mile, then reach a bridge and junction with Explorer Red Trail (loop 3) in another 0.4 mile. You have the option to turn right here and return to the parking lot. To continue your hike on Red Trail, turn left, cross the bridge, cross a small paved road, and take the path on the left.

In 1.0 mile, Red Trail arrives back at the paved road. Cross the bridge and turn left onto Blue Trail. Pass a bench on your right in 0.15 mile, then continue 0.3 mile to the junction with Green Trail. Turn left, cross a bridge, and go 0.2 mile back to the gravel road and the end of Explorer Trail. Turn left and follow the gravel road 0.2 mile back to the parking lot.

Section 4 – Avalanche Trail (3 loops; 6 miles)

With your back to the river, you'll find Avalanche Trailhead on the hill above the Taylor Randahl Memorial. Like Explorer Trail this is also a mountain bike trail, so be aware and courteous to bicyclists when hiking this route. Be sure to hike OPPOSITE the direction bikers are directed to ride on the trailhead sign. These instructions are based on Saturday directions: bikers ride counterclockwise (right) and hikers walk clockwise (left). Pay special attention while hiking uphill because bikes may be coming downhill toward you at fast speeds. Always keep your eyes open and listen while hiking on trails shared with mountain bikers.

Start at the information kiosk and take Avalanche Green Trail (loop 1) to the left. Pass a bench on your left in 0.1 mile, then cross two bridges in 0.3 mile before reaching a junction with Avalanche Blue Trail (loop 2). You can turn right here to return to the parking lot. Stay left to continue your hike on Blue Trail.

Cross a clearing and emergency access point, then cross a bridge that leads back into the woods. In 0.3 mile, pass a junction with a trail on your left that leads to Trestle Rock Multi-Use Trail.

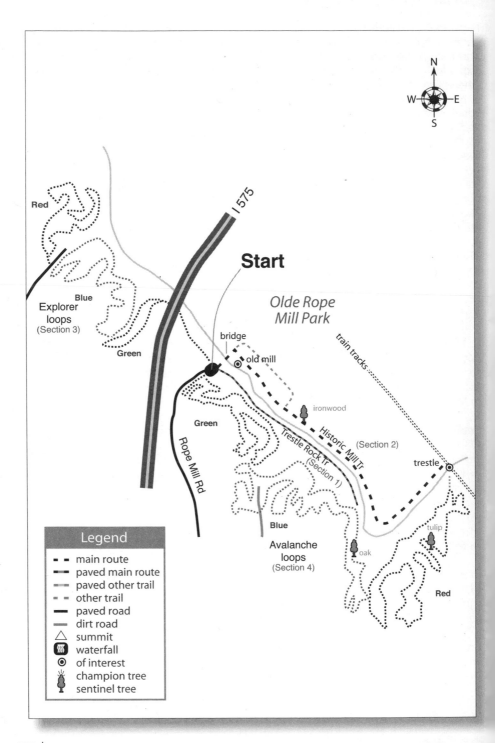

Start

Olde Rope
Mill Park

Red

Blue
Explorer
loops
(Section 3)

Green

I 575

bridge

old mill

train tracks

ironwood

Historic Mill Tr

(Section 2)

Green

Rope Mill Rd

Trestle Rock Tr
(Section 1)

trestle

tulip

Blue

Avalanche
loops
(Section 4)

oak

Red

Legend

- - main route
— paved main route
— paved other trail
- - other trail
— paved road
— dirt road
△ summit
▨ waterfall
◉ of interest
🌳 champion tree
🌱 sentinel tree

In 0.2 mile, just before passing the 360 sign, pass the sentinel white oak on the left. Then hike another 0.1 mile to reach a junction with Avalanche Red Trail (loop 3). To return to the parking lot, turn right into the clearing and take Blue Trail back. To continue your hike go left, cross a small clearing, then cross a wooden bridge with railings to re-enter the woods.

Cross a bridge in 0.3 mile, then another in 0.1 mile. In 100 yards reach a junction near the railroad trestle. Turn right to stay on Red Trail.

Cross a bridge in 0.4 mile, then pass the sentinel tulip tree on the hill to the left of the trail. In 1.0 mile, cross a bridge then reach the junction with the Blue Trail. Go left and hike a long uphill to the top of the ridge above the Little River. You'll see a view of the river on your right in 0.5 mile. In another 0.5 mile, stay right at a junction with a dirt access road.

In 0.25 mile cross a bridge, turn left into a small clearing, then turn right, back into the woods. In 0.3 mile you'll reach the junction with Green Trail. Continue straight on, pass a bench on the left, then cross a bridge. Cross another bridge in 0.6 mile, then in 0.2 mile the trail comes alongside Rope Mill Road and parallels the road for the last 100 yards before reaching the trailhead and the end of the hike.

AUTREY MILL NATURE PRESERVE & HERITAGE CENTER

Besides providing the perfect spot to picnic along a bubbling brook, this nature preserve is a wonderful place to learn—and to hike. Its network of interconnecting trails has wildlife-viewing stations and informative signs about its trees and birds. The forest is peaceful, and the hiking is not strenuous. Back at the nature center, visitors can learn about Native American and pioneer living and see reptiles and amphibians in a special exhibit.

DISTANCE FROM DOWNTOWN ATLANTA • 27 MILES

BY CAR FROM GA 400 Travel north on GA 400 and take exit 7A for Holcomb Bridge Road. Merge onto Holcomb Bridge, then turn left on Old Alabama Road in 0.6 mile. In 2.5 miles, turn left to continue on Old Alabama Road. Drive 3 miles and turn left on Autrey Mill Road, just after passing Autrey Mill Middle School. The Nature Preserve parking lot is on your left in 0.5 mile.

PUBLIC TRANSPORTATION *This hike is not easily accessible by public transportation.* Take the Red Line north to North Springs Station and board the 140 North Point/Mansell P/R bus. Get off at Kimball Bridge Road; it is 5 miles from there to Autrey Mill.

PARKING Small paved parking lot near the nature center, with more parking farther up the gravel road; GPS N 34° 01.2257, W 84° 13.9194

ADDRESS 9770 Autrey Mill Road, Johns Creek, GA 30022

These monkey statues add a little levity to your hike.

HIKE DISTANCE 1-mile loop

WHY THIS HIKE IS GREAT Trails are well-marked and maintained so you can enjoy yourself, keep an eye out for wildlife, and learn about trees without worrying about getting lost.

DIFFICULTY

Overall — Easy

Terrain — Well-maintained hard-packed soil trails

Elevation change — Some ascents and descents with only mild grades

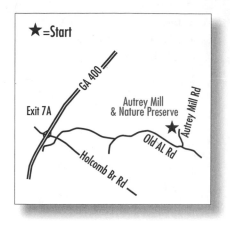

HOURS 8 am to dusk, year-round; visitor center open Monday through Saturday, 10 am to 4 pm (closed on major holidays)

DOGS Leashed dogs permitted

FACILITIES Toilets, water fountains, nature center, historic homes, Native American dwelling replicas, plenty of signage on the trails

FEES & PERMITS None

LAND MANAGER Autrey Mill Nature Preserve & Heritage Center

SENTINEL TREES

Pignut Hickory – GPS N 34° 1.1250, W 84° 13.9570
- 7'4" circumference
- This double-trunk pignut hickory is labeled with a small sign on the right side of the trail. Smaller than many in this forest, it may be one of the oldest trees in the area. Pignut hickory grows relatively slowly, adding a very small amount of girth each year. Sometimes the size of a tree means nothing about its age.

Loblolly Pine – GPS N 34° 1.1090, W 84° 13.990
- 10'4" circumference
- In contrast to the slow-growing pignut hickory, loblolly pine adds circumference faster than most native trees. This labeled specimen on the left side of the boardwalk is the largest tree in the Autrey Mill Preserve. Despite its size, it is probably no older than the surrounding trees.

Tulip Tree – GPS N 34° 1.102, W 84° 14.006

- 9'2" circumference
- Though smaller than the loblolly pine across the path, this tulip tree is one of the mature sentinel trees in this park. Tulip trees grow straight and tall until the elements (winds, lightning, etc.) cause them damage. This tree is young enough that its gnarliness factor is still low.

HIKE

Maps are posted on kiosks throughout the nature preserve. This hike starts on Forest Trail and passes between two replica Native American structures (a teepee and a log-and-mud hunting shelter), before passing a small area with monkey statues. The statues are an artist's reference to a time in the early 1900s when a circus train derailed nearby, and monkeys ran loose in the area of Autrey Mill.

In 250 feet, pass a bench and junction with Well Loop. Continue straight and cross a bridge. Just before turning right on a second bridge, notice the sentinel pignut hickory tree on the left that is labeled with a sign. After viewing the sentinel tree, turn right onto the bridge and start Miller's Trail just beyond the well.

Proceed uphill, passing a covered nature blind built by an Eagle Scout. These trails contain many Eagle Scout projects, a testament to the preserve's strong community ties. The trail soon enters a developed area. After passing the backyard of a historic home, turn left onto River Trail.

Hike downhill for 0.1 mile, then turn right to cross a bridge and make an immediate left after the bridge. You'll quickly come to another bridge and an outdoor classroom, just beyond which the trail reaches Sal's Creek. Cross several more bridges, then a boardwalk. Midway down the boardwalk, you'll find the sentinel loblolly pine (labeled with a sign) on the left and the sentinel tulip tree directly across from it. After the end of the boardwalk, turn right at the next trail junction to continue on River Trail.

In almost 0.1 mile, arrive at a junction with a powerline above. Go straight on River Trail, passing a gazebo, until you come to the junction with Forest Loop Trail. Turn left here and begin hiking uphill. In 0.1 mile, turn left at a junction and hike on, passing a circle of benches on your left.

At a junction with Wildflower Trail, turn right (uphill), passing flower beds on your right after 0.1 mile. Just beyond these flower beds is a junction near the road. Turn left and walk another 300 feet before ending your hike next to an amphitheater and the parking lot.

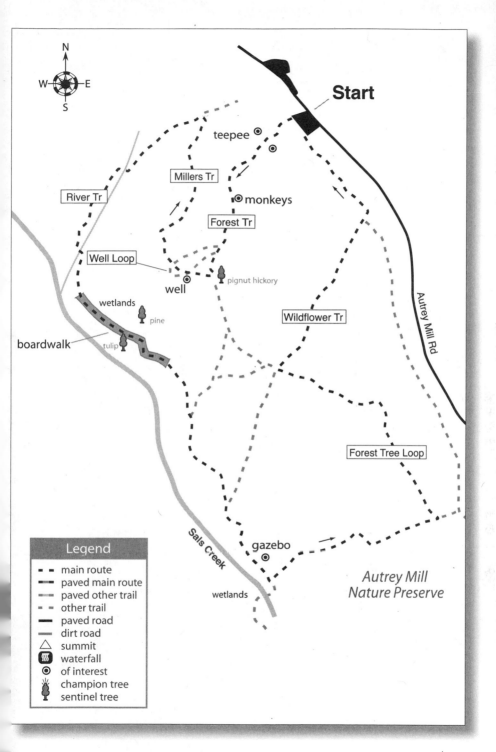

Start

N
W—E
S

teepee ◉

Millers Tr

monkeys ◉

River Tr

Forest Tr

Well Loop

well ◉

pignut hickory

wetlands

pine

boardwalk

tulip

Wildflower Tr

Autrey Mill Rd

Forest Tree Loop

Legend

- - - main route
— paved main route
— paved other trail
- - other trail
— paved road
— dirt road
△ summit
▦ waterfall
◉ of interest
♠ champion tree
♠ sentinel tree

Sals Creek

gazebo ◉

wetlands

Autrey Mill
Nature Preserve

Simpsonwood Conference & Retreat Center

Whenever you visit Simpsonwood you'll pass runners, neighbors walking their dogs, and conference-goers. This 300-acre-plus retreat center along the Chattahoochee River has done an excellent job as steward of this special greenspace. It was donated to the Methodist Church by "Miss Ludie" Simpson, whose vision was "to keep the land so that all people could enjoy God's beautiful creation." After hiking at Simpsonwood, you'll likely agree the trails do just that.

DISTANCE FROM DOWNTOWN ATLANTA • 23 MILES

BY CAR FROM I-285 Take exit 32 and go north on Buford Highway. In 2.2 miles, turn left onto Jones Mill Road which becomes Peachtree Corners Circle. In 4.3 miles turn left onto West Jones Bridge Road. Take the third left onto Jones Bridge Circle, then another left to stay on Jones Bridge Circle. The entrance to Simpsonwood is on your left. Enter and park on the left near the bath house.

PUBLIC TRANSPORTATION
This hike is not easily accessible by public transportation. Take the Gwinnett County Transit bus 35 (which connects with MARTA at the Doraville Station) to the corner of Peachtree Parkway and Peachtree Corners Circle. From here it is 2 miles to the entrance of Simpsonwood.

PARKING Paved parking area near a bath house close to the Simpsonwood entrance; GPS N 33° 59.1793, W 84° 14.5924

Simpsonwood offers a peaceful hike through a piedmont forest.

ADDRESS 4511 Jones Bridge Circle, Norcross, GA 30092

HIKE DISTANCE 2-mile loop

WHY THIS HIKE IS GREAT Simpsonwood provides a peaceful hike through piedmont forest with excellent views of the river, just across from the Jones Bridge unit of the Chattahoochee National Recreation Area.

DIFFICULTY

Overall — Easy

Terrain — Hard-packed soil trails

Elevation change — Lots of short ascents and descents; no extended climbs

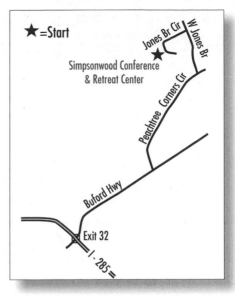

HOURS 6 am to sunset, year-round

DOGS Leashed dogs permitted

FACILITIES Toilets, benches along the trail

FEES & PERMITS None

LAND MANAGER Simpsonwood Conference & Retreat Center

SENTINEL TREES

Black Oak – GPS N 33° 59.1695, W 84° 14.6870
- 12'5" circumference
- This enormous ancient tree, the largest on this hike, greets you at the very beginning. After you pass it, the forest abruptly becomes almost exclusively young loblolly pines—an example of how clearcutting dramatically changes the nature of a forest.

White Oak – GPS N 33° 59.2942 W 84° 14.8328
- 10'3" circumference
- Just off trail to the left, this white oak is one of the larger trees in this area of old-growth forest. As you walk downhill toward the river, notice the old hardwood trees around you—tulip trees, oaks, sweetgum, and others.

"Trinity" Beech – GPS N 33° 59.1133, W 84° 14.8941

- 8'6" circumference
- This beautiful beech tree has a triple-forked trunk, the result of damage sustained early in its life. It's not particularly large for its species, but its three trunks and position on the side of a small hill along the trail give it special character.

HIKE

From the parking area near the bath house, walk down the road away from the entrance. Just past a pavilion on the left, turn right into the woods on a trail marked with a white arrow on a tree. There are many side trails on this loop, but the main trail is marked with white blazes and arrows painted on trees. When in doubt, look for white blazes.

After entering the woods, pass the sentinel black oak on your right. Continue 0.1 mile and bear right at a junction. The trail continues through a young pine forest before reaching the 0.25-mile marker and a gate, where you'll turn right. After this turn, just before reaching an old post and small trail on the right, pass the sentinel white oak on the left.

Stay left on the main trail. After the 0.5-mile marker, the trail descends toward the Chattahoochee River, passing through a small clearing, then curving left to parallel the river. The trail along the river's edge passes five benches, a suspension bridge, the 0.75-mile marker, and several spur trails to the left leading up to the retreat center facilities. Stay parallel to the river as long as you can (about 0.2 mile more). The trail on the river's edge dead-ends just after the last junction on the left. Take this left turn and look for a white blaze. The trail jogs slightly to the right while crossing a gravel road. Follow the trail right as you pass a bridge on your left.

Hike uphill as the trail curves slightly left until you reach the 1-mile marker. Go straight at the next major 4-way trail junction. Continue following white blazes to reach the 1.25-mile marker.

For the next 0.4 mile the trail winds generally uphill. After crossing a bridge, a the sentinel "Trinity" beech is just up the hill in front of you. The trail curves sharply right around this tree.

Cross a wide trail, a dirt road, and then pass the 1.5-mile marker before coming to a developed area with an outdoor chapel, picnic pavilion, and campsites. Follow the white blazes across the road, and go right at a Y-junction.

In 0.1 mile go left across a bridge and turn right. Pass a side trail on your left that leads to an open field, just before the 1.75-mile marker. Follow the trail along an elevated section of land. When you come to a T-junction, go left.

Cross a bridge, then hike generally uphill for the last 0.25 mile of the route, passing several side trails and the 2-mile marker before reaching the parking area and bath house where the hike ends.

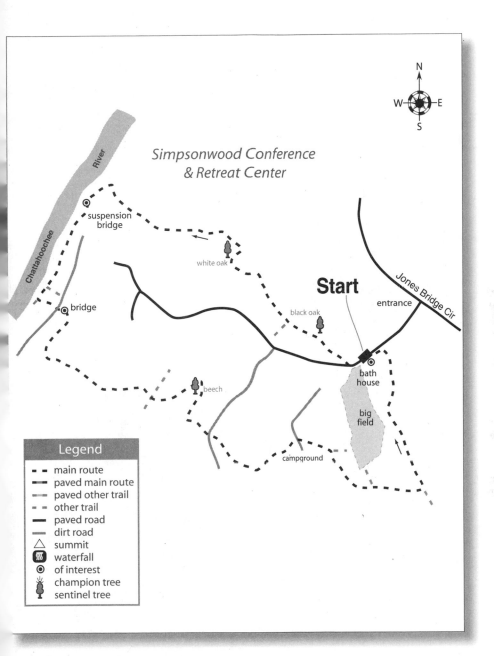

McDaniel Farm Park

This 134-acre greenspace is adjacent to the sprawling Gwinnett Place Mall, but once you're on the trails its easy to forget the bustling shopping center next door. The trails wind through fields and forests, along creeks, and through a restored 1930s farmstead area, all on handicapped-accessible trails. This parcel of land is relatively unchanged since the McDaniel family first purchased it in the 1850s and is a perfect respite from busy suburban life.

Distance from Downtown Atlanta • 25 miles

By car from I-85 Take exit 104 and go north on Pleasant Hill Road. In 0.5 mile, turn right onto Satellite Boulevard, drive 0.5 mile, and turn left onto Old Norcross Road. Immediately after a car dealership in 0.2 mile, turn right onto McDaniel Road. The park entrance and parking lot is at the end of McDaniel Road.

Public Transportation From the Doraville MARTA Station, take the Gwinnett County Transit Route 10 bus toward the Gwinnett Place Mall. Get off at the corner of Satellite Boulevard and Old Norcross Road, then walk 0.2 mile to McDaniel Road, turn right, and continue 0.3 mile to the park entrance.

Parking Paved parking lot; GPS N 33° 58.1382, W 84° 07.7035

Address 3251 McDaniel Road, Duluth, GA 30096

Hike Distance 2.5-mile double loop

This historic farmhouse is in the middle of the suburbs.

HIKING ATLANTA'S HIDDEN FORESTS

Why this hike is great

You walk through a restored 1930s farmstead and fields, along creeks, and through forest—all on accessible trails.

Difficulty

Overall — Easy

Terrain — Paved paths except for 0.3 mile of hard-packed soil trail that can be bypassed

Elevation change — Several steep but short ascents and descents

Hours 7 am to sunset, year-round; farmstead area open 10 am to 4 pm, Tuesday through Saturday

Dogs Leashed dogs permitted

Facilities Toilets, interpretive farmstead area, benches and picnic tables, trail maps at most junctions

Fees & Permits None

Land Manager Gwinnett County Parks & Recreation

Sentinel Trees

Southern Red Oak – GPS N 33° 58.1542, W 84° 07.5859

- 11'7" circumference
- One of several large oaks in this area, this tree on the left side of the path is particularly large a relic from when the farm was in operation.

Sweetgum – GPS N 33° 58.2282, W 84° 07.3135

- 11'6" circumference
- This sweetgum is significantly larger than all other trees in this area of the park. Sweetgum can be identified by its star-shaped leaves and spiky round seedpods littering the ground. Find it growing to the right of the trail.

Sycamore – GPS N 33° 58.1882, W 84° 07.4141

- 13'5" circumference
- This tree on the creek's edge, 50 feet to the right of the trail, is a perfect example of where sycamore trees like to grow—as close to water as possible. Sometimes sycamores are called "ghost trees" because the outer bark on their branches flakes off, showing the white inner bark.

HIKE

Start on the trail next to the map kiosk to the left of the restrooms, passing a side trail to the group shelter. After 0.1 mile you'll pass a bench and the sentinel southern red oak on the left. In about 75 yards turn left and hike downhill.

Reach a junction at the bottom of the hill in 0.15 mile. Stay left and cross a bridge. Stay left at the next junction, then pass a picnic table on your right after another 0.1 mile. Pass a double-trunk sweetgum tree with two cedars at its base before reaching a junction with a trail leading left to the park's maintenance area. Stay right.

Keep hiking and in 0.15 mile, when the path curves sharply to the left, turn right onto Wildflower Trail, a dirt path; it will meet back up with the main path in 0.3 mile. Alternatively you can stay on paved Cross Park Trail, which meets Wildflower again in 0.15 mile.

Wildflower Trail winds through a young pine forest before reconnecting with the main paved path. Turn right and hike 0.2 mile through a somewhat more mature forest past a picnic table and bench before reaching the sentinel sweetgum tree on the hill to the right.

Pass a picnic table after the sentinel sweetgum, then the trail curves left and descends. In 0.15 mile, go straight (toward the bridge) at a junction. Cross the bridge on Lower Meadow Trail and pass Farm Stream Trail on your left. This hard-packed soil trail leads in 0.4 mile to the farmstead area near the parking lot. Stay on the paved path which borders an open field. In 0.15 mile pass an area of picnic tables on your right that includes an outdoor classroom and a good place to wade in the creek if you are so inclined. The trail continues parallel to the creek. In less than 100 yards you'll pass the sentinel sycamore 50 feet off the trail on the right, at the creek's edge. Though this is the largest tree in this park, it is hard to spot in the summer because it is not right next to the trail, so keep your eye out. It's the first large tree in the woods on the right after passing the outdoor classroom area.

These woods also contain quite a few river birch; look for their extremely flaky bark. When you come to a junction near the first bridge you crossed, turn left and hike up the hill. Continue straight at the junction near the top of the hill. The trail will curve left past a bench. Stay left again at the gate to the farm on Upper Farm Trail.

In the last 0.5 mile of the route, the path winds around the exterior of the farmstead area, passing Farm Stream Trail on the left before ending at the parking lot to finish the hike.

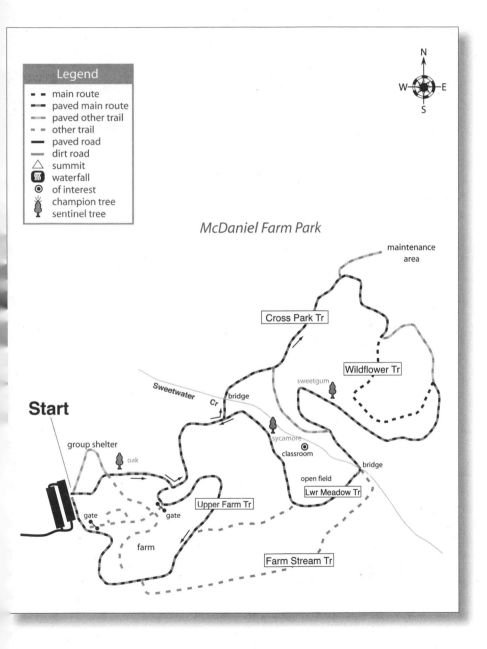

McDaniel Farm Park

Legend
- - main route
- paved main route
- paved other trail
- - other trail
- paved road
- dirt road
- △ summit
- ▨ waterfall
- ◉ of interest
- 🌳 champion tree
- 🌳 sentinel tree

maintenance area

Cross Park Tr

Wildflower Tr

sweetgum

Sweetwater

bridge

Cr

Start

group shelter

oak

sycamore

classroom

bridge

open field

Lwr Meadow Tr

gate

gate

Upper Farm Tr

farm

Farm Stream Tr

LEITA THOMPSON MEMORIAL PARK

One of the best kept secrets in Roswell, Leita Thompson Memorial Park contains several creeks, many large trees, and a well-maintained 2.5-mile loop trail. The trails are paved with crushed gravel and signed with map kiosks and mile markers, making both the walking and navigation easy. This is an excellent destination for trail running and for walking with children and seniors. Yet despite the ease of its footpath, the trail's length makes this hike enjoyable and even challenging for a hiker of any skill level.

DISTANCE FROM DOWNTOWN ATLANTA • 28 MILES

BY CAR FROM GA 400
Take exit 7B to merge onto Holcomb Bridge Road toward Roswell. Continue straight on this road for 6 miles as it changes names to GA 92, Crossville Road, then Woodstock Road. Turn right into the Leita Thompson parking area just after the Roswell Art Center.

PUBLIC TRANSPORTATION
This hike is not easily accessible by public transportation. Take MARTA 85 bus toward Roswell. Get off at the corner of Holcomb Bridge Road and Alpharetta Highway, from which the park is 5 miles farther.

PARKING Small paved
parking lot near an apartment complex (with overflow parking near Roswell Art Center); GPS N 34° 03.7987, W 84° 24.4310

It's nice to pause and reflect on your tour around the pond.

ADDRESS 1200 Woodstock Road, Roswell, GA 30075

HIKE DISTANCE 2.5-mile loop

WHY THIS HIKE IS GREAT Perfect for a hike or trail run, the even grade and crushed gravel surface of the trail allows you to focus on the forest around you instead of roots and rocks under your feet.

DIFFICULTY

Overall — Easy to moderate

Terrain — Wide, crushed gravel trails

Elevation change — Many short ascents and descents, gently graded

HOURS Dawn to dusk, year-round

DOGS Leashed dogs permitted

FACILITIES Portable toilet at trailhead, map kiosks and mileage markers throughout

FEES & PERMITS $10 day parking fee or $35 annual parking pass

LAND MANAGER City of Roswell

SENTINEL TREES

Beech – GPS N 34° 3.9300, W 84° 24.0910

- 8' circumference
- Just before crossing two bridges, look for this sentinel beech on the right about 50 feet off the trail, near the creek. In this younger part of the forest this tree stands out because of its size and location on the creek's floodplain, where beech trees love to grow. Because it is slightly off the path, it has escaped the graffiti carving that many older beech trees suffer.

Tulip Tree – GPS N 34° 4.0280, W 84° 24.2190
- 10'9" circumference
- On the left side of the trail and several feet larger in circumference than any tree around it, this is a tree worth stopping for. Tulip trees are commonly the largest in Atlanta; this one survives from a time before the forest was clearcut.

White Oak – GPS N 34° 03.7579, W 84° 24.5239
- 11'10" circumference
- The largest tree in Leita Thompson Memorial Park. Growing near Woodstock Road to the left of the trail about 50 feet, this tree was protected from axes and saws by its proximity to people's homes.

HIKE
Start at the map kiosk on the southeast side of the parking lot (next to the driveway) and begin your hike on Yellow Loop. Throughout this entire hike you will see regular mile marker signs indicating how far you've come or how far you have to go on each loop—Yellow, Blue, and Red.

After 0.25 mile, pass a map kiosk near Roswell Art Center. In another 0.1 mile, reach a junction at the edge of a field. Go right and continue for 0.2 mile to a series of two bridges and a side trail leading to a dog park. The trail then curves sharply to the left and crosses several more bridges.

Walk another 0.1 mile, then turn right at a junction with a map kiosk where Blue Loop joins Yellow and Red Loops. In 0.1 mile just before two bridges, the sentinel beech is 50 feet off the trail to the right, near the creek.

In 0.2 mile, after crossing several more bridges, pass the sentinel tulip tree on your left. This is the largest tree in this part of the park, so it should be easy to spot.

Just after the tulip tree you'll pass a cabin on your right and come to a junction with a paved maintenance road. Cross the road and go straight on the gravel path on the left bank of the pond. This quarter-mile side trail circles the scenic pond and is well worth the detour. At the end of this trail, cross the maintenance road and go straight, downhill past a map kiosk and 1.25-mile marker.

Pass two corrugated metal sheds on your right, then pass a side trail to an elementary school on your right. Continue straight and stay on the high ground.

In 0.1 mile, pass a bench and small overlook, then continue on the main trail for 1.0 mile, past two junctions with maintenance roads, until you come to a small apartment building. The trail winds and switchbacks in and out of several hollows.

Cross the apartment driveway and re-enter the woods. At the bottom of the hill, look to the left for the sentinel white oak—the largest tree in the park. From here it is 0.1 mile back to the parking lot to finish the hike.

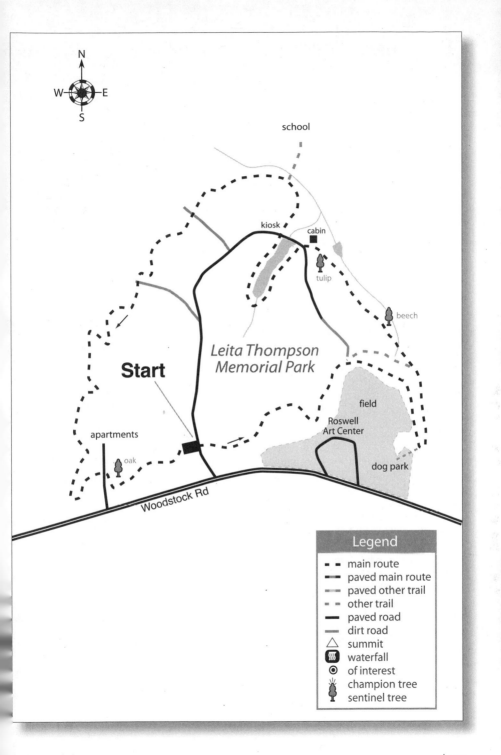

BIG TREES FOREST PRESERVE

Just off the busy thoroughfare of Roswell Road you can get a glimpse of how Atlanta looked before white settlers arrived—rolling hills, steep-banked creeks, and big trees. When this land was about to be developed into a car dealership in the 1980s, John Ripley Forbes (who also established the *Outdoor Activity Center* [p. 98] and the Chattahoochee Nature Center) spearheaded the work to save this forest. Today it stands as a testament to Forbes's memory—its full name is John Ripley Forbes Big Trees Forest Preserve.

DISTANCE FROM DOWNTOWN ATLANTA • 16 MILES

BY CAR FROM GA 400
Take exit 5B toward Sandy Springs and merge onto Abernathy Road. Drive 1.3 miles and turn right onto Roswell Road. The entrance for Big Trees Forest Preserve is on your right and shares a parking lot with the North Fulton Government Service Center.

PUBLIC TRANSPORTATION
Take the MARTA Red Line train to the North Springs Station and transfer to the 87 Roswell Rd bus toward Dunwoody Station. Get off just after the intersection of Roswell Road and Jefferson Drive, right in front of the Big Trees Forest Preserve.

PARKING Paved parking lot shared with the North Fulton Government Service Center (park toward the right rear of the lot to be closest to the preserve entrance); GPS N 33° 57.8733, W 84° 21.7746

Big Trees Forest Preserve is a testament to the memory of its founder, John Ripley Forbes.

276

ADDRESS 7645 Roswell Road, Sandy Springs, GA 30350

HIKE DISTANCE 1.25-mile loop

WHY THIS HIKE IS GREAT A perfect escape from the surrounding city and excellent for hikers of any age—and it lives up to its name, with several large sentinel white oaks.

DIFFICULTY

Overall—Easy

Terrain—Well-maintained hard-packed soil trails and a short section of paved path

Elevation change—Extended ascent and descent on Backcountry Trail

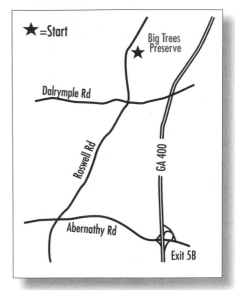

HOURS Dawn to dusk, year-round

DOGS Leashed dogs permitted

FACILITIES Toilets, outdoor classrooms

FEES & PERMITS None

LAND MANAGER Big Trees Forest Preserve

SENTINEL TREES

White Oak – GPS N 33° 57.8180, W 84° 21.8180
- 10'5" circumference
- This white oak stands alone next to the trail and is the first truly big tree you'll pass after leaving the pavement. Examine its bark and leaves for similarities to the other two sentinel trees along this route.

White Oak – GPS N 33° 57.7980, W 84° 21.8260
- 12'8" circumference
- Just to the left at a junction near an outdoor classroom, this gigantic tree is the largest and most impressive in the park, and itself is reason enough to hike in the Big Trees Forest Preserve. Take a moment to sit and marvel at it.

White Oak – GPS N 33° 57.7810, W 84° 21.8270

- 9'10" circumference
- This tree is interesting because of the resurrection ferns, which live symbiotically with white oaks, growing in its branches. These ferns look dry and dead during times of little precipitation, but become green and lush after rain.

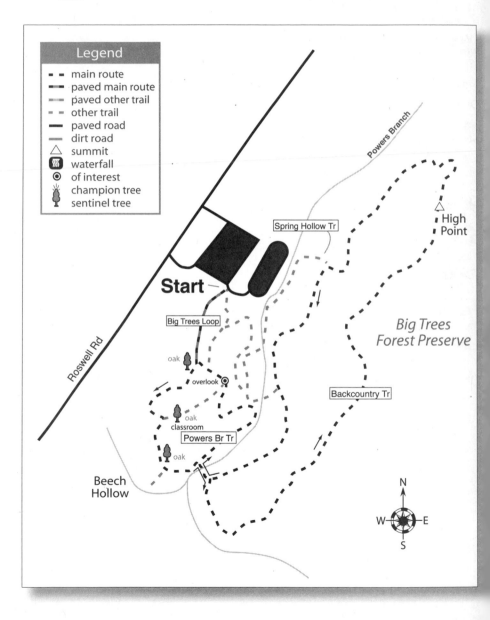

HIKE

Start your hike through the wooden gate, passing an outdoor classroom, connector trail, and information kiosk on your left. The trail is paved for the first 100 yards.

When the main path curves to the left go right onto a mulched path, passing the sentinel white oak on your right. In 100 yards, reach a junction that leads to an outdoor classroom and the second sentinel white oak to the left. Go straight past this junction.

Just before the Beech Hollow junction, pass the third sentinel white oak on your left. Bear left past the junction and the trail continues to curve left before reaching a junction with Backcountry Connector Trail. Turn right, cross the bridge, and turn right onto Backcountry Trail.

During the next 0.3 mile the trail curves left and then ascends, passing some young hemlock trees on the right, to reach the highest point in the park. As the trail begins to descend from the ridge, it curves left, right, then left again before reaching a junction with Spring Hollow Trail in 0.2 mile. Continue straight another 0.1 mile to a junction signed To Entrance. Continue straight past this trail for 0.1 mile to once again reach Backcountry Connector Trail junction. Turn right, cross the bridge, and turn right onto Powers Branch Trail.

In 100 yards at a junction with Back 20 Connector Trail near a bridge, go left and wind uphill through a privet thicket. Cross a small boardwalk, then reach Big Trees Loop Trail and bluff overlook. Go right, regain the paved path, and finish your hike at the parking lot in 0.1 mile.

Dunwoody Nature Center

You might have attended camp here or visited it on a school field trip, but surprisingly few people know the trails at the Dunwoody Nature Center. It's worth a visit! Besides the sheer joy of spending time in the woods, hiking here is fun because trees are labeled with plaques. You'll pass families walking with young children, and there is plenty of information available to learn more about forest and stream ecology if you choose.

DISTANCE FROM DOWNTOWN ATLANTA • 17 MILES

BY CAR FROM GA 400

Take exit 5A toward Dunwoody and merge onto Abernathy Road. In 0.3 mile, turn left onto Mt. Vernon Highway. Drive for 1.4 miles, then turn left onto Chamblee Dunwoody Road. After another 0.5 mile, turn right onto Roberts Drive. The entrance to Dunwoody Nature Center will be on your right in 0.3 mile.

PUBLIC TRANSPORTATION

Take the MARTA 150 Perimeter Center/Dunwoody Village bus to the corner of Chamblee Dunwoody Road and Dunwoody Village Parkway. Walk north on Chamblee Dunwoody for 0.2 mile, then stay right to continue on Roberts Drive 0.3 mile to the entrance of Dunwoody Nature Center.

PARKING Paved parking lot near the Nature Center building; GPS N 33° 57.3990, W 84° 19.9910

Take a break at one of the many benches along the trail.

ADDRESS 5343 Roberts Drive, Dunwoody, GA 30338

HIKE DISTANCE 1.25-mile double loop

WHY THIS HIKE IS GREAT One of the best places to bring kids, walk dogs, and enjoy the natural world. This park's nature and educational programs are a bonus on top of a small but scenic system of trails in the heart of Dunwoody.

DIFFICULTY

Overall — Easy

Terrain — Hard-packed soil, mulch, crushed gravel, and boardwalks with a few bridges

Elevation change — Rolling hills throughout; mild grades on all ascents and descents

HOURS 7 am to sunset, year-round; nature center open weekdays 9 am to 5 pm

DOGS Leashed dogs permitted

FACILITIES Toilets (open during nature center hours), nature center, information sheets that can be borrowed from nature center, tree house pavilion, boardwalk, picnic table

FEES & PERMITS None

LAND MANAGER Dunwoody Nature Preserve

SENTINEL TREES
White Oak–GPS N 33° 57.3842, W 84° 19.7847
- 8'3" circumference
- The forest on the east side of Dunwoody Nature Center is a young one that is slowly maturing. White oaks such as this sentinel are hardwoods that make up the backbone of a healthy mature forest.

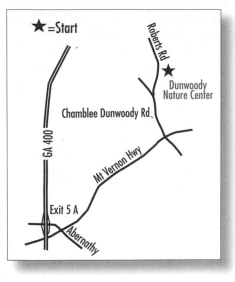

Sweetgum–GPS N 33° 57.4032, W 84° 19.9352

- 8'9" circumference
- Look for spiky, spherical seedpods on the ground, and you'll find the sentinel sweetgum tree. This species likes to grow above the floodplains of creeks—notice that this one is right at the edge of the higher ground, just above the lower area near the water.

Tulip Tree–GPS N 33° 57.3984, W 84° 19.9540

- 10'1" circumference
- It's no surprise that a tulip tree is the largest tree in the park. This species is ubiquitous in the Atlanta area and thrives in piedmont soils.

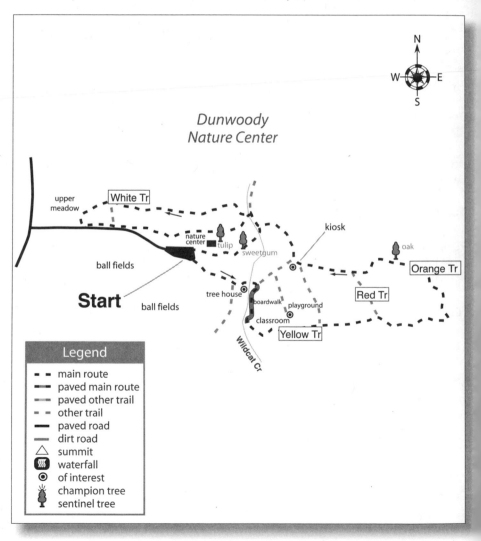

HIKE

Start your hike near the nature center building and follow the trail to the right. After leaving the pavement, pass a side trail to the baseball fields. Just after this junction you might choose to explore the tree house pavilion to your right.

Less than 75 yards beyond the tree house pavilion, turn right onto the boardwalk and walk through the wetlands. At the end of the boardwalk, hop off and turn left on Yellow Trail near an outdoor classroom. This trail leads uphill to a playground where you'll turn right to stay on Yellow Trail.

In 75 yards, Yellow Trail joins Orange Trail. Make a soft right and hike uphill. On the Orange Trail loop there are landmarks every 100 yards. First, pass a junction with Red Trail on the left. Stay left on Orange Trail at a junction with a trail that leads into an adjacent neighborhood. Enter an area with three benches and go left. As the trail passes several backyards, on your right is the sentinel white oak. You'll reach another junction with Red Trail near a picnic area. Continue straight, then go right to stay on Orange Trail. Finally you'll reach a kiosk and a junction with several trails. Ahead you can see the nature center and parking lot. Turn right onto a spur of Orange Trail.

This trail skirts the edge of a short bluff over the creek, then descends. Pass a junction with Meadow Trail, turn right across a small bridge, then go left over a larger bridge spanning the creek. White Trail starts after the bridge. Go right when the trail splits, then stay left at a small junction with a side trail that leads out of the park.

In 0.1 mile cross a bridge, then reach a junction near the upper meadow. Stay straight to reach the upper meadow's outdoor classroom and picnic tables. Go left to return to the nature center on the crushed gravel path that parallels the road.

In 0.1 mile, reach the junction with the White Trail loop. Continue straight, cross the bridge, then go right onto Meadow Trail. Cross another bridge over the creek to reach the meadow, where you'll find two more sentinel trees, the sweetgum on the left and the tulip tree on the right, near the nature center building. Walk up the wooden stairs next to the building to reach the parking lot and finish your hike.

Exploring the creeks which empty into the Chattahoochee River is always rewarding on this hike.

COCHRAN SHOALS

CHATTAHOOCHEE RIVER NATIONAL RECREATION AREA

Known mostly for flat jogging paths along the river, the Cochran Shoals unit of the National Recreation Area is also home to miles of hiking trails. This route leads you through quiet piedmont hollows, past small creeks, and along the edge of the Chattahoochee River. You can also connect this loop with the *Sope Creek* hike (p. 290) to make an epic 12-mile trek.

DISTANCE FROM DOWNTOWN ATLANTA • 13 MILES

BY CAR FROM I-75 Take exit 258 for Cumberland Boulevard and head northeast on Cumberland. In 0.7 mile, turn right onto Akers Mill Road. In 0.8 mile, turn left onto Powers Ferry Road. Go under the I-285 overpass and turn right onto Interstate North Parkway. The entrance to the parking area is on the left in 0.3 mile.

PUBLIC TRANSPORTATION Take the MARTA 148 bus to the corner of Interstate North Parkway and Riveredge Parkway. The entrance to the parking area is on the right in 0.4 mile. Or take the Cobb Community Transit 50 bus to the corner of Interstate North Parkway and Powers Ferry Road; the entrance to the parking area is on the left in 0.3 mile.

PARKING Paved parking area; GPS N 33° 54.1569, W 84° 26.6722

ADDRESS 590 North Interstate Parkway, Marietta, GA 30067 / 2069 Eugene Gunby Road, Marietta, GA 30067

HIKE DISTANCE 7-mile loop

WHY THIS HIKE IS GREAT Cochran Shoals contains one of the more extensive networks of trails in the Atlanta area, so hikers can plan any number of routes.

DIFFICULTY

Overall — Moderate

Terrain — Hard-packed soil trails

Elevation change — Rolling hills throughout; no extended ascents or descents

HOURS Dawn to dusk, year-round

DOGS Leashed dogs permitted

FACILITIES Toilets, benches, picnic areas

FEES & PERMITS $3 daily park pass—cash only at kiosk on-site (note that kiosks are often out of service)—or $25 annual park pass which can be purchased online

LAND MANAGER Chattahoochee River National Recreation Area

SENTINEL TREES

White Oak – GPS N 33° 54.3756, W 84° 27.4526
- 9'9" circumference
- This leaning white oak on the right side of the trail is the largest tree in this area of the woods. Most of the piedmont forests above the river have been logged many times. This tree began growing after the most recent logging, but its size and shape qualify it as a sentinel.

Double-Trunk Water Oak – GPS N 33° 55.0016, W 84° 26.4673
- Both trunks have 9'9" circumference
- This water oak to the right of the path likely started as two seedlings from the same mother tree and grew so large that their trunks fused to become one.

Water Oak – GPS N 33° 54.7435, W 84° 26.8517
- 12'10" circumference
- Located next to a bench and water fountain, this is the largest water oak in the park. Because it grows near an open area and has no competition for light, its trunk has grown thick and its crown is rounded and full.

BIRDS TO LOOK FOR

COCHRAN SHOALS

Fall: Canada warbler, golden-winged warbler, gray catbird, marsh wren, Philadelphia vireo, sedge wren, Swainson's thrush

HIKE

Start the hike at the payment kiosk at the far end of the parking lot. It begins on a very wide gravel path. Walk 0.5 mile, cross a bridge, and come to a junction with a small trail on the left. Pass the No Bikes barrier and follow the trail along a boardwalk through a wetlands.

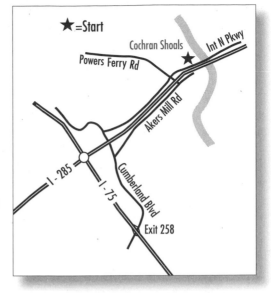

At the end of the boardwalk pass a trail on your right, then go left and uphill. Follow this very steep trail for 0.25 mile before the grade evens out on the top of the ridge, passing two trails on the right along the way.

In 0.2 mile turn left at a pipeline clearing, cross the clearing, then re-enter the woods past a No Bikes barrier. In 0.15 mile the trail makes a hard left and goes uphill. Stay left at the next junction, then pass the large leaning sentinel white oak on the right.

In 0.1 mile, the trail nears an enormous glass building. Bear right along the edge of the property, getting a glimpse of the sculpture in the building's atrium, then hike 0.2 mile more after the trail turns away from the building.

At the first junction you come to, continue straight on, then turn left and hike downhill at the next junction. In 0.1 mile cross a suspension bridge and turn right. Cross another bridge, then follow the trail until it veers to the left, away from the creek (don't stay straight on the muddy path along the sewer right-of-way) to reach a junction next to a bridge on the right. Turn right, cross the bridge, and hike 0.1 mile to a junction with a very wide gravel trail.

Turn left and continue 0.25 mile, cross a bridge, and turn left onto a small trail paralleling the creek. After 0.35 mile, reach a junction with two trails on the right. Make the soft right onto the path where bikes are allowed and begin a long, steady uphill climb.

The next junction is at an old dirt road in 1.2 mile. Cross the road and continue on the single-track trail. Stay straight at the next two junctions (the first junction allows you to connect this hike with the *Sope Creek* trails, p. 290). At the third junction (in 0.1 mile) turn right and hike downhill.

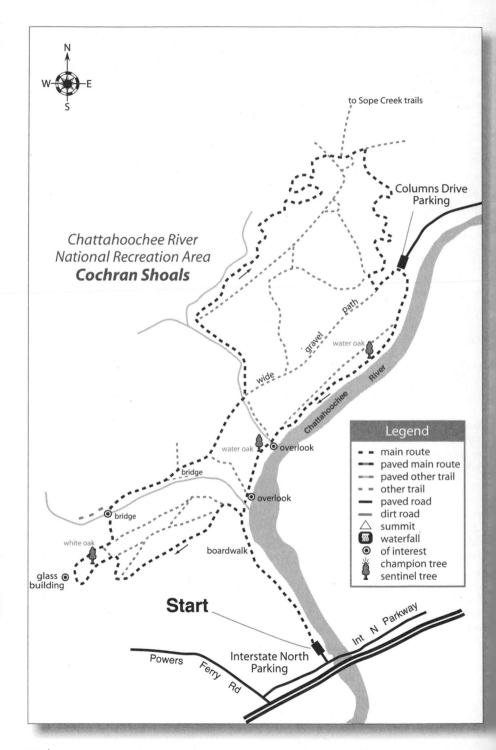

Reach a junction in 0.8 mile and turn left. In less than 100 yards, this trail leads you back to the wide gravel path. Go left toward the Columns Drive parking area, which you will reach in 0.1 mile.

At the parking area curve right and stay on the wide path for 0.2 mile before turning left onto a small trail, somewhat more secluded and peaceful, that parallels the gravel path.

In 0.2 mile, pass the sentinel double-trunk water oak on the right. Walk another 0.3 mile to where the small trail reconnects with the main path.

In 0.15 mile reach a junction near a bridge. There is an overlook platform on the left. Go straight, cross the bridge, then pass the sentinel water oak, water fountain, bench, and trash can on the right.

Continue for 0.15 mile to the next junction and overlook platform. Stay straight for 0.5 mile to return to the parking area and finish your hike.

Sope Creek

Chattahoochee River National Recreation Area

This route, while not along the banks of the Chattahoochee, still provides plenty of water-related scenery. Sope Creek and the mill ruins along its banks are impressive, and Sibley Pond is a peaceful place to stroll and contemplate nature's beauty. If you're feeling athletic, the Sope Creek loop can connect to the *Cochran Shoals* loop (p. 285) to create a 12-mile day hike.

Distance from Downtown Atlanta • 17 miles

By car from I-75 Take exit 261 toward Lockheed/Dobbins AFB. Go east on Delk Road for 1.4 mile and turn left onto Terrell Mill Road. After 1.1 mile, turn right onto Paper Mill Road. The parking area and trailhead will be on the right in another 1.1 mile.

By car from I-285
Take exit 24 and go north on Riverside Drive for 2.3 mile. Turn left onto Johnson Ferry Road, cross the Chattahoochee River, and turn left onto Paper Mill Road in 0.5 mile. The parking area and trailhead will be on your left in 2.2 mile, just after crossing the narrow bridge over Sope Creek.

Public Transportation
This hike is not easily accessible by public transportation. Take the Cobb County Transit 50 bus to the corner of Delk Road and Powers Ferry Road. From there it is 2.5 miles to the trailhead on Paper Mill Road.

Sope Creek provides plenty of water-related scenery.

PARKING Gravel parking area;
GPS N 33° 56.2660, W 84° 26.5787

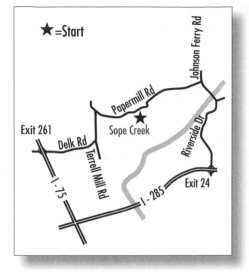

ADDRESS 3760 Paper Mill Road SE,
Marietta, GA 30067

HIKE DISTANCE 4.5-mile loop

WHY THIS HIKE IS GREAT Besides quiet
forests and a scenic pond, Sope Creek
is home to some of the most impressive
historic ruins in the metro area.

DIFFICULTY

Overall — Moderate

Terrain — Wide, well-maintained hard-
packed soil and gravel trails

Elevation change — Rolling hills with short ascents and descents

HOURS Dawn to dusk, year-round

DOGS Leashed dogs permitted

FACILITIES None

FEES & PERMITS $3 daily park pass — cash only at kiosk on-site (note that kiosks
are often out of service) — or $25 annual park pass which can be purchased online

LAND MANAGER Chattahoochee River National Recreation Area

SENTINEL TREES

Northern Red Oak – GPS N 33° 55.8656, W 84° 26.1916
- 8'10" circumference
- Though not large for its species, this northern red oak on the left of the trail
  stands out in the recently logged forest. Think for a moment about why this
  oak tree might have been spared when the area was last clearcut.

Redbud – GPS N 33° 56.4183, W 84° 26.2680
- 2'1" circumference
- This redbud leans over a ruined building. Redbuds are understory trees and never grow as large as oaks or tulip trees, but they have showy edible flowers that emerge in the early spring. Look for heart-shaped leaves in summer.

Tulip Tree – GPS N 33° 56.3025, W 84° 26.1339
- 9'2" circumference
- This tulip tree up the hill from the trail is one of the largest trees in the Sope Creek unit of the park. Erosion has exposed some of its roots, making the tree seem larger than its nine-foot circumference.

Hike

Start your hike on the wide gravel service road just past a map kiosk and metal gate. Go straight at the first junction you come to and cross the dam next to the pond. After the dam, go right to continue the loop around the pond.

In 0.15 mile cross a bridge, stay right at a junction, cross a second bridge, and go left at the next junction. After 0.25 mile pass several small trails on the right. Stay left at each junction until you reach a clearing. Pass through the clearing and walk 0.15 mile to another junction. Take the right fork. In 0.1 mile reach a junction with a much wider trail. Pass the No Bikes barrier and turn right. This trail is shared with mountain bikes, so be aware as you are hiking.

Immediately after turning right, stay left at a junction with a closed trail. Hike another 0.1 mile, then stay straight at a junction with a trail on the left.

In 0.6 mile you'll reach a junction with the trail that leads to the Cochran Shoals unit of the Chattahoochee River National Recreation Area. Continue left through an area with many young buckeye and beech trees. The trail parallels Fox Creek. Go straight and cross a bridge at a junction in 0.3 mile. After another 0.1 mile, pass the sentinel red oak on the left.

In 0.15 mile cross a bridge, then go left and uphill across from a small trail leading to an apartment complex. Continue straight at the next junction in 0.1 mile.

The trail parallels Sope Creek for 0.4 mile, crossing a bridge along the way. This is a particularly secluded and scenic section of the hike. At the next junction turn right and cross a small creek. In 0.1 mile go right at another junction. In the next 0.2 mile, pass two small trails leading down to Sope Creek on your right. Then at a major junction along a small creek, turn right to take a short detour (100 yards) for a view of Sope Creek and the mill ruins. This is a very beautiful area—don't miss it!

After spending some time on the banks of Sope Creek, retrace your steps, pass the trail on the left (the direction you originally came from), and take the right fork at the next junction in 50 feet.

In 0.2 mile go right at a junction that leads downhill to a mill ruin. At the ruin go left to follow the path between two buildings. The small tree leaning over the ruin on the right is the sentinel redbud.

To continue on an optional spur to the ruins on the far side of Sope Creek, cross the guardrail at the edge of the road and very carefully cross the Paper Mill Road bridge over Sope Creek, turning right onto a wide gravel path after the bridge. This path leads 0.3 mile to the mill ruins and Caney Creek. Just before reaching the ruins you'll see the sentinel tulip tree with exposed roots up the hill on the left.

After visiting the ruins, retrace your route back to the other side of the creek and uphill to the junction with the main trail. Turn right at this junction, then stay straight at a junction with a small trail on the right leading down to the road.

In 0.15 mile the trail curves left and reaches another junction. Turn right, then right again at a second junction in less than 0.1 mile. This trail leads 0.1 mile back to the parking lot and the hike's end.

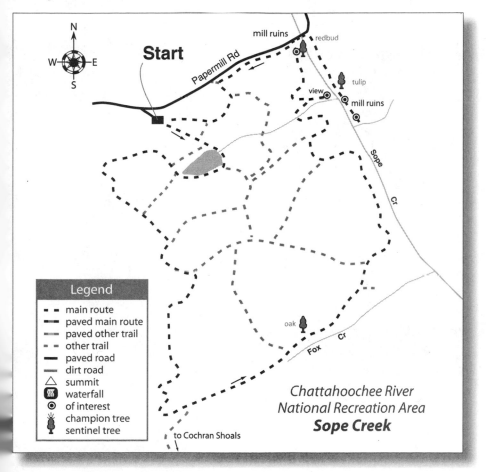

The old farm road makes for a peaceful hike.

Johnson Ferry South

Chattahoochee River National Recreation Area

Though not as well-used as its neighbor Johnson Ferry North, this unit of the Chattahoochee River National Recreation Area offers a secluded picnic area and peaceful walking along the riverbank. The trail follows the path of an old farm road along the banks of the Chattahoochee. Large trees grow at the river's edge, and wild blackberries abound in the young forest that is quickly replacing the once cultivated fields.

Distance from Downtown Atlanta • **19 miles**

By car from I-285 Take exit 24 and go north on Riverside Drive for 2.3 miles. Turn left onto Johnson Ferry Road, cross the Chattahoochee River, and make the first left onto Columns Drive. The entrance to the parking area and trailhead is on the left in 0.7 mile.

Public Transportation *This hike is not easily accessible by public transportation.* Take the MARTA 87 bus to the corner of Roswell Road and Abernathy Road. Follow Abernathy Road (which becomes Johnson Ferry Road) west for 1.9 miles. Turn left on Columns Drive, and it's 0.7 miles more to the trailhead on the left.

Parking Gravel parking area; GPS N 33° 56.2425, W 84° 24.8026

Address 4650 Columns Drive SE, Marietta, GA 30067

Hike Distance 1.6 miles out & back

Why this hike is great It's a peaceful out-and-back route along the banks of the Chattahoochee with a picnic spot as an added bonus.

Difficulty
Overall — Easy
Terrain — Wide gravel and hard-packed soil trails
Elevation change — Almost no elevation loss or gain

Hours Dawn to dusk, year-round

Dogs Leashed dogs permitted

Facilities None; toilets at nearby Johnson Ferry North trailhead

Fees & Permits $3 daily park pass—cash only at kiosk on-site (kiosks are often out of service) or $25 annual park pass which can be purchased online

Land Manager Chattahoochee River National Recreation Area

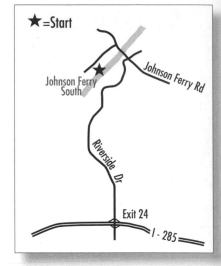

Sentinel Trees

Water Oak –
GPS N 33° 56.1405, W 84° 24.8724
- 13'2" circumference
- One of several large trees near the water's edge, this water oak is a particularly impressive specimen and the largest tree in the area.

Water Oak – GPS N 33° 56.1213, W 84° 24.8982
- 11'3" circumference
- The farm that once existed on this site did not clear the large timber from the banks of the Chattahoochee. As a result, many older hardwood trees still stand here, including this water oak.

River Birch – GPS N 33° 56.4112, W 84° 24.6102
- 11' circumference
- Smaller than the sentinel water oaks, this river birch is one of the largest of its species in the metro area. River birches have flaky, papery bark, but this tree is so old and large that you have to look high up on its trunk to find it.

Hike
From the parking area, turn right and walk through the clearing toward the pavilion. Continue past the pavilion for 0.1 mile. Just before leaving the clearing you'll see two small side trails leading to sentinel water oaks. The first side trail leads to the larger of the two.

After visiting the sentinel trees, retrace your steps to the parking area. Pass the parking lot and continue on the trail that parallels the river. In 0.2 mile, pass the enormous sentinel river birch 20 feet off the trail on the right.

Be on the lookout in the summer for wild blackberries growing on the edges of the trail. Walk 0.3 mile farther to a junction on the right. Continue on the main path for another 0.2 mile to the end of the trail. Turn around here and retrace your steps 0.6 mile to the parking area to finish the hike.

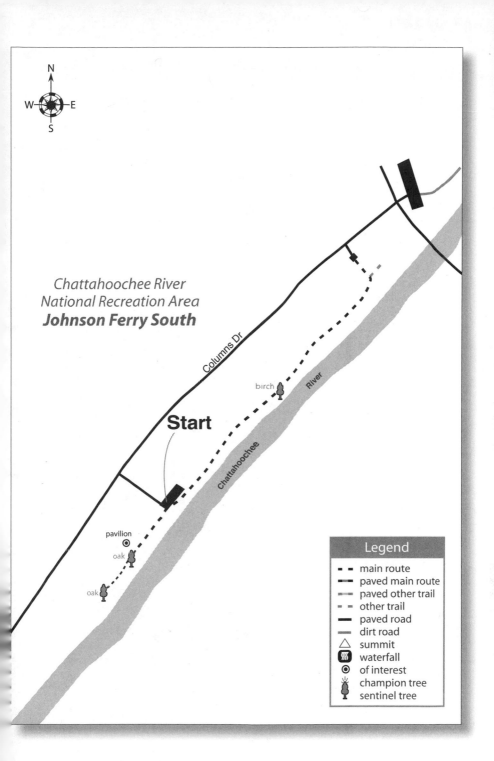

JOHNSON FERRY NORTH

CHATTAHOOCHEE RIVER NATIONAL RECREATION AREA

This trail is popular for good reason. An easy loop allows hikers to stroll along the riverbank and explore a rocky stream in a secluded hollow and provides a great place for a jog, a family outing, or a dog walk. The more adventurous can extend their hike to the north along a pipeline clearing for a good view of the Morgan Falls dam upstream.

DISTANCE FROM DOWNTOWN ATLANTA • 19 MILES

BY CAR FROM I-285 Take exit 24 and go north on Riverside Drive for 2.3 miles. Turn left onto Johnson Ferry Road, cross the Chattahoochee River, and make the first right into the Johnson Ferry North parking area.

PUBLIC TRANSPORTATION
This hike is not easily accessible by public transportation. Take the MARTA 87 bus to the corner of Roswell Road and Abernathy Road. Follow Abernathy Road (which becomes Johnson Ferry Road) west for 1.9 miles to reach the trailhead.

PARKING Paved and gravel parking areas; GPS N 33° 56.7811, W 84° 24.2624

ADDRESS 161 Johnson Ferry Road, Marietta, GA 30068

HIKE DISTANCE
2-mile loop

Small cascades are at the far end of the route.

WHY THIS HIKE IS GREAT Offering a superb riverside walk and easy access, Johnson Ferry is suitable for all ages and ability levels.

DIFFICULTY

Overall — Easy

Terrain — Gravel and hard-packed soil trails with a short boardwalk

Elevation change — Little or no elevation gain or loss

HOURS Dawn to dusk, year-round

DOGS Leashed dogs permitted

FACILITIES Toilets, picnic area

FEES & PERMITS $3 daily park pass—cash only at kiosk on-site (kiosks are often out of service)—or $25 annual park pass which can be purchased online

LAND MANAGER Chattahoochee River National Recreation Area

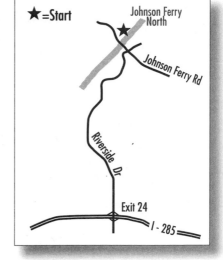

SENTINEL TREES

Ironwood – GPS N 33° 56.8897, W 84° 24.0874
- 5'8" circumference
- Knarled and twisted, this tree leans out over the river to adapt to its location. Ironwood does not grow as large as its look-alike beech; this is one of the largest known specimens in metro Atlanta.

Water Oak – GPS N 33° 56.9853, W 84° 24.0084
- 11'6" circumference
- The trail curves to the left just beyond this water oak. The largest tree along this trail, this oak has stood on the banks of the Chattahoochee River for many, many years.

Twin White Oaks – GPS N 33° 56.9556, W 84° 24.1143
- 10'4" and 9'3" circumference
- Once used as a property boundary (notice the barbed wire that has grown into the tree on the left side), these twin white oaks growing on the hill to the right of the trail are relics of the time when this park was farmland.

Hike

Start hiking at the far end of the parking lot. Pass a metal gate and continue on a wide gravel path. Reach a junction in 0.15 mile, followed immediately by a second junction. Turn right into the woods (do not continue straight along the pipeline clearing).

In 100 yards, just as the trail comes parallel to the river, you will find the sentinel ironwood tree leaning out over the river on the right.

Hike 0.15 mile past a pipeline clearing and a bench to the sentinel water oak where the trail curves left. Just beyond the water oak reach the pipeline clearing again; turn right, then right again into the woods. Hike another 0.2 mile before the trail connects with the pipeline clearing one more time. Turn right, cross the creek, then turn right into the woods.

Continue 0.2 mile, then go left at a junction and walk another 100 yards to a junction with the pipeline clearing. If you cross the creek on the pipe you can follow the clearing to a place where there is a view of the Morgan Falls Dam. This path is not part of the park and can be overgrown in summer months.

Pass the pipe, follow the main trail for 100 yards and go straight at the next junction to stay parallel to the creek on this spur trail. Continue straight again at a junction near a sewer access point. At the next junction, go straight across a small creek. The next junction will lead you across the main creek. Here you can turn around and retrace your steps or pick your way down the creek on rocks. This is a scenic area with rock overhangs and several small cascades.

Retrace your steps to the junction near the sewer access point. Go right to meet up again with the main loop trail. Turn right and walk 0.5 mile before reaching the twin sentinel white oaks on the hill on your right.

Beyond the sentinel trees 100 yards, go left on a short boardwalk that leads to a trail junction at the pipeline clearing. Turn right, then go right at the next fork to return to the parking lot in 0.15 mile and end your hike.

BIRDS TO LOOK FOR

Johnson Ferry North

Winter: American woodcock
Spring: blackpoll warbler, blue-winged warbler, common yellowthroat, Tennessee warbler

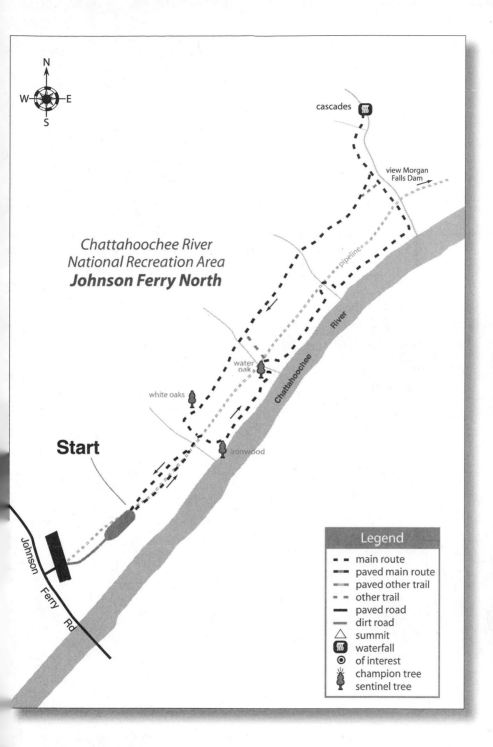

Chattahoochee River
National Recreation Area
Johnson Ferry North

Start

cascades

view Morgan
Falls Dam

pipeline

Chattahoochee River

water oak

white oaks

ironwood

Johnson Ferry Rd

Legend

- - - main route
▬▬▬ paved main route
▬▬▬ paved other trail
- - - other trail
▬ paved road
▬▬ dirt road
△ summit
🌊 waterfall
◉ of interest
🌳 champion tree
🌳 sentinel tree

Ice, wind, lightning, and other natural phenomena cause trees like the "moose tree" to form ever-evolving and interesting shapes.

GOLD BRANCH

CHATTAHOOCHEE RIVER NATIONAL RECREATION AREA

Though it is one of the lesser-known units of the Chattahoochee River National Recreation Area, Gold Branch is one of the best. Nestled in a relatively undeveloped area of Roswell, Gold Branch terrain includes rolling hills covered with hardwood forest and waterside trails teeming with birds and other wildlife. This stretch of the river is just upstream from Morgan Falls Dam; the water is still, marsh grasses flourish, and ducks, geese, herons, and kingfishers abound. It is unusual to see such natural diversity in a 3.5-mile hike.

DISTANCE FROM DOWNTOWN ATLANTA • 22 MILES

BY CAR FROM I-285 Take exit 24/Riverside Drive, go north on Riverside for 2.3 miles, and turn left on Johnson Ferry Road. Cross the bridge over the Chattahoochee River and drive 1.8 miles before turning right onto Lower Roswell Road. Continue 2.3 miles on Lower Roswell Road before turning right into Gold Branch Recreation Area. If you reach the intersection with Willeo Road and Timber Ridge Road, you've gone too far.

PUBLIC TRANSPORTATION *This hike is not easily accessible by public transportation.* If you take the 85 Roswell/Mansell Rd bus and get off at the intersection of South Atlanta Street and Azalea Drive you can walk 1.7 miles on Roswell Riverwalk Trail (parallel to Azalea Drive) until it ends at Willeo Road. Go left for 1.4 miles on Willeo Road (which has no sidewalk), turn left on Lower Roswell Road, and walk another 0.6 mile to the Gold Branch entrance on your left. Consider bringing your bicycle to ride from the bus stop.

PARKING Gravel parking lot at the trailhead; GPS N 33° 59.064, W 84° 23.117

ADDRESS 6156 Lower Roswell Road, Marietta, GA 30068

HIKE DISTANCE 3.5-mile loop

WHY THIS HIKE IS GREAT You'll hike through mature hardwood forests, lush wetlands, and along riverbanks. The hike is invigorating, and the scenery is always changing. Wildlife abounds.

DIFFICULTY

Overall — Moderate

Terrain — Mostly hard-packed soil with a boardwalk and a few bridges; some rocky and narrow trails

Elevation change — Trails climb up and down small hills; at mile 2.3 there is an 0.5-mile steady climb from the bank of the river to the hills above.

HOURS Dawn to dusk, year-round

DOGS Leashed dogs permitted

FACILITIES No toilets; trail maps posted at most junctions

FEES & PERMITS $3 daily park pass — cash only at kiosk on-site (kiosks are often out of service) — or $25 annual park pass which can be purchased online

LAND MANAGER Chattahoochee River National Recreation Area

SENTINEL TREES

Sourwood – GPS N 33° 58.7495, W 84° 22.5807
- 4'5" circumference
- The larger of two mature sourwood trees on the left side of the trail, this sentinel can be identified by its curved trunk and the deep furrows in its bark. You can often find its dried compound flowers littering the ground.

Tulip Tree – GPS N 33° 58.4472, W 84° 23.0055
- 12' circumference
- This tulip tree, the largest in the park, has been through a lot! Its lower trunk is significantly larger than the upper trunk due to major fire damage. Walk up the hill from the trail 30 feet to visit this tree, and you'll find the back side is burned out and hollow.

Mockernut Hickory "Moose Tree"– GPS N 33° 58.7070, W 84° 23.1220
- 5'6" circumference
- The bends and twists of this tree might remind you of a duck, moose, deer, dog, or other animal. Sadly, its unusual shape put too much pressure on its twisted trunk, and it has cracked open. Its insides are now exposed to the elements, and it will soon die. Happily, a younger mockernut hickory (probably an offspring of this one) is growing directly to the left and will likely take the older tree's place in the canopy.

HIKE

Begin your hike by entering the woods at a trailhead in the far (southeast) corner of the parking area near the information sign. The path descends quickly in 0.1 mile to a boardwalk over a quiet creek. After crossing the boardwalk turn to the left at an obvious fork in the trail and walk up the rise, continuing on this trail up and down small hills, through a beech grove next to a wetlands. In 0.25 mile after crossing two wooden bridges, take a right fork in the trail which leads you up a hill to a map post. From here take the trail to the left to continue hiking along the edge of the wetlands on your left. Keep an eye out for birds, including great blue heron, as you hike this section of trail.

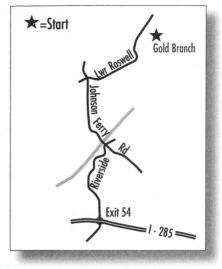

In 0.2 mile you'll come to another fork in the trail. Stay on the path to the left to continue your hike along the water's edge. This next section of trail is the most confusing and difficult of this route, but as long as you keep the water on your left you'll be going the right direction. In just over 200 yards the bank becomes very steep, and the trail narrows and splits. Take the higher trail on the right and pass a series of small trails you'll see below to your left. The trail eventually drops down off the steep hillside to follow the water's edge. Look for cattails and other marsh grasses on the far bank.

After 0.5 mile you'll reach another trail junction with a map post. Take the left fork and hike uphill steeply for 0.1 of mile to reach another junction and map post. This is an easy turn to miss, so keep your eyes peeled for the map post where you'll make a sharp left turn downhill and then over a wooden bridge.

Not far beyond the bridge the trail climbs up a steep staircase of roots. Use your hands to pull yourself up; you may find segments of rope left by past hikers to hold onto. A trail relocation is being planned to avoid this obstacle. The trail again becomes fairly flat and easy to walk. In 0.2 mile you'll pass the sentinel sourwood tree on your left. Hike another 0.3 mile to the next trail junction and map post for a nice spot to view the river and take a snack break.

From here take the left fork at the trail junction. The trail curves around an inlet, over a log bridge, and along the edge of the water. In 0.1 mile you can see all of the way across the wide river. The trail becomes narrow and rocky but in another third of a mile you gain a view of Morgan Falls Dam. The spiny succulent yucca plant lines the trail at places. Soap can be made from its root, but please don't disturb the plants, even if you're feeling dirty.

Very soon the trail curves right, away from the water, and begins ascending into the hills. After walking up a short set of stairs you'll see the sentinel tulip tree 30 feet off the right side of the trail. Stay on the main trail; you'll see several faint side trails leading to the development to the southwest. But a third of a mile after the trail begins to climb, one of these small trails leads 50 feet to a ruin of an old car left in the woods. It is always intriguing (and sometimes disturbing) to come upon the ruins of human technology after spending time hiking in a pristine nature preserve. Beyond the car you'll see another piece of bullet-riddled metal on your left, followed by a natural marvel on your right. This bent and twisted hickory tree is unmistakable and draws the eye even more than the rusted car. One local hiker says his daughter dubbed it the moose tree. Spend some time looking at the tree from all angles. Imagine the storm that must have caused the damage many years ago!

A quarter-mile past the moose tree you'll reach a trail junction and map stand. The route continues along the ridge to the left where you'll find another trail junction and map post in 300 yards. Stay left and hike another 0.1 mile to yet another junction and map (it's hard to get lost on this portion of the hike!) where you'll turn left and hike steeply downhill for almost 0.2 mile.

The last junction and map stand you'll come to is the first one you saw on this route. Continue straight across the boardwalk, then back uphill on the trail to the parking area to end the hike.

INSIDER TIP

FINDING SOLITUDE AND SPOTTING WILDLIFE AT GOLD BRANCH

Because Gold Branch doesn't have the same volume of human traffic as Cochran Shoals or Island Ford, there's a better chance for solitude and encountering more wildlife here. Come in the morning and keep your eye out for deer, turtles, and waterfowl. Late in the day, deer, fox and other small mammals are active. At dusk, listen for bird calls. You might be lucky enough to see a barred owl in the trees or flying silently through the canopy.

HIKING ATLANTA'S HIDDEN FORESTS

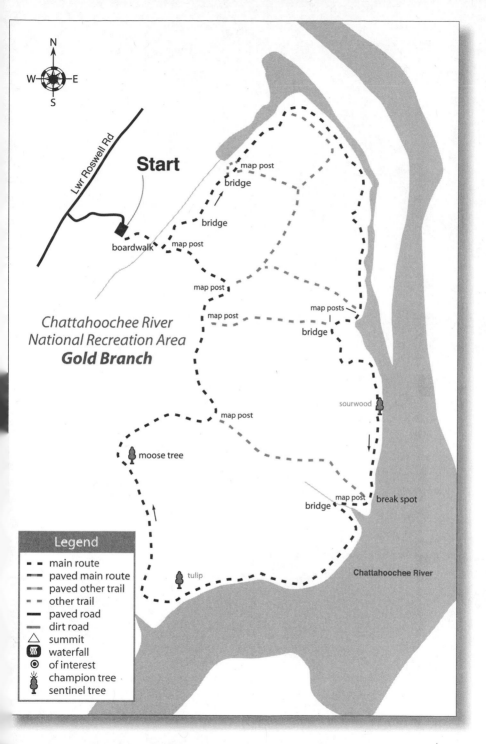

Rolling piedmont hills make for a gorgeous hike, all within the heart of Roswell.

VICKERY CREEK

CHATTAHOOCHEE RIVER NATIONAL RECREATION AREA

The Vickery Creek trails offer an excellent loop hike, scenic views, several man-made waterfalls, and historic ruins, all within the heart of Roswell, Georgia. Accessible from Waller Park and the Roswell Mill Shopping Center as well as the Chattahoochee River National Recreation Area parking lot, these trails are well used and provide many routes for exploration. Though this greenspace is a young forest, the steep banks of Big Creek and the rolling piedmont hills make for a fantastic hike, especially in the heat of the summer when you can dip your feet in the water.

DISTANCE FROM DOWNTOWN ATLANTA • 21 MILES

BY CAR FROM GA 400 Take exit 6 for Northridge Road, then go west and make an immediate right onto Dunwoody Place. In 1.3 mile, turn right onto GA 9 (Roswell Road/Atlanta Street). In 0.5 mile, cross the Chattahoochee River and turn right onto Riverside Road. In 500 feet, turn left into the Recreation Area entrance to reach the parking lot.

PUBLIC TRANSPORTATION Take the MARTA 85 bus to the corner of GA 9 (Roswell Road/Atlanta Street) and Riverside Road. Turn right on Riverside Road; the entrance to the parking area is 500 feet on the left.

PARKING Partially paved parking area; GPS N 34° 00.4483, W 84° 21.0617

ADDRESS 259 Riverside Road, Roswell, GA 30075

HIKE DISTANCE 4.5-mile lollipop loop

WHY THIS HIKE IS GREAT The creek and hills that surround it are a gorgeous place to go hiking. You'll see the famous Roswell Mill ruins and can dip your feet in the creek if you get tired.

DIFFICULTY

Overall — Moderate

Terrain — Hard-packed soil trails

Elevation change — Rolling hills throughout the park with no extended ascents or descents

HOURS Dawn to dusk, year-round

DOGS Leashed dogs permitted

FACILITIES None at the Recreation Area parking lot; toilets available at Roswell Mill Shopping Area, maps posted at many trail junctions

FEES & PERMITS $3 daily park pass—cash only at kiosk on-site (kiosks are often out of service)—or $25 annual park pass which can be purchased online

LAND MANAGER Chattahoochee River National Recreation Area

SENTINEL TREES

Big Leaf Magnolia – GPS N 34° 00.6758, W 84° 21.0837
- 2'8" circumference
- On the left, just before reaching a trail junction, this big leaf magnolia is the largest and oldest of the many in this area of the forest. In the summer, you can recognize the species by its enormous leaves—the largest of any native plant in Georgia. This specimen also has a carving on its bark.

River Birch – GPS N 34° 00.6820, W 84° 21.5456
- 7'9" circumference
- Across the trail from a rock outcrop is a large, leaning river birch. This tree is surrounded by thorny vines, so don't get too close. You can identify river birch by its papery and flaky bark at the top of the trunk.

Big Leaf Magnolia – GPS N 34° 00.9124, W 84° 20.7359
- 7 trunks; largest has 1'9" circumference
- Though none of its trunks are as large as the first sentinel big leaf magnolia you passed on this hike, this tree is notable for the large number of trunks growing from the same node.

Hike

Maps are not posted at all trail junctions, so be sure to refer to the map in this book if you get confused.

Start hiking at the far end of the parking area and reach a junction in less than 75 yards. Turn right, climb the stairs, and follow the trail as it switchbacks up onto the ridge. Reach a bench where the trail flattens out on the ridgetop in 0.15 mile. Walk 0.3 mile farther, passing another bench and the first sentinel big leaf magnolia with carving on its trunk, to reach a junction. Turn left.

Stay straight at the next junction in 0.1 mile, then go left at a second junction in another 0.1 mile.

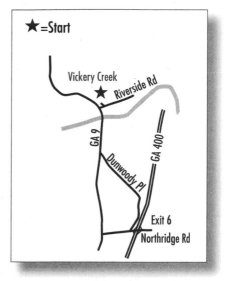

In 0.1 mile, pass a bench and small cut-off trail to the right that leads to a dam. You will have another opportunity to visit the dam later in the hike. Stay straight for 0.2 mile to another junction. Go left and hike steadily downhill for 0.2 mile to one more junction.

Turn right and follow the trail along the bank of Big Creek. Pass a sewer pipe crossing the creek in 0.15 mile. In another 0.1 mile, pass the sentinel river birch on the left next to a very short creek access trail and across from a rock outcrop on the right. Just past the birch, take a left where the trail splits.

This will take you closer to the creek, near some large flat rocks at the water's edge and some small beach areas. The paths reconnect in 0.1 mile near a sewer pipe that crosses the creek below old Roswell Mill. Follow a small trail alongside the pipe that parallels the creek to reach a large covered bridge.

After passing underneath the bridge, turn right and scramble up a steep path to a set of concrete stairs next to the bridge. You can reach the Roswell Mill Shopping Center and historic mill buildings by crossing it; at the other end are two markers explaining the history of the mills in this area as well as the construction of the covered bridge itself. To continue on the route, walk up the concrete stairs and go straight for 50 yards to a junction with a wide trail. Turn left here before reaching the map signpost that is situated a little farther up along the trail.

In 0.2 mile, reach a junction with a spur trail that leads 100 yards downhill to the dam. The water of the creek now rushes over the top of the dam. This is the best place to visit the dam and waterfall.

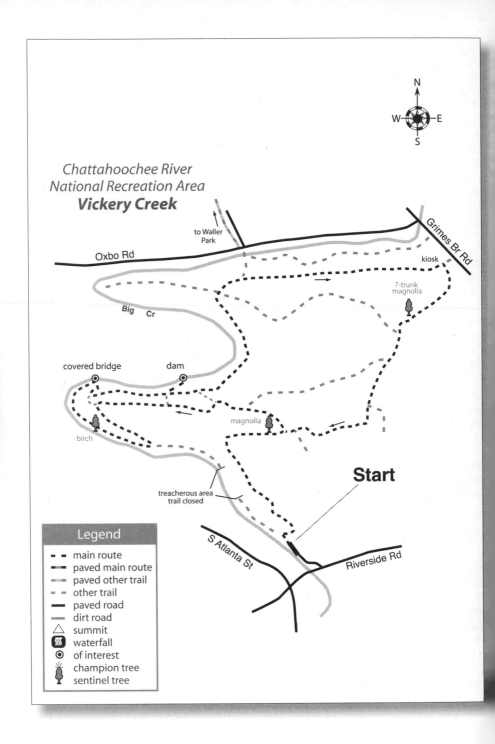

Chattahoochee River
National Recreation Area
Vickery Creek

to Waller Park

Oxbo Rd

Grimes Br Rd

kiosk

7-trunk magnolia

Big Cr

covered bridge

dam

birch

magnolia

Start

treacherous area
trail closed

S Atlanta St

Riverside Rd

N
W   E
S

Legend
- - main route
- - paved main route
- - paved other trail
- - other trail
— paved road
— dirt road
△ summit
♨ waterfall
◉ of interest
♣ champion tree
♣ sentinel tree

Return to the spur junction and turn left. Pass a small cut-through trail on your right and hike 0.1 mile to the next junction. Turn left.

Cross a small bridge in 0.2 mile then walk another 0.15 mile to a junction. Go straight, and come to another junction in about 100 yards. To the left is a trail that crosses a bridge over Big Creek and connects with a multi-use path that leads to Waller Park. Go straight and hike 0.5 mile to a junction with an information kiosk. Turn right and hike 0.2 mile to reach the second sentinel big leaf magnolia tree. As the trail ascends a small hill, this sentinel tree with seven trunks is on the right.

At a junction after the sentinel tree, stay straight. In about 100 yards, turn left at the next junction. In 0.15 mile, go left again at a junction. Go right at the next junction in 0.2 mile, pass a trail exiting on your left, and then take a left at the following junction (which is the same as the second junction you came to on this hike).

Follow this trail 0.5 mile back to the junction near the parking area and turn left to return to where you started, ending the hike.

Island Ford

Chattahoochee River National Recreation Area

The Park Service planted their park headquarters at Island Ford for a reason: it is one of the largest and most beautiful units of the National Recreation Area. Trails extend for several miles along the banks of the Chattahoochee, which widens and rolls over shoals here, but hikers also get to walk through scenic piedmont forests, beside creeks, and past large granite outcrops. Having recently added nearly 3 miles of new trail, Island Ford now boasts one of the longer hikes in the metro Atlanta area.

DISTANCE FROM DOWNTOWN ATLANTA • 21 MILES

BY CAR FROM GA 400 Take exit 6/Northridge Road and go west onto Northridge Road. Take an immediate right onto Dunwoody Place, then drive 0.6 mile before turning right onto Roberts Drive. Continue 0.6 mile and turn right onto Island Ford Parkway. Drive 1.2 mile to the parking area where the road ends at the visitor center.

PUBLIC TRANSPORTATION Take the MARTA 87 bus to the corner of Dunwoody Place and Roberts Drive, then walk 0.6 mile to the park entrance. It is 1.2 mile from the park entrance to the visitor center, but you can also begin your hike from the parking area next to the entrance gates.

PARKING Paved parking area near the visitor center; GPS N 33° 59.2353, W 84° 19.5454

ADDRESS 1978 Island Ford Parkway, Atlanta, GA 30350

HIKE DISTANCE 6.25-mile triple loop

Canada geese on the Chattahoochee.

WHY THIS HIKE IS GREAT One of the longest hikes in the Chattahoochee River National Recreation Area trail network, offering both rolling piedmont terrain and riverside hiking.

DIFFICULTY

Overall — Moderate

Terrain — Mostly hard-packed soil trail with few roots and rocks

Elevation change — Several extended uphill climbs with a fairly even grade

HOURS 7 am to dusk, year-round; visitor center open daily 9 am to 5 pm except December 25

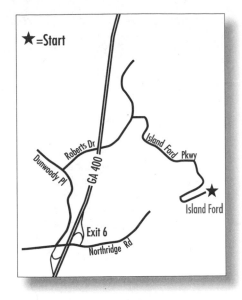

DOGS Leashed dogs permitted

FACILITIES Visitor center, toilets, picnic tables, trail maps posted at most junctions

FEES & PERMITS $3 daily park pass—cash only at kiosk on-site (kiosks are often out of service)—or $25 annual park pass which can be purchased online

LAND MANAGER Chattahoochee River National Recreation Area

SENTINEL TREES

White Oak – GPS N 33° 59.4611, W 84° 19.6424
- 10'9" circumference
  Viewed from afar, trees often don't seem very large. As you approach this white oak you will be impressed by its girth. See if you can wrap your arms around it—don't be ashamed to call yourself a tree hugger!

Tulip Tree – GPS N 33° 59.7536, W 84° 19.7264
- 10'1" circumference
- This tulip tree isn't as big around as the white oak, but it certainly wins in the gnarliness category. Notice how much larger it is than all others around it.

Northern Red Oak – GPS N 33° 59.7628, W 84° 19.7772

- 9'7" circumference
- This northern red oak has a trunk that was crooked from the start. Growing on a steep hillside near the creek, it had to compensate for the slope of the land by bending and growing wider at its base.

HIKE

Park near the visitor center and start your hike in the far corner of the parking lot (away from the building). After 0.1 mile turn left at the first junction, cross the road, then turn left on the trail at the pond's edge. It quickly emerges from the woods near a maintenance parking area. Stay right, following the water's edge.

In 0.1 mile turn right, then walk down the stairs and across a bridge before following the trail back along the other side of the pond. At the far end of the pond turn left, walk up the stairs, cross the road, then climb another set of stairs to a parking area. Turn right and re-enter the woods.

In almost 0.2 mile, reach the Chattahoochee River and turn left. Hike 0.2 mile to the next junction and turn left to join a trail paralleling Summerbrook Creek. Hike uphill and cross the creek. Just after crossing the creek the trail passes the sentinel white oak on your right.

You will reach the next junction in 0.3 mile. Go right here and walk down the ridge through a much younger forest until you reach a trail junction in another 0.3 mile. Turn left (don't go up the stairs) and in 75 yards look for the sentinel tulip tree just up the hill on your left. The trail soon crosses another creek and then passes the sentinel northern red oak below the trail on your right. Hike another 0.3 mile to reach a parking area and junction with Cowert Trail.

Turn right to begin this 2.75-mile lollipop loop trail. In 0.1 mile, cross Island Ferry Road and continue straight. The trail generally descends for the next 0.9 mile, crossing a bridge after 0.4 mile, then another in 0.2 mile. The loop starts at a trail junction near the river. Turn right and follow the river. In 0.3 mile, the trail goes left and ascends steeply. In 0.3 mile, pass a junction with a small trail that leads to Roberts Drive, then hike another 0.15 mile back to the beginning of the loop. Turn right and hike 1.0 mile back to the parking area, turn left and hike 0.4 mile to the trail junction with the stairs.

This time, walk up the stairs and turn left. In 0.1 mile this trail arrives at Beech Creek, turns right, and becomes significantly wider and flatter. Hike another 0.1 mile past a small trail on your left to a junction where you will follow the river back to the visitor center.

Along the way you'll pass a large boulder that has climbers' chalk marks, bridges over Summerbrook Creek, and a picnic area near the boat ramp. The paved path uphill to the visitor center will return you to the parking area to end the hike.

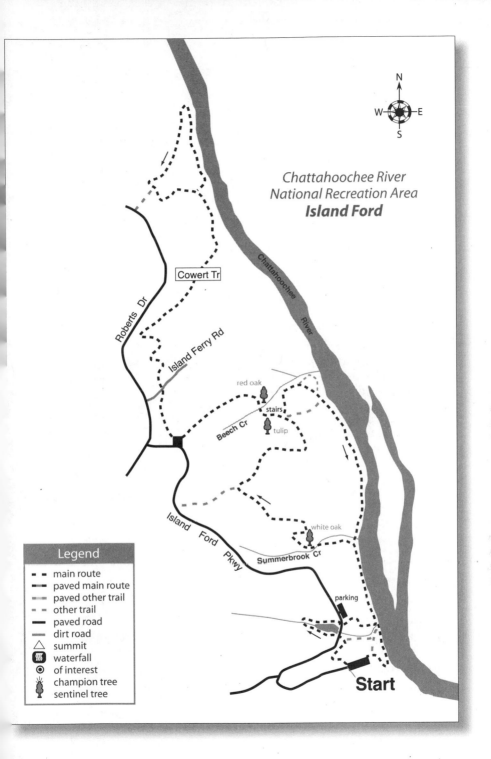

Chattahoochee River
National Recreation Area
Island Ford

Cowert Tr

Roberts Dr

Island Ferry Rd

Chattahoochee River

red oak

stairs

Beech Cr

tulip

Island Ford Pkwy

white oak

Summerbrook Cr

parking

Start

Legend
- - main route
— paved main route
═ paved other trail
- - other trail
— paved road
— dirt road
△ summit
♨ waterfall
◉ of interest
🌲 champion tree
🌲 sentinel tree

Jones Bridge

Chattahoochee River National Recreation Area

This protected area of land in the midst of multi-million-dollar housing developments has many miles of hiking trails and a storied past; half of Jones Bridge itself (visible from the trail) was actually stolen in the 1940s. And if you venture beyond the first mile of riverside trails you'll reach a remote area of interconnecting routes that wind over piedmont ridges and through an old-growth oak forest along the river's edge.

Distance from Downtown Atlanta • 26 miles

By car from GA 400
Take exit 7A to merge onto Holcomb Bridge Road toward Norcross. Drive 4.5 miles, then turn left onto Barnwell Road. Drive 1.5 mile and turn right at the sign for the Jones Bridge unit of the CRNRA. Drive 1 mile to the second parking area at the end of this road.

Public Transportation
This hike is not easily accessible by public transportation. Take the MARTA 185 bus to the intersection of GA 400 and Holcomb Bridge Road. From there it is 3.7 miles to the Jones Bridge parking area.

Parking
Park in the second parking area; GPS N 34° 0.073, W 84° 14.375

Address
9131 Barnwell Road, Johns Creek, GA 30022

Hike Distance
5.25-mile lollipop loop

Early mornings sometimes bring fog to the riverbank.

WHY THIS HIKE IS GREAT Jones Bridge is a perfect escape for anyone craving time beside the Chattahoochee River. This historic place has stories to tell, and you can create your own on your hike.

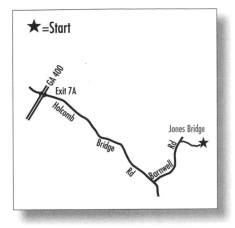

DIFFICULTY

Overall — Moderate

Terrain — Hard-packed soil trails with some wooden footbridges

Elevation change — Mostly level trails with some significant elevation change section in the middle

HOURS Dawn to dusk, year-round

DOGS Leashed dogs permitted

FACILITIES Toilets next to parking, boat ramps, observation platform, picnic tables

FEES & PERMITS $3 daily park pass—cash only at kiosk on-site (kiosks are often out of order)—or $25 annual park pass which can be purchased online

LAND MANAGER Chattahoochee River National Recreation Area

SENTINEL TREES

Tulip Tree – GPS N 33° 59.9950, W 84° 14.5385
- 10'2" circumference
- Because riverbank trees were the last to be cut down for development or farming, trees at the water's edge are often larger than those on ridges. This sentinel is in a grove of many trees of similar size.

White Oak – GPS N 33° 59.7165, W 84° 15.1576
- 10'10" circumference
- Near the crest of the ridge, this white oak stands out as the largest tree in the area. Its crooked limbs and thick, flaky bark give the tree a decidedly ancient look.

Water Oak – GPS N 33° 59.2049, W 84° 15.2667
- 10'8" circumference
- In a section of the trail along the river that is home to many old trees, mostly oaks, this large and impressive water oak stands alone.

HIKE

Begin your hike at the second parking area (the first parking area is for vehicles hauling boats only). The trail begins past the back gate of the parking area and winds uphill on an old road. In 0.15 mile the trail curves right and continues uphill to the crest of the ridge, then descends.

The trail exits the woods in a small field near the river. At the first map post, turn left and rockhop across the creek, continuing through a picnic area to where the old Jones Bridge is located and then circling back in 0.2 mile to a footbridge in the clearing. Jones Bridge spans only half of the river because a rogue salvage company stole the other half in the 1940s. When you finish your hike you can read more of this amazing story at the information kiosk near the parking lot.

After viewing the bridge and returning to the footbridge in the clearing where you rock-hopped across the creek, continue straight, passing an observation deck on your left. Stay left on the trail that parallels the river.

In 0.15 mile pass a side trail to the parking lot and continue straight across another footbridge.

In 0.2 mile, pass the sentinel tulip tree on your right, then cross another bridge in 0.1 mile.

Walk 0.15 mile to yet another footbridge, then reach the boat trailer parking lot. Cross the footbridge on the opposite side of this parking lot to continue on the route.

Hike 0.3 mile, then turn right to climb steps and follow a switchback to the crest of the ridge. The trail immediately dips back down to a private gravel road. Cross this road and hike uphill for 0.1 mile before passing the sentinel white oak on the left, just before a small footbridge.

Take the left fork at the junction just beyond the bridge and hike 0.25 mile, passing under some powerlines, to reach the next junction. At this junction, go left and downhill, then turn left again at the next junction.

The next 0.75 mile of trail parallels the river through an area of many large old oak trees.

After almost 0.5 mile, the trail curves right and meets a junction. Turn left; the trail curves back to the river's edge, passing the sentinel water oak on the right in 0.1 mile. In another 0.2 mile, you'll reach another junction. Turn left and then left again at another junction in less than 0.1 mile.

On this section of trail you'll pass an elaborate rope swing over the river—using this swing is not recommended. At the next junction in 0.1 mile go right. The trail will enter a small field and reach another junction where you should turn left. You'll enter a larger clearing, pass another junction, and come to a picnic table on your right. If you continue straight, there is a pond at the top of the hill. Just past the picnic table the route turns right on a faint trail through the field. Pass another picnic table at the far end of the field and enter the woods.

Cross a footbridge, then come to a junction in 0.1 mile. Turn left and reach the edge of a pond where you'll walk across the dry spillway. In 0.1 mile stay left at the next junction and continue 0.1 mile to a junction where you'll stay straight. In 0.3 mile the main trail turns right. Turn left and pass a wooden barrier to take a small trail that connects back to the main trail in less than 0.1 mile. Turn left, cross the footbridge, and retrace your steps 0.5 mile back to the boat trailer parking area, then continue another 0.5 mile to the trail on the left leading back to the main parking area to finish.

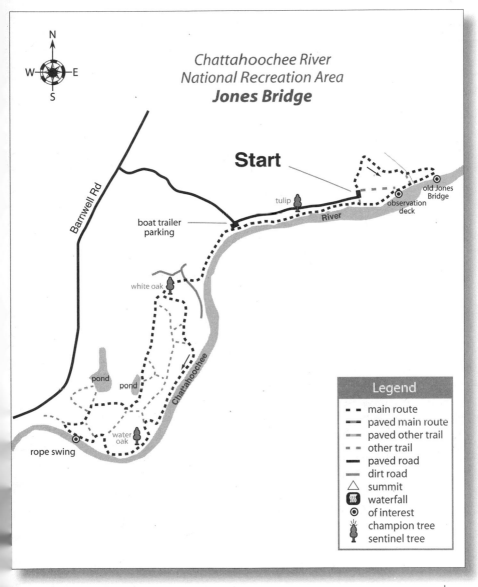

Chattahoochee River
National Recreation Area
Jones Bridge

Start

Barnwell Rd

boat trailer parking

tulip

River

old Jones Bridge

observation deck

white oak

pond

pond

Chattahoochee

rope swing

water oak

Legend

- - main route
— paved main route
— paved other trail
- - other trail
— paved road
— dirt road
△ summit
▧ waterfall
◉ of interest
♣ champion tree
♣ sentinel tree

APPENDICES

Appendix A

Hikes with Special Features

Hikes with Special Features

APPENDIX B

CHAMPION TREES

STATE CHAMPIONS

Basswood	Tanyard Creek Park & Northside Beltline	. . . 90
Pin Oak	Piedmont Park & Eastside Beltline	 85
White Ash	Tanyard Creek Park & Northside Beltline	. . 90

CITY CHAMPIONS

Basswood	W.D. Thompson Park	 106
Black Cherry	Herbert Taylor Park	 48
Eastern Red Cedar	Glenlake Park & Decatur Cemetery	 79
Ironwood	Hahn Woods & Lullwater Preserve	 44
Loblolly Pine	Hahn Woods & Lullwater Preserve	 44
Osage Orange	Atlanta Memorial Park	 110
Pawpaw	CRNRA East Palisades	 59
Pignut Hickory	Glenlake Park & Decatur Cemetery	 79
Red Bud	Frazer Forest & Deep Dene	 73
River Birch	Atlanta Memorial Park	 110
River Birch	CRNRA East Palisades	 59
River Birch	South Peachtree Creek Trail	 39
Silver Maple	Herbert Taylor Park	 48
Sourwood	Cascade Springs Nature Preserve	 102
Virginia Pine	Glenlake Park & Decatur Cemetery	 79
Willow Oak	Constitution Lakes Park	 27
Winged Elm	Outdoor Activity Center	 98

APPENDIX C

LAND MANAGEMENT AGENCIES

NATIONAL PARKS

Chattahoochee River National Recreation Area
1978 Island Ford Parkway
Sandy Springs, GA 30350
678-538-1200
www.nps.gov/chat

Kennesaw Mountain National Battlefield Park
900 Kennesaw Mountain Drive
Kennesaw, GA 30152
770-427-4686
www.nps.gov/kemo

STATE PARKS

Panola Mountain State Park
2600 Highway 155 North
Stockbridge, GA 30281
770-389-7801
www.gastateparks.org/
PanolaMountain

Sweetwater Creek State Park
1750 Mt Vernon Road
Lithia Springs, GA 30122
770-732-5871
www.gastateparks.org/
SweetwaterCreek

CITY PARKS

City of Atlanta Office of Parks
233 Peachtree Street NE
Atlanta, GA 30303
404-546-6813
www.atlantaga.gov/index.
aspx?page=250

City of Chattahoochee Hills
6505 Rico Road
Chattahoochee Hills, GA 30268
770-463-8881
www.chatthillsga.us/Parks.aspx

City of Decatur
509 N McDonough Street
Decatur, GA 30031
404-370-4100
www.decaturga.com

City of Roswell
38 Hill Street
Roswell, GA 30075
770-641-3705
www.roswellgov.com/index.
aspx?nid=104

City of Sandy Springs
7840 Roswell Road
Sandy Springs, GA 30850
770-206-2035
www.sandyspringsga.org/City-
Departments/Recreation-and-Parks/
Parks-and-Facilities

City of Woodstock
108 Arnold Mill Road
Woodstock, GA 30188
770-517-6788
www.woodstockparksandrec.com

County Parks

Clayton County Parks & Recreation
2300 Highway 138 SE
Jonesboro, GA 30236
770-477-3766
www.claytonparks.com

Clayton County Water Authority
1600 Battle Creek Road
Morrow, GA 30260
770-960-5200
www.ccwa.us

Cobb County Parks & Recreation
1792 County Services Parkway
Marietta, GA 30008
770-528-8800
www.prca.cobbcountyga.gov

DeKalb County Parks & Recreation
404-371-2000
www.dekalbcountyga.gov/parks

Douglas County Parks & Recreation
6754 Bankhead Highway
Old Douglas County Courthouse
Douglasville, GA 30135
770-489-3918
www.celebratedouglascounty.com/

Fulton County Parks & Recreation
141 Pryor Street
Atlanta, GA 30303
404-612-4000
www.fultoncountyga.gov/fcprd-home

Gwinnett County Parks & Recreation
75 Langley Drive
Lawrenceville, GA 30046
770-978-5270 (trails hotline)
www.gwinnettcounty.com/portal/gwinnett/
Departments/CommunityServices/
ParksandRecreation

Preserves, Foundations & Land Trusts

Arabia Mountain
National Heritage Area
3787 Klondike Road
Lithonia, GA 30038
770-492-5231
www.arabiaalliance.org

Atlanta Memorial Park Conservancy
PO Box 551009
Atlanta, GA 30355
www.atlmemorialpark.org

Autrey Mill Nature Preserve
& Heritage Center
9770 Autrey Mill Road
Johns Creek, GA 30022
678-366-3511
www.autreymill.org

LAND MANAGEMENT AGENCIES

Big Trees Forest Preserve
PO Box 422571
Sandy Springs, GA 30342
770-673-0111
www.bigtreesforest.com

Blue Heron Nature Preserve
4055 Roswell Road
Atlanta, GA 30342
404-345-1008
www.bhnp.org

Clyde Shepherd Nature Preserve
PO Box 33247
Decatur, GA 30033
678-951-0105
www.cshepherdpreserve.org

Dunwoody Nature Preserve
5343 Roberts Drive
Dunwoody, GA 30338
770-394-3322
www.dunwoodynature.org

Frazer Center
1815 S. Ponce De Leon Avenue
Atlanta, GA 30307
404-377-3836
www.frazercenter.org

Murphey Candler Park Conservancy
1560 Brawley Circle
Brookhaven, GA 30319
www.murpheycandlerpark.org

PATH Foundation
PO Box 14327
Atlanta, GA 30324
404-875-7284
www.pathfoundation.org

Southern Conservation Trust
192 McIntosh Trail
Peachtree City, GA 30269
770-486-7774
www.sctlandtrust.org

The Atlanta Beltline
86 Pryor Street, Suite 300
Atlanta, GA 30303
404-477-3003
www.beltline.org

The Olmsted Linear Park Alliance
PO Box 5500
Atlanta, GA 31107
404-377-5361
www.atlantaolmstedpark.org

West Atlanta Watershed Alliance
1442 Richland Road SW
Atlanta, GA 30310
404-752-5385
www.wawaonline.blogspot.com

UNIVERSITIES

Emory University
201 Dowman Drive
Atlanta, GA 30322
404-727-6089
www.emory.edu

Mercer University
3001 Mercer University Drive
Atlanta, GA 30341
678-547-6000
www.mercer.edu

OTHER

**Simpsonwood Conference
& Retreat Center**
4511 Jones Bridge Circle
Norcross, GA 30092
770-441-1111
www.simpsonwood.org

Stone Mountain Park
1000 Robert E Lee Boulevard
Stone Mountain, GA 30083
770-498-5690
www.stonemountainpark.com/activities/
recreation-golf/Hiking-Trails.aspx

Photo Credits

Cover photos by the author, Mary Ellen Hammond, Jim Parham, and David Foster [www.davidfosterimages.net] (front) and Jim Wilson (back). Author photo (opposite) by Robert Armstrong.

Interior photos by the author except as follows:

Pam Higginbotham: pp. 40, 80, 86, 146, 170
Ben Fowler: p. 254
Mary Ellen Hammond: pp. 13, 19, 44, 58, 179
Bill Holland: pp. 72, 78
Gene Koziaria: pp. 220, 240, 300
Bob Lough: pp. 222, 308
Laura MacNorlin: p. 149
Jim Parham: pp. 200, 323
Karen Skellie: p. 196
Jesse Stewart: pp. 68, 290
Gary Thompson: p. 98
Regina Willis: pp. 38, 235, 248, 284
Jim Wilson: pp. 17, 24, 28, 34, 96, 130, 154, 194, 232, 250, 286

About the Author

Jonah McDonald is an Atlanta resident and a former Appalachian Trail thru-hiker. As an educator and naturalist, he has designed and taught wilderness and outdoor programs for several Atlanta-area independent schools. McDonald is the founder of Sure Foot Adventures, an outdoor guide service offering hiking, camping, backpacking, and outdoor education programs throughout the Southeast. He has spent countless days exploring the greenspaces of metro Atlanta.

As a professional storyteller, McDonald performs for groups of all ages. He also conducts a Bicycle Tour of the Battle of Atlanta for the annual B*ATL Festival. He has served on the board of the Friends School of Atlanta, the Southern Order of Storytellers, and the American Friends Service Committee.

Beyond his passion for hiking, McDonald raises chickens in his backyard, enjoys basketball and rock climbing, throws boomerangs, is the proud companion of a Catahoula leopard dog, and wants to learn to ride a unicycle.

Visit the Companion Website for Hiking Atlanta's Hidden Forests

New trails are constantly being built, trees die, and park rules change. Please visit www.hikingatlanta.com for a current list of trail updates, including a space for readers to post hike comments, and additional information on hikes and greenspaces that do not appear in this book.

MILESTONE PRESS

OUTDOOR ADVENTURE GUIDEBOOKS

HIKING GUIDES

* *Hiking Atlanta's Hidden Forests*
  by Jonah McDonald

* *Hiking the Carolina Mountains*
* *Hiking North Carolina's Blue Ridge Mountains*
  by Danny Bernstein

* *Day Hiking the North Georgia Mountains*
* *Waterfall Hikes of North Georgia*
* *Backpacking Overnights:*
  NC Mountains & SC Upstate
  by Jim Parham

* *Waterfall Hikes of Upstate South Carolina*
  by Thomas E. King

* *Family Hikes in Upstate South Carolina*
  by Scott Lynch

MOUNTAIN BIKE GUIDES

* *Off the Beaten Track*
  Mountain Bike Guide Series
  by Jim Parham
    Vol. 1: Western North Carolina-Smokies
    Vol. 2: Western North Carolina-Pisgah
    Vol. 3: North Georgia
    Vol. 4: East Tennessee

ROAD BIKING GUIDES

* *Road Bike Asheville, NC*
  by The Blue Ridge Bicycle Club

* *Road Bike North Georgia*
* *Road Bike the Smokies*
  by Jim Parham

MOTORCYCLE GUIDES

• *Motorcycle Adventure Series*
  by Hawk Hagebak
    Book 1—North GA, East TN, Western NC
    Book 2—Asheville, Blue Ridge Parkway,
    NC Highcountry
    Book 3—VA Blue Ridge, Shenandoah Valley,
    WV Highlands

FAMILY ADVENTURE

• *Natural Adventures in the*
  Mountains of North Georgia
  by Mary Ellen Hammond & Jim Parham

ROCKHOUNDING

• *A Rockhounding Guide to*
  North Carolina's Blue Ridge Mountains
  by Michael Streeter

Can't find the Milestone Press guide that you want at a bookseller near you? Don't despair—you can order it directly from us. Call us at 828-488-6601 or shop online at www.milestonepress.com.

Great Hikes
of the Southern Appalachians

Put the hikes from this book on your phone.

iPhone or Android

Taking a hike doesn't get much easier! With hundreds of routes to choose from in Western North Carolina, Upstate South Carolina, North Georgia, and metro Atlanta, this mobile app helps you search and select a hike, get to the trailhead, and find your way on the trail. All hikes are adapted from Milestone Press's best guidebooks, so you know they're created by expert hikers and tested by countless users. Watch for updates as more routes are added to the list! Once you've purchased and installed the GPS-enabled hikes on your phone, all your trail information is fully functional, with no wi-fi or data connection required.

All your favorite hikes from this and other Milestone Press guidebooks are now accessible on your smart phone.

* Hundreds of hikes to choose from in the mountains of North and South Carolina and Georgia, as well as the Atlanta metro area

* GPS-enabled so you always know precisely where you are on the trail and en route to the trailhead

* Look for **Great Hikes of the Southern Appalachians** at the Apple App or Google Play store.

* Downloading the app is easy. Just scan the QR code with your iPhone or android for direct access to **Great Hikes**.

An App for iPhone or Android